THE QUICK AND THE DEAD

RICHARD VAN EMDEN has interviewed over 270 veterans of the Great War and has written twelve books on the subject including *The Trench* and *The Last Fighting Tommy* (both top ten bestsellers). He has also worked on more than a dozen television programmes on the First World War, including *Prisoners of the Kaiser*, *Veterans*, *Britain's Last Tommies*, the award-winning *Roses of No Man's Land* and *Britain's Boy Soldiers*, *A Poem for Harry* and *War Horse: The Real Story*.

THE QUICK AND THE DEAD

Fallen Soldiers and Their Families
in the Great War

Richard van Emden

BLOOMSBURY

LONDON · BERLIN · NEW YORK · SYDNEY

First published in Great Britain 2011
This paperback edition published 2012

Copyright © Richard van Emden 2011

The moral right of the author has been asserted

Bloomsbury Publishing Plc
50 Bedford Square
London WC1B 3DP

www.bloomsbury.com

Bloomsbury Publishing, London, Berlin, New York and Sydney

A CIP catalogue record for this book is available from the British Library

ISBN 978 1 4088 2245 6

10 9 8 7 6 5 4 3 2 1

Typeset by Hewer Text UK Ltd, Edinburgh

Printed in Great Britain by Clays Ltd, St Ives plc, Bungay, Suffolk

Dedicated to the memory of Joyce Crow, née Sherington (1909–2008), and her brother, Private Robert Arthur Sherington, killed during the Battle of the Somme, 9 October 1916.

And to Leonard Sutton* of Hillside, Reading, who lost four of his five sons in the war: Lieutenant Eric Sutton MC, aged twenty-one, killed 8 April 1916; Second Lieutenant William Sutton, aged twenty, killed 13 November 1917; Second Lieutenant Alexander Sutton, aged nineteen, killed 2 January 1918; Lieutenant Eustace Sutton, aged twenty-two, killed 24 March 1918.

And to Captain Leonard Noel Sutton, wounded 1918.

---

* Leonard Sutton owned a large late-Victorian house called Hillside, and a company, Sutton Seeds, that still specialises in the packaging and selling of commercial seeds. Hillside, now one of Reading University's halls of residence, was within sight of the home in which I grew up. I walked past Hillside every day and noticed the wrought-iron railings and the tall brick entrance that still bears the name of the house.

I knew nothing of its history until last year when, by chance, I discovered that Leonard Sutton had owned the house where he lived with his wife, Mary, and their five sons and one daughter. Mary Sutton died in 1900 leaving Leonard, then thirty-six, to bring up six children under the age of ten. All five boys went on to serve in the Great War and four were killed.

After the war, Leonard Sutton became a Governor of the Royal Agricultural Society, vice-president of the Royal Berkshire Hospital, president of Reading Chamber of Commerce, and vice-president of the Royal Horticultural Society; he was also three times Mayor of Reading. Before his death in 1932, he was elected vice-chairman of the NSPCC. Perhaps his loss made him throw himself into his work. He certainly knew more than anyone ever should about cruelty, pain and suffering.

The dreaded word 'gas' was sounded along the line. Instantly 'tin hats' were flung off and gas-masks donned, a feat which was performed quicker than it takes to write, for we thoroughly believed in the oft-repeated maxim that in a gas attack there were but two kinds of men – *the quick and the dead.*

– Henry Russell, Slaves of the War Lords

CONTENTS

INTRODUCTION

Should you find yourself in Eastbourne with an hour or two to spare, you might care to visit the little Musgrave Museum in Seaside Road, a street that runs behind and parallel to the seafront parade of shops, restaurants and hotels. It contains the life's work of George Musgrave, an independent and, as he describes himself, single-minded man. His museum is an eclectic collection of items, from coins to paintings, from newspapers to cameras, from pottery to wax models – in truth there is no obvious link; it simply seems to offer items of cultural interest that George has collected from across the globe. The visitors' book shows a steady trickle of interested and appreciative – if occasionally bemused – tourists who have looked around during the spring and summer months when the museum is open.

Just inside the front door of the museum is the link that binds everything together. It is a wooden, glass-fronted stand in which is a photograph of a soldier, the pencil drawing of a train, the picture of a little boy, and above them the words, *The Dad I Never Knew*. A brass plaque, known as a 'death penny', is also in the stand. Given by the government to bereaved families, it confirms that this particular soldier did not return from war.

The collection is George's act of devotion to a lost father, mortally wounded in France in 1917. Indeed, everything in the building has been brought together by this ninety-six-year-old man so as to leave a lasting memorial to a soldier now ninety-four years dead. And that small difference of two years is important. George has no memory of his father, but the train, drawn under fire in the trenches, was crucial in fusing forever the bond between them. 'To little George for his birthday from Daddy' is the accompanying note. It is one thing for a mother to tell a son that his late father loved him, quite another to have tangible and irrefutable proof.

The Musgrave Museum lends credence to the idea that the Great War's rippling influence remains with us today, and absorbing stories have continued to excite media interest for their mixture of tragedy, poignancy and simple curiosity. In December 1998, the *Guardian* ran an article about the meeting, eighty years on, of a brother and sister separated by war. After their father was killed in November 1917, Albert and Daisy Bance were placed in different children's homes by their mother who herself died shortly afterwards. The siblings were reunited only after a long search by relatives who discovered Albert living in Canada, where he had been sent when he was fourteen. The two were brought together in an emotional meeting at Montreal airport. 'There were all these people standing there and there was Albert with a lovely bouquet of flowers. I just put my arms around him and started crying,' Daisy is reported to have said. Aged eighty-five, she then returned to England where she died peacefully the following March.

That same month, in the Thames Estuary, fisherman Steve Gowan was hauling in his catch of cod and Dover sole when he saw an old ginger-beer bottle in the nets with what appeared to be a piece of paper inside. After prising off the rubber stopper, he found a message written by a soldier as he left for war in September 1914: 'Dear wife, I am writing this note on this boat and dropping it into the sea just to see if it will reach you. If it does, sign this envelope on the right hand bottom corner where it says receipt. Put the date and hour of receipt and your name where it says signature and look after it well.' The message ends, 'Ta ta, sweet, for the present. Your hubby.' The writer asks the finder to 'kindly forward the enclosed letter and earn the blessing of a poor British soldier on his way to the front'.

The soldier, Private Thomas Hughes of the Durham Light Infantry, was killed thirteen days later. Widowed with a two-year-old daughter, Elizabeth Hughes would later remarry and in 1919 emigrate from her home in Stockton-on-Tees to New Zealand. *The Times* printed the story when it was discovered that the daughter, Emily, was still alive and in May 1999 Steve took the letter to Auckland and handed it to the then eighty-six-year-old.

'Thomas Hughes had sailed from Southampton so the bottle had bumped along the sea floor, carried along by the tides and currents for over a hundred miles to reach the Estuary,' explained Steve. 'It had got to the stage where one edge was really thin and it would not have been long before it would have broken.' Even then, it was lucky not to be smashed, for, as the fishing net opened, it was almost certainly cushioned by the catch tumbling to the deck.

Two years later, in 2001, Emily made her one and only trip back to Britain to meet relatives she had never known and to give the bottle to the Durham Light Infantry Museum for safekeeping.

If the picture of the train made George Musgrave's father come alive to him, the recovery of the bottle transformed Emily's feeling about her father. 'I was overwhelmed by the whole experience. All of a sudden my father was real to me rather than just my mother's memories.'

More than 350,000 children lost their fathers during the Great War, and the vast majority have themselves since died. George Musgrave is one of a rapidly diminishing band, all now at least in their early nineties, who were left to forge their lives not only without the guiding influence of a father but all too frequently in the teeth of unremitting and abject poverty. After 1918, the mood was to honour the dead but also to forget the war, to move on and be grateful to those whose noble sacrifice had guaranteed everyone else's life, liberty and freedom. Loss was so general, so communal, that survival was reward enough.

This book is about the families of those who did not come back from the war. It is an examination of how they fared during the conflict and in the immediate aftermath of peace, primarily through the eyes of the last survivors of that war – the children and the siblings of those who died. Of the generation above, the wives and parents, there are none left, although remarkably, at the time of writing, there is still one surviving fiancée of a soldier killed in action. Nevertheless, the thoughts and feelings of wives and parents are included, drawn from the few memoirs, diaries and letters left to posterity.

Yet this is far from just a book about life on the home front. The experiences of families at home are set firmly within the context of the war overseas. The soldiers' optimism and excitement, coupled with the trepidation they felt when they went off to war, the fear and anxiety they experienced at returning to action after a spell of leave – such emotions were as widespread as they were harrowing. Through their own letters and diaries it is possible to get a sense of the concerns they felt for their loved ones back home as they undertook the daily chores of soldiering.

The expansion of the British Army was a colossal undertaking. In 1914, there were fewer than 300,000 regulars but by late 1916 onwards, two million men would be serving in France and Belgium at any one time.

Arms and ammunition were obviously needed, but there was also the supply of food for men and animals, water for both, fuel for the motorised vehicles, stores of clothes and equipment, materials for the trenches, wood for the duckboards, sandbags, medical facilities, sawmills, pumping stations, engineering works, billets, a postal service: the list appeared endless. Simply giving men ten days' leave on an annual basis was a major operation, with tens of thousands of soldiers being issued with passes and the need for a transport infrastructure to get them home and back again.

It was against this backdrop that the British Army had to deal with the administration of casualties. The wounded were taken off to hospital; the dead – where there was a body at all – went to the burgeoning cemeteries behind the line. Either way, information had to be gathered and relayed to families back home. With casualties during major operations running into many thousands per day, the paperwork was phenomenal. And for every notification of a casualty there was usually a reply, perhaps many replies, from distressed families hoping for news of loved ones in hospital or of husbands and sons simply missing in action.

On the battlefield, the dead had to be collected and buried. In the trenches, burial was often rudimentary, whereas behind the lines cemeteries were opened with increasingly strict rules governing the location of new burial grounds and the manner of interment. Personal effects had to be removed and returned to families back home, final statements of accounts prepared.

More than at any other time in modern history, the access to clear and accurate information was supremely difficult. It was a problem that beset each offensive, when those who decided the order of battle, who made the deployments and the battle strategy, were effectively blind once the operation was under way. Long gone were the days when men like Wellington could with their own eyes review a battle practically in its entirety. Yet advances in communications were still haphazard: wireless communication was in its infancy, telephone lines too easily cut, so that a critical message had to be brought by runner, dog or pigeon through shellfire and quagmire. The fog of war confused, misdirected and concealed vital information, and so it was with the collection and dissemination of news about loved ones missing or believed killed. 'I had a suspicion,' wrote one officer in the front line, 'that many of the dead who lay unburied for so long were not reported dead – but simply as "missing".' His suspicions were right. An examination of officers' papers confirms that the unknown whereabouts of many sons and husbands was the cause of protracted searching, too often in vain.

The administrative responsibility by which news was dispersed to anxious families back home will feature strongly in this book: how eyewitness accounts were sought from survivors in order to piece together what had happened. In conjunction with this, I will explore how the dead were treated on the battlefield by both comrades and enemy, and how personal effects were sent home.

The losses of the Great War and the casualties suffered in each offensive still cause much heated debate among historians and the wider public alike, and a culture of blaming the most senior officers is still ingrained in the British psyche. My intention is neither to condemn nor to exonerate anyone, but to shine a little light into the well of anxieties and fears that are inevitable when a nation is at war. During this conflict, every class of society was represented in the front line and all suffered to a greater or lesser extent.

In Britain we remember each year those who died in war and recall their sacrifice. The act of remembrance is a way for us to acknowledge the lessons of history, and, by learning, we pay the dead the best tribute of all. Nevertheless, the veterans themselves warned against fixation with the dead. Old soldiers such as John McCauley spoke for many when he said, 'In honouring the dead, forget not the living. Remember us, but remember too, those who survived,' while Harry Patch was more direct: 'We say on Remembrance Day, "They shall grow not old, age shall not weary them . . ." All right, remember the dead, but I also remember the people left behind, mourning.' This book is dedicated to those who mourned, such as Joyce Crow and Lily Baron. Joyce died two months short of her hundredth birthday in 2008, a lifetime longer than her sibling, Arthur Sherington, killed on the Somme in

1916. Joyce always thought of Arthur and celebrated his short life through her vivid recollections.

Like Joyce, Lily Baron remembered her loved one, this time her dad, killed at Bourlon Wood in November 1917. Lily, born in 1912, had distinct memories of him and his last leave at home, and in the summer of 2010, just short of her ninety-eighth birthday, she visited France and entered the wood at the point where he died to lay a wreath and say a prayer. Her wreath was adorned, appropriately, with lilies and a card on which she had written 'Thank you for five years of real happiness – I've missed you all my life.' Lily died in December 2010.

Donald Overall, now aged ninety-eight, went to France in September 2007, to the south of Arras where his father was buried in June 1917. As flight engineer in a Halifax bomber, Donald had flown over northern France on many occasions during 1944 and 1945. He had stared down into the night's inky blackness and thought of his father 'down there', and the promise he made himself one day to visit. At the grave of his father, he recalled with emotion:

> I'm an old man, I am supposed to be tough, I thought I was hard, but I'm not. He's my dad. I miss him. I missed him as a boy and I miss him as an old man. It is very important that I have come back, can you understand? I feel closer now than I have ever been. That time he carried me to bed was the last time and this is the next time, ninety years. I don't know how much longer I will live but I will never forget him. I would have come here, I wouldn't have cared if it was snowing, because it meant something.

George Musgrave is younger, with no such recollections, only the picture of a train. He has spent a lifetime honouring his father, but he remembers, too, how much his mother struggled to keep the family together. There is no memorial for her or any monument to recognise her dedicated work, nor those like her. And nothing either for Joyce, Lily, Donald or George or all the other children whose formative years were forged by war and whose lives have been altered through loss, and rarely for the better. Though these four children had different lives – family circumstances and, most pointedly, income dictated that – all four were typical of their peer group, for as children all four never quite believed their loved ones were dead and thought that they might yet walk through the door again one day.

Children were both passively and actively participant in that war, and their stories are just as valid when it comes to the history of the conflict as anyone else's. While writing this book, I have been astonished and moved not just by the variety and intensity of some of their stories but by the depth of emotion that the Great War still stirs in them. For this reason, at the start of each chapter I have included an inscription dedicated – and originally paid for – by the families of the dead. Such dedications appear at the foot of perhaps half of all Commonwealth War Graves' headstones and I have selected a number that express something of the loss these families suffered.

The war hugely influenced the lives of the children of Britain, for good or ill, and it continues to do so for those few thousands of our citizens who can still recall that time. And in the sense that its influence must cascade down the generations, then we, too, are children of that war for, at least in part, it has made us what we are today.

Richard van Emden, June 2011

I

A Call to Arms

'We kissed his cheek
We little thought
It was our last goodbye'

55342 Private Edward Fellows
14th Royal Welsh Fusiliers
Died of wounds 27 August 1918, aged thirty-one
Buried Puchevillers British Cemetery

'I wish you could have known my son as he was to me, I wish all fathers could know their sons as I knew John,' wrote Sir Harry Lauder, the music-hall entertainer, of Captain John Lauder, killed in 1916.

The doting pride Sir Harry and his wife, Ann, had for their son was almost tangible. 'Have I told you how my boy looked?' he implored readers in his memoirs, *A Minstrel in France*, published two years after his son's death.

He was slender, but he was strong and wiry. He was about five feet five inches tall; he topped his Dad by a hand-span. And he was the neatest boy you might ever have hoped to see. Aye – but he did not inherit that from me! Indeed, he used to reproach me, often-times, for being careless about my clothes . . . When he was a wee boy, and would come in from play with a dirty face; how his mother would order him to wash; and how he would painstakingly mop off just enough of his features to leave a dark ring abaft his cheeks, and above his eyes, and below his chin . . . I linger long, and I linger lovingly over these small details, because they are a part of my daily thoughts.

Four years earlier, John had stepped off the boat in Melbourne, Australia, to be greeted by his parents. It was July 1914 and John, a territorial officer, had been granted permission to miss that summer's annual training to travel abroad. His father had been touring since the end of March, performing to packed audiences in Sydney and other towns and cities, cementing his reputation as an artist of world-class renown.

While overseas, Sir Harry had been aware of the shooting in Sarajevo of Franz Ferdinand, the Archduke and heir to the Austro-Hungarian throne; both he and Ann had felt sorry, sorry in particular for the Archduke's wife, Sophie, who was also killed by an assassin's bullet. 'And then we forgot it. All Australia did,' he wrote.

It had been months since he had seen his son and there was plenty to talk about, not least the success of the tour. 'Maybe we did not read the papers so carefully as we might have done,' he admitted, for the diplomatic fallout from the assassination was leading rapidly towards a European conflagration. The killings by a Serbian nationalist had enormous, wider regional significance: secret treaties and alliances guaranteeing one country's support for another in the event of war were holding firm. Germany was going to back Austria in its dispute with Serbia; Serbia called for and received support from its traditional ally, Russia. Russia was in alliance with France, and Britain had an 'understanding' with France: the ramifications for Sir Harry's son had not yet encroached on his father's consciousness, though they were about to.

Arthur Sherington was a very talented artist. Although he had never been to Australia, he worked in the graphics department of the office of the Agent General for Western Australia in London. He had been brought up in England but born abroad, in

Georgetown, British Guyana, the home of his mother, Letitia. His father, Offord Sherington, was a journalist and editor of Georgetown's *Daily Chronicle*. However, in early 1892 he had returned home with his wife and young son to try to establish himself as an editor in London. The family settled in Hornsey where, in years to come, he and Letitia were to have six further children including Joyce, the youngest, born in 1909.

'We all knew that Arthur was my mother's favourite child,' acknowledged Joyce,

> and we were pleased about it too because he was a lovely chap; good looking, charming, great fun, such a nice disposition, and always ready to play with his younger siblings, like me. We all looked up to him for he was a very fine artist, particularly in pencil.
>
> The time I remember him most was Saturday teatime. We lived in a house with big square rooms and a great big kitchen with a large table and I remember all my brothers and sisters coming in with muddy football boots and netball bags and we all sat round and had tea together and then we played silly family games such as tapping out the rhythms of different tunes. Arthur's favourite was 'The Cornish Floral Dance'.
>
> In the winter, on Sundays, we used to pull the curtains and Arthur would tell a story. 'When we lived in Warwickshire . . .' he always began. It was years before I realised Warwickshire was a real place. Each story was beautifully complete in itself, perfectly ordinary happenings about perfectly ordinary people, but somehow these stories had an importance to us even though we knew he made them all up.

By August 1914, twenty-three-year-old Arthur had become the main breadwinner in the house. His father had been working for Chappell, the music publishers, but serious ill health had almost crippled him, leaving the family in a difficult financial position. For this reason Arthur resisted any temptation to enlist, at least for the time being.

The Peels, like the Sheringtons, lived in London, struggling financially, too, but that was about all they had in common. Esther's father was a drinker and part-time poacher, prone to sudden mood swings and frequent violence.

Dad used to say he'd rather go poaching than work and so when he felt like it he'd take me to a place called Three Hills. 'You sit down and make a daisy chain,' he would tell me before disappearing off, always coming back with something, very often it was a lamb, sometimes a rabbit. He had a poacher's jacket on, the pocket of which went all the way around and when he got something hidden in there we'd go to one of the back streets where a mate of his lived, to skin whatever he'd got and burn the evidence.

Any money Dad had was spent down the pub. He was a boozer, and my mother used to say, 'Go and ask your dad to come home,' and I used to go to the pub, sit on the step and the men used to say, 'Hello, nipper, are you waiting for your dad?' and I'd say, 'Tell him to come, his dinner's ready,' but of course he would only come when he was ready. Once Mother threw his dinner on the garden because he was so late, and I remember Dad beating our cottage's pebble-dashed wall with his fist. Blood was all pouring down his fingers but he was so drunk I don't think he could feel the pain. I know I was there trying to stop him and at the finish he'd go in and probably gave my mother a thump in the face, knock her out of the way and go to bed. Another time Dad was sitting on the sofa and I was sitting on his lap. Dad had been to the pub and Mum was frying some food, then something happened, something was said, and he pushed me off his lap and went up to my mother and punched her straight in the face. They were always rowing. Home life only improved when Dad had gone in the army. When he was leaving I said to him, 'What are you going away for?' and he said, 'Well, I've got to go and kill those Germans and when we've killed them all I'm coming back.' I am not sure Mum was that pleased at the prospect.

In time the British Army would find all three of these men in its ranks, three of a truly motley collection of recruits, men who would never have been drawn to the services were it not for war and the desperate need for vast numbers of civilian recruits.

The popular memory of the great patriotic rush to the colours that long summer of 1914 has tended to obscure one inescapable and unpalatable truth: no matter in which direction anyone cared to look, the headlong charge to enlist Britain's young men into the services created a vast and as yet untrained army and with it a social, military and administrative mess of epic proportions.

Hours after the outbreak of hostilities, the newly appointed Secretary of State for War, Lord Kitchener, appealed for the formation of a New Army made up of civilian volunteers. His call to arms was a remarkable and unparalleled success and therein lay the problem. He knew that to embark on conflict with Germany the small regular British Army would need to expand, and rapidly. Instead of the 100,000 volunteers he asked for (he knew he would need one million over time), the public response was so emphatic that the army was swamped by a tidal wave of eager recruits, 750,000 in the first two months of the war, nearly 1.2 million by the end of the year. The Regular Army's pre-war annual recruitment was around 30,000 men; 33,000 enlisted on one day alone, 3 September, so what on earth was it to do with twenty-five times that number almost simultaneously beating a path to its door? It was a severe headache from which it took the army months to recover. Who was going to train these troops? How were they going to be equipped? Where on earth would they be housed? Who would feed and pay them?

In peacetime, the public's view of the army was generally negative: most people did not want their sons to serve alongside those they saw as little more than 'thieves and vagabonds'. The army had always attracted its share of down-and-outs, the hungry, men temporarily down on their luck. It also attracted Barnardo boys looking for a home, deserters wishing to return to the fold, and of course it appealed to boys who had always wanted to soldier. But now it had men and boys drawn en masse from every echelon of society, including civilians who held down full-time jobs in the very industries that would be required to crank up their output if Britain were to fight an international war. They came from coal mining (115,000 miners enlisted in the first month of war) and agriculture, industries concerned with the extraction of iron ore and lead, and businesses rooted in manufacturing, such as textiles and carpentry.

'It is impracticable even for an angel from Heaven to meet all the wants of these new and vast forces with the desirable rapidity,' wrote The Times military correspondent in November 1914. To give some idea of the challenge facing the services, it is worth noting that, as reported in The Times on 7 November, the peacetime army annually ordered 245,000 pairs of boots, 250,000 service dress jackets and 43,000 greatcoats. In the autumn of 1914 it placed an order for 6.5 million boots, 1.5 million greatcoats, 5.25 million service dress jackets, not to mention 11 million shirts, 5 million pairs of trousers and 4.5 million pairs of puttees, as well as cardigans, towels, caps, pants and socks. It was anticipated that another round of orders would be necessary after just six months. Such were the immediate shortages that entrepreneurs entered the fray. One middleman who had obtained 5,000 jerseys for 3/11d. (three shillings and eleven pence – the equivalent value of about £8.50 today) offered them to the War Office for 4/5d. The War Office refused, so the man sold them to a Territorial Association, which could contract locally for clothes, for 6/11d, turning in today's money a quick £32,000 profit. Such speculation only tempted others to hold on to their surplus stock in the hope of higher prices, exacerbating the situation further.

For every army recruit crammed into a hastily erected bell tent, there was an additional administrative nightmare being played out in offices all over the country and none was greater than the provision of Separation Allowances to wives and their children.

Six weeks after the outbreak of war, the Prime Minister, Herbert Asquith, announced (*The Times*, 18 September 1914) that Separation Allowances would be increased. As from 1 October, a wife would be guaranteed to receive a minimum 12/6d. a week. (twelve shillings and sixpence – the equivalent of about £27 today), up from 11/1d., including a maximum allotment of 3/6d. from her husband's army pay. A wife with one child would be guaranteed 15/- (fifteen shillings) as opposed to the previous 12/10d., and every additional child would benefit from a further 2/6d. (£5.40 today).

When the allowances were announced, one wife with three children was reported to have said: 'It seems too good to be true, a pound a week and my husband away.' This might have seemed a lot of money to one whose husband had rigidly controlled the purse strings, but allowances were not intended to cover more than half a family's expenditure and she might have come to regret her exuberance when she was subsequently forced out to work.

The rapid expansion of the army led to severe payment problems to servicemen's families. To be fair, the army pay offices did everything they could to alleviate the difficulties. They rapidly recruited staff, growing from their peacetime establishment of 300 employees to nearly 3,000 by mid-October. However, new staff would not reach the required levels of efficiency without training, and training took time and resources.

Personal records for those serving in the Regular and Territorial armies had been completed in peacetime, making payments relatively easy to administer, but the wives of men serving on the Army Reserve (former regular soldiers recalled from civilian life) were greatly disadvantaged. Many had married after their husbands had been placed on the Reserve and the army had no paperwork on the altered circumstances. Press advertisements were taken out instructing these wives how to claim their allowances but, according to the army, many wives in their ignorance sent in marriage and birth certificates without including any clue as to the regimental identity of the husband. In Kitchener's New Army, details of marriage were taken on attestation and information forwarded for verification and payment, but the sheer numbers involved ensured this all took time. Newspapers claimed that some wives had not received a penny in six or even eight weeks, and there were accusations in the press that women had been forced to pawn household goods to eke out what little money they had.

Reservist Nelson Newman had served in the Royal Fusiliers between 1901 and 1909 before marrying Edith Cocking in the summer of 1910. Aged thirty, and after five years in civilian life, he had dutifully returned to his regiment on news of war, being given the rank of lance corporal and serving with the 6th (Reserve) Battalion, Royal Fusiliers, soon joining the 4th Battalion in France. After returning to the regimental depot, he wrote regularly to Edith and his children. His letters in the weeks before he embarked for overseas service on 21 September 1914 refer constantly to the problem of allowances and pay in the British Army:

Well Ede, don't forget that if there is anything going from the different distress funds that they are setting up, put your name down as you are as entitled to some as anyone else . . .

I am not sending you any money as they only gave me four shillings. I know you will think this is a lie dear but as true as I am sitting writing this, it is the truth. In fact god, you will soon have to send me some as I tell you, if things go on like this I am going to pack up and come home . . .

I am glad to hear you got some out of that distress fund, that is right girl, get as much as you can and don't forget to play the fund up as we are earning all you get here, I give you my word . . .

Whatever you do dear, as I said, don't go short of food [even] if
you have to get rid of half of our stuff as I hope to have a bit
enough to get another lot if I come back which I hope I do.

Lance Corporal Nelson Newman was killed on 26 October
1914.

There was one further and unexpected complication to the
payments system. The army and, indeed, the government were
surprised to discover just how many claimants were not in fact
married but nevertheless had children. After brief political soul-
searching, these women were also paid where evidence of an
'established' home existed. This was not a sign of progressive poli-
tics at work; rather, it was clear to the government that if so many
people were living out of wedlock, only the guarantee of an allowance would facilitate their recruitment.

All in all, and with the benefit of hindsight, it was something
of a blessing that at least some married men had read of the confusion and been put off enlisting in the forces until the government
sorted out the issue of Separation Allowances and recruits'
accommodation.

In Australia, the only allowances that concerned John Lauder
were those associated with luggage. He had barely set foot in
Melbourne when, on 4 August, Sir Harry's birthday, a bluntly
worded cable arrived: 'Mobilise. Return'.

John's eyes were bright. They were shining. He was looking at us,
but he was not seeing us. Those eyes of his were seeing distant
things. My heart was sore within me, but I was proud and happy
that it was such a son I had to give my country.

John Lauder immediately set about returning to Britain. He
took a train to Adelaide where he could pick up a steamer bound
for Britain; his parents would also catch a steamer, but in this case
for New Zealand. They would not meet again until January when

the then newly promoted Lieutenant Lauder was training in Bedford.

It would still be several weeks before John Lauder could get home. By the time he reached Britain, not only had the Regular Army been heavily engaged against the numerically superior might of the German army at Mons, it had been forced into an exhausting retreat almost to the gates of Paris. In the event, the army marched to the south-east across the rivers of the Aisne and the Marne where, in early September, and with the aid of the French, it had managed to throw the Germans back. Stalemate followed, ushering in trench warfare. Soon after, the Territorials began to arrive to support – no one would say prop up – the depleted ranks of the Regular Army, and these part-time soldiers would continue to stream across the Channel, though it would be several months before John Lauder's battalion, the 8th Argyll and Sutherland Highlanders, was ordered overseas.

News of the Regular Army's heroic retreat from Mons inspired a second great wave of enlistment so that the New Army became New Armies numbered K1, K2 and K3. In September 1914, the urgent call for men was played out at recruitment rallies everywhere, though it would be the best part of a year before the first of the New Army battalions was ready for overseas service. Many of these units were formed of men local to one town or another and became popularly known as Pals Battalions, groups of like-minded men who worked together, played sports together, went to the same church and who chose to enlist together. No longer was the army pulling in only the poor and hungry, but men eager to serve, to see something of the world and to escape the drudgery of their lives in foundries, fields and mills. The brother of seven-year-old Len Whitehead was one of the first to go.

Everybody was terribly excited, and there was nobody more excited than my elder brother George. He was going, he said, 'first thing tomorrow morning'. Dad didn't want him to enlist, he tried to persuade him against going so soon – stop to see the harvest in. But George was keen to go and here was his chance, and he went into my mother's bedroom – she was not very well at the time – and he picked up a stick which she used to rap on the floor if she wanted anything. 'This is how I shall strut about the London parks,' he said, jokingly of course. It was the glamour of it all, nobody gave it a second thought that they might never come back.

The next day we watched him set out with a parcel tucked under his arm, with his towel and shaving gear. He went up the farm chase, which was about half a mile long, and he was gone to the nearest village railway station at Rayne. The village was so empty, it seemed so, you see there were so many young men although they didn't all go together, they went in sort of dribs and drabs – they would meet perhaps in an evening – there was a reading room, a place where they would meet and say, 'Right, we're off,' perhaps five or six of them. 'Meet at the village pump tomorrow morning and we'll go,' and they did of course. We were very proud to say he'd gone. 'You know my brother, he's in the 9th Battalion of the Essex Regiment,' you see. Other children had got people in more glamorous regiments but we didn't care, we'd got a brother soldiering.

Among those who joined up were tens of thousands of lads aged seventeen, many sixteen, and some younger still, all well under the stipulated age of nineteen. These boys were some of the first to go. Single and with few if any responsibilities, they became caught up in the adventure of the occasion, and the promise of a life less repetitious. Other lads wished to escape difficult family lives. Whatever the reasons, they were enlisted by recruiting sergeants, who were paid for every recruit and were often happy to wave through a fit and enthusiastic volunteer. For the most part these lads did not suffer the physical ailments that afflicted many men who worked long hours in heavy industry, while parents, too, were willing to let sons go in the mistaken belief that the war would not last very long – it might end before Christmas – and no boys would be fully trained within a year.

Edwin Maindonald lied about his age to enlist when he was just seventeen. A clerk from Vauxhall in south London, he was the elder brother of Mabel, known to everyone as Madge. She doted on him but their mother died in March 1915 and the family home changed for the worse. Edwin decided he would escape and enlist at Chelsea Town Hall.

Before Mum died we were a happy family. I was always well dressed because my mother used to make my clothes and we had enough money to be comfortable. My father brought his wages home, which a lot of men didn't. I was always nice and clean; we had good meals, and every year we used to go to Guernsey for a holiday to see my grandmother.

Mum's death ruined everything because people don't realise how much the woman runs the house. Dad was so pent up, he was terribly upset, they were very happy together and when she died the house became a house of misery. I think my brother couldn't stand it, really, and two months later he ran away to war. He altered his birth certificate – which my family had a habit of doing – and he went. I was upset. He was one of the gang and I didn't want him to go in the army but what had I got to say about it, nothing.

For married men, doing their duty to their country did not always sit well with their loved ones, some of whom saw enlistment not as a patriotic and welcome act but rather as a dereliction of duty – to their families. That was certainly the feeling among members of Mary Morton's family, although family disputes hardly helped matters. Growing up, Mary had always felt a certain tension between her father and his mother-in-law, known to Mary as Granny Stirrat, an austere and dour lady.

Daddy only visited the Stirrats for Mama's sake, she felt it was their duty. The Stirrats did not seem to like Daddy either. Among the family wedding photographs arranged on the high mantelpiece, we noticed Daddy's was kept behind the others, though Mama was the prettiest bride of them all, in a large hat, a tiny-waisted dress with many frills all round the hem. They thought their youngest and prettiest daughter had thrown away her chances of a better marriage; he was not what they wanted for her at all, and said they were not surprised when he joined up, just to avoid his responsibilities.

The glamour of the uniform, and the dullness of his job and married life all conspired to send him post-haste to the recruiting office. The Stirrats were appalled. Mary, my mother, was expecting his third child. They called him a 'bounder'.

A powerful sense of duty was ingrained in lads who enlisted. Even if they were not inclined to accept all the lurid stories of German atrocities that gained currency across Britain, they still believed in the nation's just cause to stand up to aggression and to uphold the rule of international law. If they had any sympathy with this, then they would not stand back and watch from the sidelines. Letitia Sherington would later recall how her son Arthur made up his mind to go.

He had no illusions of glory to sustain him. What he said was: 'I don't think it's any less wrong or futile, but I can't sit at home knowing that every mouthful of food I eat is brought to me because another man is willing to die.'

It was honour, too, that drove Peter Miller to the recruiting station. Peter, a committed Christian and son of a prominent London Methodist preacher, had grown up and adopted the family tradition of pacifism; that remained his position for a while, but suddenly one day that stance changed, according to Emily, his elder sister.

Shortly after the war broke out, we sat in the house discussing the matter, as my brother was wondering whether he, in fact, ought to volunteer. We were talking, whether it would be right or wrong to join, to go and kill people, and of course we said no, it was wrong. 'Thou shalt not kill.' We were in mid-discussion when my brother suddenly stood up and said, 'You know, Mother, supposing people were to come into this room,' and he pointed, 'come in that door and attack you and Emily.' He said, 'I've got to go, the Germans are coming here, we all know the stories they are telling. I've got to protect you from them. I'm not a conscientious objector; I'm here as a defender and I've a right to defend you.' That was my brother's attitude. We didn't want to go and fight anybody, we wanted to live in peace. However, we weren't allowed to because of Germany, it wasn't our fault.

Arthur and Peter may have felt the moral imperative of enlisting, but George Whitehead was never in any doubt and he was already involved. His battalion might not have been the most glamorous in the British Army but it was not short of volunteers ready to fill its ranks. The 9th Battalion, a New Army battalion, reached establishment so rapidly that a 10th and then an 11th were formed within weeks. It quickly became apparent that the earlier a New Army battalion was formed, the more likely it was to get hold of any pre-existing resources and to receive any new kit as suppliers fulfilled their government contracts. George Whitehead's prompt action in joining the 9th meant he was better off than those village lads who waited, if only a week or two, and ended up in the 10th, for this battalion was in a state of near rebellion.

Nothing was happening in the 10th Essex, and therein lay the problem. The men were so hungry and fed up with sitting around that they approached one of the few officers to demand some changes. He was in the orderly room, a bell tent, and so sick and tired was he with telling the men that all that could be done was being done that in the end he simply rolled up his sleeves and offered to fight all-comers if that's what it took to win them round.

'The grievances, indeed, were legitimate,' wrote the officer:

These ardent patriots had poured into recruiting stations in numbers which upset all calculations. Trains were plentiful enough, and the sole object of the overworked recruiting staffs was to get the eager thousands somewhere outside London – it mattered little where. And so a mixed and muddled mass of humanity found itself on the downs of Shorncliffe provided with numberless bell tents but with no other assets than the garments in which they stood.

The experience of the 10th Essex was replicated time and again in Kitchener's New Armies and from one end of the country to the other. 'No one knows exactly how order was eventually evolved out of chaos,' he continued, 'or comprehends the miracle of organization which was performed by a microscopic handful of regular officers and NCOs.'

These regular NCOs were raised from whatever rank they were to company sergeant major on the spot, while any civilian with even the scantiest military knowledge was elevated among his peers. 'A straw hat or a bowler determined the choice of Lance Corporal,' wrote the officer, 'while a really clean white collar in addition to a decent hat was the sure passport to the rank of Corporal.'

The brand new officers knew little about warfare either, although they at least were dressed in khaki, having paid for their own kit. They often learned the art of soldiering from the manuals that were sold in bookshops, and they relied heavily on those CSMs who could point them in the right direction. Such officers, armed only with apparent self-confidence, grew into the job and would, over the next few months, mould something akin to a football crowd into a decent battalion.

After weeks at sea John Lauder had rejoined his territorial unit and was training with his men in Bedford when his father and mother returned from their tour of Australia and New Zealand. At the first opportunity they travelled to see their son who, they found, had unexpectedly matured.

> There were curious changes in the laddie I remembered. He was bigger, I thought, and he looked older and graver. He had a great responsibility. The lives of other men had been entrusted to him, and John was not the man to take a responsibility like that lightly.
>
> I saw him the first day I was at Bedford, leading some of his men in a practice charge. Big, braw laddies they were – all in their kilts. He ran ahead of them, smiling as he saw me watching them, but turning back to cheer them on if he thought they were not fast enough. I could see as I watched him that he had caught the habit of command. He was going to be a good officer.

A good officer would help recruits who were not natural-born soldiers to enjoy army life, men like Private Peter Miller and Private Arthur Sherington. Through their letters, their families glimpsed their development from civilian to soldier, from inefficiency to efficiency, and felt, too, the inexorable approach of the day when their boys would have to go overseas, as extracts from their letters testified:

Private Peter Miller, 2/8th Essex Regiment
This morning our company had some physical drill. One of the exercises was a tug of war, with a rope about as thick as a telegraph pole. Talking about telegraphs, I have found that if one asks the local newsboy for a *Daily Telegraph*, one's superiority over half-penny readers [the tabloids] is acknowledged by 'Sir!' The D.T. seems to have ousted all other penny newspapers at the camp.

Private Arthur Sherington, 3/5th London Regiment (London Rifle Brigade)

Since I have been down here, I have done all kinds of fatigues from unloading coal wagons to cookhouse, which is chiefly cleaning out greasy dixies. This is far better than doing drill on the Square day after day. I think they like to vary the monotony by a few fatigues sprinkled here and there.

By the way, I tried to get measles the other day as there is five days' leave attached to it, but it didn't come off.

Private Peter Miller

I and two others went to Walton on the Naze to have our blankets fumigated at the hospital. All the blankets for the Company went in motor transports, so we had a pleasant ride. The blankets were put in a huge oven and literally baked by steam for three quarters of an hour to kill all germs and in fact make them generally better to sleep on. We had lunch at a restaurant and a bath in the hospital.

Private Arthur Sherington

I make my third epistle to the family at large. Would you mind sending down my football knickers together with a pair or two of pants if such be reasonable and also if you can spare it, another towel and last but not least those two thin cotton vests.

I have made arrangements for my washing to be done in the village, but this has to be kept quite quiet as we are not supposed to send it there on account of the various diseases to which the said villagers are subject.

Private Peter Miller

Yesterday afternoon a few of us were watching a sergeant playing with a machine gun, when an officer rushed up and said that the British had broken through 20 miles of front. Later, the evening paper reported 20 miles; now this morning the distance has come down to 16 miles. Perhaps tomorrow it will have dropped still lower(!) Still if any progress is made it is better than standing still; and the end of the war may come in our time.

The 'France' rumour, which obtained much credence a fortnight ago, has subsided, some people are trying to start an 'India' rumour.

Private Arthur Sherington

We get up horribly early in the morning and spend our time chiefly cleaning Government property such as equipment, not forgetting the gas pipe – known to civilians as the soldier's best friend – or rifle . . . We also do 'night-ops' twice a week which sounds exciting but isn't. That is about all – you see it goes on day after day and I get very fed up with it anyhow. This is very unexciting – but quite healthy – so that I can place my hand over my heart and say that I am quite brown and quite fit.

Private Peter Miller

I hope you do not get many disturbing dreams about me. I assure you I am perfectly well. It is said we are to have a series of manoeuvres next month lasting quite a long time, after which we may or may not go to the front. The officer I was with on Wednesday said he would not be surprised if we were still in khaki two years from now.

Private Arthur Sherington

Although it seems years since I saw you last – in reality only a week has passed. Nothing has happened except that all my pals or nearly all will be off to France on Wednesday. As far as I know we shall finish our firing by next week and shall get our four days' leave soon after so I hope to be up again fairly soon . . . Don't think there is anything further to report except that the grub is steadily going from bad to worse.

Private Peter Miller

We have not gone yet. But it may be any day – even any hour – that we shall move . . . I am going into the danger zone, trusting in God; so I am not afraid. All the same, the possibility of getting killed is there, and you will understand how I feel. Thank you for your expressions of comfort. There is no need for you to worry, for I am sure it is a matter of destiny.

Private Arthur Sherington

A large draft went off today and we are now in the next batch . . . As far as I know we shall probably go at the end of this week or early next. Anyhow I will let you know of course. Of the boys very few indeed are left and so I shan't be so very sorry when we pack up.

Private Peter Miller

We are going tomorrow. Where or how we do not know. It is thought we shall go straight to France.

2 August 1916

Reverend Peter Miller (father)

Had a P.C. from Peter – from Folkestone – he left for France on Monday – 31st July – may God keep him, and bring him back safely.

*   *   *

Few soldiers, if any, could have accepted the prospect of going to war without some hesitation and deep-seated anxiety. Just how a man felt depended on many variables: whether he had been out before, whether he was a reluctant or keen soldier, and, perhaps more than anything, whether he was married with children. Private Stephen Graham, serving with the Scots Guards, watched one middle-aged private, having been warned for overseas duty, sending a telegram to his wife to come down to see him. She left the children at a neighbour's house and went straight away to say goodbye. After she had left, Graham observed as the man grimly and quietly disposed of his spare kit, 'making his will and doing all those final things that precede the going to the Front'.

The following day the man was told he would not be leaving with the draft after all and his reaction to the news is interesting as a photographic negative of his previous emotions.

> Joy curiously suffused and transfigured his usually inexpressive countenance, and a generous flow of life-blood rushed through his veins. He wired his wife again. The unopened parcel which she had brought him the day before he now opened, and distributed among us shortbread and home-baked scones. He was not one who gave away things as a rule. But now a light-heartedness seemed to possess him and smiles flickered across his face.

One man who was set to go with the draft was Sergeant Five. After an evening out he had come back into barracks in a conversational mood and, recalls Graham, 'sat by the embers of the fire talking to himself for hours about his wife and little ones: "I believe in God and all that; I'm not afraid to die," said he, "but the question I ask is, if I die, what are they going to do? What will the army do for *them*? Why, nothing, of course. That's just it. There are too many widows and orphans."'

If soldiers were fortunate, they might receive a few days' embarkation leave, but this was a privilege not a right. Neither the Sheringtons nor the Millers saw their boys before they went abroad. Either way it was typical of the men who were going overseas to sprint off a few lines to reassure their families that all was well. On 10 July 1915 Private Hugh Smith wrote to his mother, Sarah, that he was all right, before adding every reassurance he could think of. In his letter he was right about leaving soon – he landed in France four days later – but everything else he jotted down as a comfort to her was spectacularly wide of the truth.

Don't fret yourself about what I am going to tell you but I think we shall be going away before long. It's a question whether we shall get any farther than the base and even if we do it won't be for long [wrong]. It has come from good authority that the Germans are just about done up [wrong] and I see according to this morning's papers that they have been knocked out all together in Africa [wrong], and now the Turks have turned on them [wrong]. I reckon another week or two will see the finish [wrong]. Well, whenever we go we shall go in good spirits. Our chaps are quite excited at the thought of it and you know if we only land on the French coast we shall get a medal [right].

Private Hugh Smith was killed fifteen months later.

Soldiers' thoughts are well documented. Rarely recorded is the experience from the other side: the feelings of those who had to part with their husband or son, those made utterly powerless to influence events. One of the few to leave such a record was Marie Leighton, the mother of Lieutenant Roland Leighton, an officer in the Worcestershire Regiment, to be immortalised after the war in the memoirs of his fiancée, Vera Brittain. In great detail, she recalled in her book, *Boy of My Heart*, the first time the son she had given the childhood nickname Little Yeogh Wough left home for France.

Marie remembered how that day in early April 1915 she had watched as Roland finished his packing before both of them stopped for tea. Roland would have to leave in ten minutes.

He spoke quite bravely and with an attempt at his usual gaiety, but it was easy to see that there was something not quite right about him. Eagerly though he had striven to go, he yet was not going without a pang. But it was not the coward's pang – Heaven be thanked! There was nothing of fear in it.

Downstairs in the kitchen department of the house there was a great and unwonted silence that made itself felt even in our rooms.

The servants knew and were sorry. One of them had known him for eight years, another for four and yet another for two; and their unnatural silence and stillness had a meaning which struck a chill to my heart.

Then, the ten minutes being over, he got up and kissed us good-bye all round. A curious look came on his face as he saw the tears in his father's eyes brim over. He went out very suddenly, walking a little blindly. He would have no one go to the station with him. For one thing, he was not going there immediately, and, secondly, he always hated being seen off by anyone that he loved.

Sir Edward Poulton had not been able to communicate what he really wanted to say to his son, Ronald Poulton Palmer, the preternaturally gifted England rugby captain and heir to the Huntley & Palmers biscuit business in Reading and, as it happened, a good friend of the Sutton family of Hillside.

'It was impossible to speak of the thoughts that were within us,' wrote Sir Edward. 'He knew how dearly he was loved; he knew the fears we felt. Speech was not needed to tell him this, and so he talked, as he had always done, of the things that had interested him in his work and he well knew would interest us.'

Sir Edward was devoted to his young officer son and it is noteworthy how Marie Leighton's childlike terms of endearment for Roland were not peculiar to her family but shared by others. The Victorian era is often characterised today as austere, even brutal, in its attitude towards children. While this is not entirely without foundation, it is certainly not to be taken as typical. Sir Edward, for one, was anything but patriarchal and unfeeling.

The signs and symbols of affection between parents and children were not abandoned as Ronald grew up. As it had been between my father and me, so it was between me and my sons. In neither generation could any point be recognized in which a love that grew with the passing years was willing to be denied its symbolic expression. The last time we kissed each other was in Piccadilly Circus where we said 'Good-bye', and I turned away with a heavy heart to return to Oxford, he to Chelmsford for the last few days in England. And not only in this but in other ways he was always the same to his parents. On any of his visits to Oxford from his work at Reading or Manchester or from his training at Chelmsford, he would warmly embrace us, always calling us by some endearing diminutive, literally most inappropriate to his father, but seeming to be all the sweeter on that account.

Sir Harry Lauder bade farewell to his son at Bedford, to where he and his wife had raced on receiving news that he was due to leave. John, Sir Harry believed, was keen to go, although he was sober with the knowledge of what he would face. The stories of German atrocities were believed by the Lauders, but his father thought that the shocking tales had also made John more determined.

We did not know whether we would ever see him again, the bonnie laddie! We had to bid him good-bye, lest it be our last chance. For in Britain we knew, by then, what were the chances they took, those boys of ours who went out.

'Good-bye, son – good luck!'

'Good-bye, Dad. See you when I get leave!'

That was all. We were not allowed to know more than that he was ordered to France.

Roland Leighton had passed out of his teens only days before he embarked for the Western Front, and, to Marie, watching her son go beyond all parental protection was excruciating. It must have felt like no time at all since her son was just a boy and the daily lengthening casualty lists in *The Times* of the killed and wounded were a constant reminder of the dangers men faced. Others who watched their sons leave spoke of a feeling of numbness or panic. Cynthia Asquith, married to Herbert 'Beb' Asquith, son of the Prime Minister, wrote of being 'curiously narcotized and unimaginative'; she could not believe her husband was going to France and that she was watching him leave. Teenager Florence Billington, girlfriend of Private Ted Felton, 'went all sort of haywire, hysterical,' she recalled. 'I had to do something, to get rid of the feeling of depression, so I went to a friend's house and we danced and danced, to try and get rid of the gloom.'

Florence had promised her boyfriend that they would get engaged when he came home. Before he embarked for the Western Front, Ted, a territorial in the King's Liverpool Regiment, had confided in Florence that he had the feeling he would not return. Florence knew nothing about war and all she could say to Ted was to look on the bright side, that there would be better days in store and she would wait for him.

> He was quite convinced he was going to be killed, that he knew in his heart he would not come back. I told him to shake off the depression by thinking of me, just think of the future, the future and us, and that as soon as the war was over we would make a life together, but he took some convincing. He wouldn't have felt it nearly as much if he'd gone before he met me, but I think meeting me made him wish that he didn't have to pay the sacrifice.

Ronald Poulton Palmer was just as sure about his fate, but remained calm. He said nothing about his feelings to anyone in his family, but he confided in a friend, William Temple. When they met in mid-March 1915, Ronald told him that he had already lost several good friends in France.

> Then he said, 'It makes a future life pretty essential, doesn't it?' I asked if he had any sort of doubt about it. 'No,' he said, 'because then life would be absurd.' We were silent for a long time.

Then he said, 'I don't want to be killed yet; there is such a lot I wanted to do, or try anyhow.' I asked if he felt that he would be killed. 'Oh yes,' he said, 'sure of it.' I said nothing and again there was a long silence. Then he suddenly said, 'Of course it's all right; but it's not what one would have chosen.'

Six weeks later Ronald was dead, the first officer in the battalion to die.

The soldiers entrained for France, converging on the Channel ports, normally Folkestone. Typically battalions were seen off in towns and city centres by waving crowds and bands playing stirring tunes: in 1915 Norman Cliff recalled passing over Waterloo Bridge with the band playing 'The British Grenadiers' as tearful relatives 'trotted alongside and occasionally a baby [was] held out for a father to kiss'. It did not matter too much at what stage of the war they left: there would be the usual shouts of 'Good luck, boys', 'Keep your heads down', 'Come back safe', as if the men had any choice in the matter; Cliff wondered just who did have return tickets.

'It was night when we passed through London and children and women came on to the verandahs of the slum tenements and cheered us,' recalled Private Reginald Kiernan, leaving England in March 1918:

Their cheers sounded shrill and faint over the noise of the train. Many were in nightclothes, and we could see them dimly, and their little rooms, by the light of their tiny gas jets.

In the yellow light in the carriages the men sprawled in all sorts of queer, curved positions. They lay against each other, asleep. Some were curled up on the floor, their heads on their new packs. They snored and slavered and broke wind. They were exhausted with singing and excitement. The racks were full of packs and brown, shining rifles, all oiled, straight from the armourer's store.

In the morning Kiernan found himself in Dover where he and the rest of his draft were marched down to the docks to board a ship. As they did so a woman approached them dressed in widow's black. 'Finish it off this time, boys,' was all she said.

Maybe it was better at this point not to have any emotional connection with civilians at all. Private Ernest Parker, drafted to France at the end of 1915, knew the men's families were waiting to wave them off at one London terminus but the draft had instead made its way through the city's tunnels and onwards to the coast, leaving the men 'bitterly disappointed, yet relieved of the ordeal of parting'.

Six days after Roland Leighton had said goodbye to Marie, the family received an early morning telegram sent by their son from Folkestone. 'Am crossing to-night' was all he had written. Marie's reaction was instantaneous.

> I buried my face in the pillow and sobbed and sobbed and sobbed. For it is in the beginning that the great Fear comes and grips and chills.
>
> 'Oh, Little Yeogh Wough!' I cried out in my heart. 'I have guarded you so much always – so much! – and now I can't guard you any more. Now already your glad young feet are marching over French ground, carrying you on – on – perhaps to your death.'

The soldiers had finally gone and it would be many months, perhaps more than a year, before they might be seen again. And so began, wrote Marie Leighton, a different life for those left behind, a life of what she called 'heart hunger'.

> We hungered to hear the boy's laugh, to hear the peculiar call he gave when he wanted his younger brother to help him with his dressing, or his half-mischievous, half-playfully tender inquiry of his father as to whether he could have the first supply of the hot bath water. We wandered about like lost souls until his first letter came.

'The war was in our house as it had never been before. I could think of nothing but my boy,' Sir Harry Lauder said of his son.

Every day some little incident comes up to remind me of my boy. A battered old hamper, in which I carry my different character make-ups, stands in my dressing room. It was John's favourite seat. Every time I look at it I have a vision of a tiny wide-eyed boy perched on the lid, watching me make ready for the stage. A lump rises, unbidden, in my throat . . .

The way Sir Harry and his wife Ann compensated for the distress of separation, and their fears for the future, was to remember these vignettes from John's childhood; these 'and a hundred other little incidents, were as fresh in my memory as if they had only occurred yesterday. His mother and I recalled them over and over again.'

It was only twenty miles to France but it might as well have been a world away. Disembarking soldiers were not normally sent straight up to the front line unless there was an emergency. Most spent a week or two at one of the transit camps dotted along the French coast. It gave the men ample time to tell their families that they were not in danger, not yet anyway. From the moment of departure there would be no official information as to how a loved one was faring, or where he was, unless he was killed or wounded.

Families were in the dark. An offensive might be under way but was he part of it? Newspapers reported successful engagements, advances capturing land and prisoners, but there was nothing about which regiment or division was involved. Families relied for information on their loved ones whose letters were in any case severely censored, although some soldiers devised codes or made certain literary allusions that would indicate where they were or what they might be about to do.

The first indication the Leightons received that Roland had reached the danger zone was one 'vivid sentence', recalled Marie.

'It has given me a thrill to-night to see the German flares go up like a truncated dawn,' he wrote.

No doubt there would have been certain characteristic turns of phrase in a soldier's letters, a particular expression or term of private affection that meant it was possible to 'hear' a loved one's voice as well as read his words. That closeness was rewarding, but as families were necessarily reliant on what their loved ones chose to tell them, there was a tendency to try to glean extra information by reading more into phrases or specific words than the writer had ever intended to suggest.

'He [Roland] says in his last letter "that he has learnt much and gained much and grown up suddenly and got to know the ways of the world",' wrote Marie.

This has made me curiously uneasy. I have a fear that it may cover up something – some experience that I should not have liked him to go through. And yet – while he can still sign himself Little Yeogh Wough, I know that he is not lost nor utterly spoiled. I know that in spite of the new life and its duties and horrors, there is even yet a good deal of the old life left in him. He is still the 'old Roland'.

John Lauder's letters were cheery. He told his parents as much as he could say without contravening the censor's rules. He described how, in early 1915, the Germans were still in the ascendancy, that their guns even now held sway on the battlefield, but the British guns were catching up. There was never a word of complaint but nonetheless Sir Harry was restless. 'I suppose it was because they [the letters] left out so much, because there was so great a part of my boy's life that was hidden from me.'

It was not just what was written in letters home that was so important in easing fears but how frequently they arrived. If anything, it was easier not to receive a letter on a regular basis as a lengthy silence was not then misinterpreted as something ominous.

'They [letters] came as if by a schedule,' wrote Sir Harry.

> We knew what post should bring one. And once or twice a letter was a post late and our hearts were in our throats with fear. And then came a day when there should have been a letter, and none came. The whole day passed. I tried to comfort John's mother! I tried to believe myself that it was no more than a mischance of the post. But it was not that. We could do nought but wait. Ah, but the folks at home in Britain know all too well those sinister breaks in the chains of letters from the front! Such a break may mean nothing or anything.

Letters home were full of appeals for some chocolate, a little money, perhaps some home-made cake; pleas for such titbits were reassuring because they were mundane and casual. These requests were fulfilled by families who were delighted that they could at least do *something* to help, anything to alleviate their loved one's discomfort in the trenches. Nevertheless, not every request was received with glad equanimity.

Traditionally, there has been a focus on how civilians could never appreciate the horror of combat, the misery of trench life, or the pain of injury. That was true, but equally the soldiers could not appreciate the plight of the civilian who, contrary to all natural instincts, could do no more to save their dear one from death or injury than they could fly to the moon. When Roland Leighton asked his mother to forward a small silver identification bracelet to France, did his request give him pause for thought? Why should it? As his mother wrote, 'On the face of it there is nothing very tragic about a flat bit of silver with a man's name and regiment engraved on it.' It was what it meant that made the request so painful.

> I knew what it stood for as I looked at it. It stood first and foremost for the fact that the boy who in himself was all earth and all heaven to me was in the army only one among many thousands – perhaps

among many hundreds of thousands. It stood for a fearful confusion in which masses of men might get inextricably mixed up so that none could know who this fellow was; and it stood for a field on which there were many dead lying, and for grim figures walking about among those dead and depending for their identifications on some token worn by the still shapes whose lips would speak no more. All this passed through my mind while I packed up the little disc and chain.

John Lauder and Roland Leighton were remembered through their associations with people who were then, or who became, more famous than themselves: Sir Harry Lauder and Vera Brittain. Yet fame or reputation was of no relevance here. In their capacity as officers, John and Roland served in the front line as did any other soldier in the army, and their families' private fears were as universal as they were heartfelt.

2

A Life Less Ordinary

'God alone knows
How I miss you dear one
As it dawns another year'

23531 Private David Hughes
6th Dorsetshire Regiment
Killed in action 24 August 1918, aged twenty-six
Buried Mill Road Cemetery

It was not healthy for a man to think too longingly about his home and family; there was no knowing where such thoughts might take him emotionally. Here and now, in a trench, was the reality that mattered, and here and now was where he would stay.

Out in the open, cold, sloshing about in mud; even out of the line, billeted in freezing huts or sleeping in tents, there was not much to remind a man of a warm fireside, the smell of home cooking or the sound of children, unless, of course, it was to make him think of what he was missing.

Private Frederick Voigt recalled the fractious nature of life when, in the middle of winter, twelve men shared a bell tent behind the lines. Muddy boots would trample over other men's blankets, and latecomers would have to wedge themselves anywhere they could sleep, with knees drawn up for the rest of the night. 'Any attempt at forcing them down would be sure to create a disturbance and lead to a furious dispute and an exchange of insults and obscenities.' Anyone who moved would cause a commotion, and anyone who could not sleep was liable to stir, roll over and fidget; it was unforgettable misery for anyone who was there. Voigt listened to the grumblings.

Gorblimey – when's this bastard life goin' ter end! When I think o' Sunday mornin' at 'ome wi' breakfast in bed an' the *News O' the World* wi' a decent divorce or murder, I feel fit ter cry me eyes out. Bloody slavery, soldierin'! An' what's it all for? Nothin' at all – absolutely nothin'! . . . Draggin' us out 'ere inter this bloody misery – it makes me blood boil . . .

In quieter moments, when boredom set in, a volunteer might wonder and grimace (or ruefully smile) at his own self-inflicted predicament and then his thoughts might drift home and to memories of life as it once had been.

In a period of inactivity, Private Thomas Hope examined his comrades at close quarters.

Webster and Taffy are talking in low tones, both very serious look-ing. Mac is lying across my feet; his eyes are closed, but by this time, like myself, he is very much awake. Two of the others are scribbling on a field postcard and exchanging confidences, while yet another, a new recruit, is reading a letter, evidently his last from home, and appears to be the most unconcerned of the lot.

Try as I like, however, my mind will dwell on the folks at home, and I wonder if I will ever see them again. Such morbid ideas are foolish, and I try to concentrate on other things, but home seems to be uppermost in my mind and I recall with tender thoughts the day my brother and I crawled into the dog kennel to smoke our first cigarette, mother's surprise at seeing what she thought was the kennel on fire and the smoke escaping from every join in the woodwork, the pail of water which came splashing in on top of us as she attempted to extinguish the flames, then the sorry spectacle we made as dejectedly we crawled out, sick and wet, and 'Fall in on top at the double' brings me back to the present and makes home seem very far away.

The British Army was never keen to leave men to their own devices for long. There was always plenty to do in or out of the trenches, carrying up supplies, fixing, building, repairing, cleaning. It was under cover of darkness that most work was carried out. It made sense in every way: inactive soldiers were cold soldiers, and working at night kept the blood circulating and passed the time quickly. Even so, soldiers could not help but think of their loved ones, and of the gulf between their lives and their own. Lieutenant Geoffrey Fildes was serving in the Ypres Salient when he was ordered to take a fatigue party to pick up supplies at a Royal Engineer dump.

An hour later and he and his men were struggling through a glutinous communication trench. Very lights lit up the night sky; rifle shots, and the splutter of machine-gun fire continued without a moment's rest.

At this moment, I wondered whether at night people at home were giving any real thought to what was passing in this dark and sinister wilderness. Away in London, hundreds were filling the theatres; the plays would be in full progress, perhaps the second act had just opened; and here were we, glued half-way up to our knees in a slough of graveyard fluid, listening to a running fire of rifle shots – and the same moon up there was looking down on us all alike.

It was the moon that endangered men's lives; in particular a full moon with its gentle, luminous glow that could highlight to the enemy the movement of a working party, detection of which might invite a rain of shells or trench mortars. It was that moon 'looking down on us all alike', that officer and artist Captain Bruce Bairnsfather captured in one of his more famous paintings. A girl looks from her bedroom window at the night's milky light and muses about her boyfriend or husband. 'And to think that it's the same dear old moon that's looking down on him!' Bert, on the other hand, placing barbed wire in no man's land, is altogether less impressed. 'This blinkin' moon will be the death of us,' he grunts.

Once Bert was safely back in the trench, he might well have had the same flights of fancy as his girl in England; other soldiers certainly did. Private Thomas Williams watched lapwings as they passed over his head in 'scattered pairs, small parties and larger flocks'. He understood enough about birds to know that 'in a few hours' time those same lapwings might be wheeling over English fields. My thoughts went with them to the level fens of East Anglia and the North Country mosses that I knew so well . . . I dozed off to sleep. My dreams were of English fields, horses at work ploughing and the spring cries of the peewits.'

In the same vein, Lieutenant Henry Lawson enjoyed being on duty at dawn when nature awoke with the brightening day. 'Those were hours of happiness as though the whole realm of nature was mine,' he wrote. 'Closing my eyes, I might entrance myself into the belief that I was still at home in Surrey fields on a golden May morning.'

Most men thought in terms far less cerebral than Private Williams or Lieutenant Lawson. Yes, there was a sense of longing, but it was as much a desire to get back to Blighty and escape the sordidness of their current life. 'I'm getting properly fed up and sick of this damn job, but it's no use grumbling, I'll have to stick it,' one sergeant, Robert Constantine, grumbled in a letter home. He was taking a risk with his complaints; as Private Voigt warned, a man had always to be careful what he said.

The C.O.'s been down on people writing things in letters. Lewis wrote home that he'd starve on the rations we get if it weren't for the parcels his people send him. The C.O. had him up. He told him to make complaints through the proper channels in future and gave him seven days [Field Punishment] Number 2. He has to collect and empty the latrine buckets every morning before breakfast . . . Of course, he's a bloody fool to write in that strain – our rations aren't so bad, considering. Thompson was up for the same sort of thing. He wrote he'd seen a thing or two out here and when he got back home he'd open people's eyes a bit about the war and the army. All bluff, of course. He got five days for his trouble.

Platoon officers censored the letters of every man under their command, although they varied greatly in their determination to strike out anything that might be construed as helpful to the enemy. Many skimmed over letters, not wishing to read personal messages, although the men, knowing these letters would be read, felt inhibited about disclosing too much. In compensation, green envelopes were issued to other ranks on an irregular basis. These envelopes were sealed by the soldier and, except for a sample few, were not opened by the censor at the base. This allowed men to say what they wanted in confidence, on the proviso that they signed the envelope guaranteeing they had written nothing untoward. Letters from the front survive in great numbers, treasured by families. Letters from home to the Western Front are far less common. These were eagerly anticipated by soldiers who read and reread them but a man had enough kit to carry without every spare pocket, every corner of his haversack, being stuffed full of old correspondence, and many eventually disappeared into the latrine as toilet paper.

Once letters were read and pictures of children and wives shown off and appreciated, men talked to each other about their hopes and desires for the future. 'She's one in a thousand, my gal,' said a man named McCarrick to Grenadier Guardsman Norman Cliff, a recent arrival in the trenches. 'I've been a rough handful,' he confided, 'and she and the poor kids have had to suffer. But it won't be again if I have a chance. If it was only for myself, I shouldn't care two brass tacks whether I came through or went under, but for the sake of the wife and bairns I hope to get through. You ought to see the kids, man. Come and see us when this is over.'

It was not Connie Mortlock's husband, Herbert, who was so much the worry as her young son, Hubert, who was proving a handful. In her letter dated August 1916, she hinted not only at the financial necessity of going to work but an emotional need, too. Coping with everything at home was not easy but she was keen to reassure her husband in France, and looking forward to resuming married life in the near future:

Dear Bertie

Thank you very much for the 3/6 which I received in your last letter. I am very glad to hear you are out of the trenches. You don't say for how long though. I suppose it is the usual few days 'rest'. Never mind, the war can't last much longer I shouldn't think. I am going to a job next week at Chiswick. I don't know whether I should be kept. I will write and let you know how I get on. I feel as if I must go out to work. I simply don't seem able to settle down at home. I expect I shall be different when you come home again and things are a bit settled.

Hubert is a perfect terror. He was not very well on Sunday so I took him to the doctor who told me to keep him very quiet and not let him rush about or get excited. I wish he had the job of keeping him quiet. He would have to tie him down I'm thinking. He [Hubert] is a lot better now. I am also a lot stronger, in fact I am as strong as a horse . . .

With lots of love from your loving wife and son Connie and Hubert xxx

One of the great frustrations of soldiering on the Western Front was that a man was unable to support his family as he would wish, or to rectify any domestic issues at home. Private Jack Rogers' girlfriend Elsie Carter was working in a munitions factory in Shepherds Bush and had even moved in with Jack's widowed mother. Elsie had written regularly but then the frequency dwindled and eventually no letters arrived at all. Jack's sisters wrote to say they had seen Elsie out with other men, that she was staying out all night and that his mother had warned Elsie about her behaviour. Elsie had threatened to move out. Jack wrote to her in desperation.

> I wrote saying I hoped she would stay at my mother's and I'd try and get home and we'd get engaged to be married, but I never heard from her, she never answered the letter, so I never wrote again. It was a betrayal, it wasn't fair, but of course a lot of this sort of thing went on behind the soldiers' backs. I wasn't the only one.

To the soldier's mind, to be let down by a girlfriend was despicable in the circumstances and it was naturally hard to see any other point of view. To a young girl, never knowing when, if ever, she would see her boyfriend again must also have been difficult. Handling the pressure of constant worry would have been a problem, as would the feelings of separation and the sense of emotional drift that time and space might cause. Elsie Carter was barely out of her teens and working in munitions; she would have been surrounded by men whose skills in a crucial war industry might well have exempted them from service and whose income from inflated war wages meant there was money to burn. In such circumstances, staying loyal to a boyfriend with whom a relationship might have been only a recent development was perhaps too much for a soldier realistically to expect.

Girlfriends were not the only ones under a cloud of suspicion. If letters and parcels from wives began to dry up, too, soldiers' worst fears would go into overdrive. During the war, more than 16,000 married women had their Separation Allowances halted for inappropriate or immoral behaviour. It was often for excessive drinking, but it might also be for infidelity. Private Thomas Hope found himself in conversation with one soldier who was roundly cursing those at home:

> ... politicians and civilians get the full blast of his vitriolic tongue; then to vindicate his outburst, he tells us he has just heard that his wife has given birth to twins and he hasn't been home for fourteen months. We add our own views on the waywardness of women as we open the tins of Maconochie rations he generously provides.

Divorces would soar almost threefold during the war, albeit from a low base, while the incidence of bigamy also rose dramatically. In 1912, 2.75 per cent (34 out of 1,232) of cases held at the Central Criminal Court concerned this crime; by the penultimate year of the war this had risen to 13.35 per cent, and by 1918 it had jumped to almost 20.2 per cent, seven times the pre-war level. In April 1918, the Court dealt with almost as many cases of bigamy as it had done for the entire year of 1912, the incidence among women working in munitions and other war-related industries being noticeably high.

Domestic problems apart, home news and parcels were greatly appreciated by the soldiers. In late 1916, *The Times* reported that for every letter a soldier wrote he received four in return; the paper also noted that it took on average three days for letters to reach men in billets and four days in trenches. These reported facts only serve to highlight the enormous pressure under which the Army Postal Service operated. By mid-June 1915, this service was handling 7,000 sacks containing 500,000 letters and 60,000 parcels every day between Britain and her troops abroad. By August 1916, it was handling 1.55 million letters a day and 110,000 parcels to its troops all round the world, 1.1 million letters to the men on the Western Front alone. In addition, the post daily dealt with 37,000 free newspapers (June 1915) given by newspaper proprietors for troops in the field to keep them in touch with domestic issues.

Manufacturers quickly realised that their products could be repositioned to a buying public anxious to help its boys abroad. Items were redesigned and/or repackaged so that soldiers could carry them in their haversacks, from a small portable Tommy cooker to cough medicine, from indelible pencils to an upside-down pipe that allowed the soldier to smoke in the trench without giving away his position. The 'famous' (self-proclaimed) Zam-Buk was sold for a shilling a pack. This was a two-inch-wide tin that was 'compact first-aid for every kit-bag'. It contained an antiseptic agent of 'remarkable power', remarkable, so it said, for its soothing and healing powers. 'Zam-Buk is the most opportune and thoughtful gift to make to your friends and relatives at home and abroad,' promised the newspaper advert. When it came to food, Bovril was offered as concentrated nourishment for men 'undergoing physical strain at the Front or in training'; Oxo built up stamina and provided 'strength to resist fatigue', while Marmite was obtainable at half the normal price to troops.

As well as families sending parcels to their own kith and kin, it was possible for complete strangers to send 'comforts', too. These were either made up by the sender and posted for distribution to a designated unit in the field, or, for a fee, one of the many organisations set up to help soldiers would pack a parcel containing such items as soap, Bovril, cigarettes, boiled sweets and matches. In September 1915, the War Office set up the Department General of Voluntary Organisations (DGVOs) to coordinate all the comforts flowing overseas, with depots opened to receive gifts from across Great Britain, creating a 'comforts pool' from which distribution could be made. It also launched its own appeals, such as its call in November 1917 for the women of Britain to knit one million items of all kinds for the men that Christmas.

The public response to supplying comforts to the men was generous and unrelenting, and slightly awkward, too, for the army, which felt that the regular appeals for socks and shirts, for example, implied that it was not doing enough for its own men. Yet any embarrassment was as nothing compared to the effect on morale when a parcel arrived from home, especially when it came from children. A primary school in St Albans posted a parcel to a soldier from its local unit, the Hertfordshire Regiment. Inside was a note that read:

> Dear soldier, we are sorry that you are cold at night so we are sending you a blanket. We mean to send one every week because you are so brave and taking care of us and our dear country. We send you our love and pray to God to end the war soon and bring you safe home. Your loving little friends. Garden Fields School (girls). PS we are not going to buy sweets till the war is over but save our money for blankets and tobacco.

While it was good to know that civilians cared, soldiers would not be soldiers if some did not see a way of manipulating people's generosity to their advantage. It was not unkind, and no one was hurt; it was just a way of working the angles to improve their lot, as Private Charles Heare recorded when he and the rest of the men from his battalion were out on rest in Poperinge, near Ypres.

> We all had our photographs taken and exchanged them with one another as well as addresses of girls. All the boys then send letters and photographs telling these girls of lonely soldiers short of smokes. I had no end of letters and cigarettes. The letters said how sorry they were to hear I was short of cigarettes, but as I didn't smoke I had my suspicions as my friend Black used to say 'more fags for me'. One girl in Cheltenham wrote to me thanking me for my photo, sending me cigarettes and saying how sorry she felt that I had lost all my brothers. I caught Black this time and so his cigarettes ended.

In August 1918, Albert Le Pla, a corporal serving with the Suffolk Regiment, found the body of Private Albert Athill along with some photographs and a card with his home address. Armed with these, he decided to write to let Athill's mother know the bare circumstances of her son's death. 'I daresay you will wonder who this surprising letter is from and more so being a perfect stranger, but it is with my deepest sympathy and sad regret . . .'

Despite being surrounded by comrades, it was entirely possible for a man to be lonely, a feeling exacerbated by the arrival of mail when everyone else received letters and he had none. Parcels from the DGVO 'pool' helped matters considerably and civilians were encouraged to write to soldiers overseas with the hope of making a connection with someone they could correspond with. Soldiers, especially those with no close family, were often happy to reciprocate when the opportunity presented itself, particularly if it resulted in free 'smokes'. Of course it was not possible to write speculatively unless a name and address could somehow be obtained.

It was not abnormal for a soldier to write on behalf of another but what was different was Le Pla's repeated appeals that she should write back. It gives the impression of a man keen to strike up a correspondence after two years' service overseas. 'I daresay you will thank me for the duty I have carried out . . . I would be awfully pleased to hear from you indeed and to know that you have received the articles that I send, *and also anyone connected with your family* [my italics]. My address is 325515 Cpl Le Pla 1/4th Suffolk Regt, D Company, 16 Platoon. BEF France . . . A letter from you at your earliest and most convenient time would be greatly accepted.' It is likely that Mrs Athill replied and thanked Le Pla for his kindness; whether any friendship was struck up is not known. Corporal Le Pla survived the war.

Naturally, family correspondence was of primary interest and there was an upside to civilians' ignorance of the war: they could not write about it. They might mention the latest reports in the newspapers; they would pass on news of how other lads in the village or street were faring. There would be the prayers offered for the continued safety of loved ones, but in essence the letters were often round-ups of family affairs, the tittle-tattle of daily life and all its seemingly petty inconsequentialities. The more a letter chirped on about nothing in particular, the more the soldier could nestle back into the fold of home for a few minutes at least.

'You say the news from home must seem trivial compared with my experience out here,' wrote Private Frederick Noakes. 'Please don't get that impression. Out here news of home is like food and drink to us, however trivial. Indeed, this life is like a dream and the old life is the only reality. We live on memories. Our constant thought is – what are they doing at home?'

Twenty-one-year-old Emily Miller was an excited letter writer and never baulked at passing on family trivia to her brother Peter. In early September 1916 she was bemoaning the foul weather that meant she could not wear her pretty summer dresses. 'Can't you send some sunshine over?' she asked her brother. 'Dadda' was soon to move on to a new parish, she told him, and she, Emily, had recently attended a service given by her father at a nearby military camp, for 'Anglicans and non-con combined'. Other than the men, there had been six New Zealand nursing sisters to keep her company. Yet all this was a preamble to the most important news, namely the family gossip.

Did Ma tell you the latest? The reconciliation between Angus [Emily's younger brother] and the GJ? G is like a blessed baby, he hangs around Angus. He came down the other evening, but Angus was busily enjoying himself with Douglas [the Millers' youngest boy], and by and by I walked in with David [Emily's boyfriend, later killed in France]. G would not deign a glance, but I made him say Good-evening and forced an introduction with David. I saw him on Sunday morning, but was met with strong indifference. Well! Ma is allowing Angus to go with this depraved

specimen of humanity for a week to a place on the Thames somewhere near Oxford – name is something like 'feed-em' or 'tuck-in',
I can't quite remember . . .

The letter ambled on happily for four pages, ending on the
recent downing of a Zeppelin over Cuffley in Hertfordshire.

Unfortunately I was too tired to get out of bed and look, but the
rest of the household heard the explosion and actually saw its
descent in flames, they say it was a wonderful sight. You should
have heard the cheer that went up – people didn't seem to care one
bit, all yelled with one accord and sirens and hooters volunteered
their feeble support . . . Dadda was speaking to an aviator yesterday and he said he had actually seen the Iron Cross and watch of
the Commander of the Zeppelin . . .

After more references to the weather and that even the family
dog, Gripp, was getting 'fed up' with it, Emily signed off: 'Heaps
of love, in which everyone joins, and none more so than your
loving Sister.'

The downing of a Zeppelin had been a cause for national celebration, being the first brought down over British soil. Like Private
Williams, who had watched lapwings flying west, soldiers could look
up on occasion and see from their trenches the high path of a Zeppelin
overhead, and know what was heading towards their friends and
families: they were, of course, impotent to do anything about it.

In this case the Royal Flying Corps had come to the rescue and
the pilot responsible for the successful attack, Captain Leefe
Robinson, was awarded the Victoria Cross. Zeppelins had brought
fear to the streets of London as well as to many provincial cities,
though out of all proportion to the damage wrought and the
deaths caused. Emily promised to send Peter the report of the
action in that day's *Chronicle*.

*   *   *

As Emily's letter began its journey to France, Peter Miller wrote a letter home to his mother. After arriving in France he had seemingly spent the best part of a month at a base camp before being sent to join the 2nd Sussex Regiment on the Somme. On 5th September he was billeted in an empty house badly knocked about by artillery fire and he and the other new men around him were gradually becoming accustomed to the noise of gunfire. His letter was brief; he did not know when he would write again but he said optimistically, 'When you look for my name in the papers, look among the decorations.' This reference to medals demonstrated that Peter probably already knew that his battalion was about to go into the front line trenches to take part in an attack. The objective would be the enemy trenches that ran close to High Wood. Square shaped and heavily defended, this piece of land, identified by its ghastly tree stumps, had been fought over for the previous six weeks and still lay partly in enemy hands. For good reason the wood had won a fearsome reputation.

Peter's letter referred to being 'at the line' though not in the line, which would usually have meant the trenches. 'At the line' still meant in danger, for anyone within several miles of the trenches was at grave risk from long-range shells or the activities of enemy aircraft. These might drop a bomb or bombs, however speculatively, on men sleeping in ramshackle billets, such as Peter's shell-damaged house, or further back in tented encampments where they could cause carnage.

Grave danger either in the line or at the line caused men great mental anguish and fear. If possible, it was advisable to clear one's mind of any thoughts, negate any feelings or emotions, but this could not always be done. Private Frederick Voigt was resting in a tented encampment behind the lines. As darkness fell, the order for 'Lights Out' was given. Candles were extinguished and a hush descended. In the dark, any noise would seem to be amplified.

'Soon we heard the familiar buzz,' wrote Voigt.

'At first it only came from one propeller, but others arrived and the sound multiplied and increased in volume, and at the same time it rose and fell in irregular gusts and regular pulsations. Anti-aircraft firing burst out suddenly and for a few minutes there was a blending of whining, whistling, rushing sounds overhead punctuated by faint reports. The firing ceased, but the droning noises continued louder than ever.

I was unable to control my imagination. I saw my comrades and myself blown to pieces. I saw the clerk in the office of the C.C.S. [Casualty Clearing Station] write out the death-intimations on a buff slip and filling in a form. I saw a telegraph boy taking the telegram to my home. He sauntered through the garden gate and knocked at the front door. The door opened . . . but I could not face the rest, and with a tremendous mental impulse I turned my mind away to other things.

When men went over the top, the descent into living hell was even more rapid and in the ensuing chaos and rush of adrenalin, the mind was prone to playing peculiar tricks. Private Norman Cliff inexplicably recalled the soothing contents of a letter from home, as attacking Germans swarmed around him. 'Ten thousand shall fall at thy right and ten thousand at thy left,' the letter had quoted, 'but it shall not come nigh thee.' Even under the stress of combat, the sentiments annoyed Cliff, with their suggestion that he might find comfort in his own survival when all around him died. These examples of uncontrolled thought appear to imply that the mind was protecting itself from the prevailing horrors, taking refuge in the security of home, sometimes even of child-hood. Private Robert Renwick was in an assault on Delville Wood when, as he dodged from shell-hole to tree stump, he suddenly saw himself back at school. 'Our schoolmaster was coming down his garden path to the wicket to call us in and line us up.' It was an image that was shockingly vivid and one he remembered all his life. Thomas Kehoe had a comparable experience. As a boy he had read stirring adventure stories such as *Treasure Island*; indeed, such stories of derring-do had drawn him into enlisting in the first place. Still a mere boy, he had lied about his age and been sent to France in 1917. In his memoirs he recalled going over the top and being wounded. Shot in the thigh, he was forced to drop to the ground as the Germans counterattacked and drove back the survivors of his battalion.

'After a long time I heard steps and some Germans passed by a few yards off. They prowled about in plain sight.' The fear pushed Kehoe to the point of passing out. Suddenly

> I was back home, sitting up in bed reading about Jim Hawkins, and hurrying over the pages for fear my mother would come stealing in and take the candle away.
>
> The room dropped away into the dark, and I was Jim Hawkins himself, sitting on the cross-trees of the good ship *Hispaniola*, with Israel Hands below me coming up the mizzen-shrouds holding a dirk in his teeth.

Near death, a soldier's thoughts returned to his family. Second Lieutenant George Atkinson of the Royal Engineers recalls how, during an attack in late 1918, a man named Cox was badly wounded. 'Just before the end he sobbed like a child: "My wife and kiddie, oh God! Sir, what's going to happen to them? Poor kid, poor kid." And then he died.' Another officer, Hugo Morgan, recalled the death of one of the men under his command. He came across the man who five minutes before had been joking and laughing with his comrades but now lay dying, wounded badly in the head. 'What are the words he is muttering? "Give my wife . . .," says the dying man with a supreme effort and the movement of his white and blood-stained face ceases; he lies there lifeless.'

The sight of a strong, sentient being reduced in a moment to a lifeless corpse made men acutely conscious of their own mortality. 'There but for the grace of God go I': a phrase that passed through the minds of many soldiers, sobered by the knowledge that at any second their turn could come.

'As we look at his inanimate figure,' wrote Morgan,

> we think of a little cottage in England, where his wife is giving supper to four happy children and telling them, with smiles on her face, that Father will be coming home on leave in a few weeks' time. Little does she dream of the cold still figure, laid out on the fire-step and the group of comrades sighing as they turn away. The stretcher-bearers, grown accustomed to their task, reverently fold the arms across in front, lift the body on to the stretcher, and carry it away down the trenches. Thus he passes out of our midst and we carry on as before, but with a remembrance.

Consideration of the family was, by force of circumstances, but a transitory thought, a fleeting concern that seemed only to emphasise the chasm between the mundane nature of death on the Western Front and the enormity of its consequences at home. Lieutenant Geoffrey Fildes, serving with the 2nd Coldstream Guards, had gone to investigate the damage to the trench system after a particularly severe German bombardment when he came across a casualty.

> In the open fire-bay beside the solitary traverse lay a huddled mass. He, at least, would never 'grouse' or jest again. On him, flies were already gorging themselves. I knew the poor fellow, and as I covered his awful remains with a ground-sheet, a vague recollection of some matter concerning him came to my mind. Then I remembered: it was an increase of his allotment to his wife.

Men were aware of being privy to an intimate and powerful knowledge. 'I always went to look at bodies to see if I knew people,' recalled Fred Hodges, a nineteen-year-old corporal in the Lancashire Fusiliers. 'Twice I saw a dead officer and I picked up the corner of the ground sheet under which he lay and I thought, "Your parents don't know you're dead." Aren't these queer thoughts? I knew what his own people at home didn't know.'

The dead, particularly those very recently killed, who lay slumped here and there in myriad poses presented a sickening sight, but men became hardened to it over time. Hodges' curiosity about the dead was common. Soldiers were often astonished at corpses remaining upright in the pose of firing a rifle, or sitting apparently asleep, but still there a day later. Men pondered over the possible scenarios in death as if it were an everyday brainteaser.

Fascination could tip over into the macabre. There were those who seemed inured to the sights of death: men who appeared to revel in the environment they found themselves in. Lieutenant John Glubb met Corporal Percy Cheale, an old regular soldier, whom he described as having a combination of an utter disregard for danger and a 'morbid love for the dead'. The 7th Field Company, Royal Engineers, with which Glubb served, had taken a great number of casualties, including many recent reinforcements; identification would be difficult in the circumstances but Cheale had volunteered to help. When he had finished going through the pockets, he went to speak to the second-in-command and said, 'Excuse me, Sir, did you notice this young feller? Don't he make a lovely corpse?'

Glubb had no doubt Cheale thoroughly enjoyed his work, clearing the dead from the roads and fields in front of High Wood on the Somme. His attentions were oddly fatherly. He would examine each one, as Glubb saw, 'after which he would carry them away, wrapped in an affectionate embrace. He would always allude to them as property owners (owning six feet of soil), and talked cheerfully of the day when he would become one.' Cheale was awarded the Military Medal and survived the war.

The soldiers' reaction to the sight of corpses depended on the body. That of an enemy soldier was, by and large, marked by indifference; the body of another British soldier drew a little more compassion. When death came to friends, and worse still close friends, the attitude was entirely different. The dead were part of an extended family, a temporary one but with a closeness and affection that in some ways paralleled that of home.

'Friendships are made quickly here,' acknowledged Private Thomas Hope, of the King's Liverpool Regiment.

> We learn to prize a man, not for the sort of citizen he was, but for the kind of comrade he can be. Social status means nothing in a front-line trench – a thief can be as good as a deacon. Mutual attractions or opposites draw us together, hardships shared strengthen the little circle formed, the shadow of death welds it tog' her in unbreakable bonds, while comradeship imparts the touch of colour which enhances its beauty. When death invades one of these circles its presence becomes a family affair; the smaller the circle, the more personal it is. And so it is with us. We have come to know and love each other as brothers, jealous of the virtues, tolerant towards the little weaknesses each one possesses, and now that our own circle has been broken, death means something more than just another 'gone west'.

In Hope's case he lost a great friend, Mac, although his attitude to another man, a corporal hit at the same moment as Mac, is also interesting. Hope's only emotion was for his friend; he could spare nothing for the corporal.

Hope had been part of a small carrying party going to a point well behind the lines to pick up materials to mend a signallers' dugout that had taken a direct hit. On their way back they heard the noise of a shell making its 'whobbling, whistling' way before, in the instant before impact, the whistle turned to a terrifying shriek as the shell landed almost on top of them.

'Corp's hit!' I yell back, as I make towards the prostrate figure.

'Where've you got it, Corp?'

I am still a yard off the corporal's body, when Webster's voice calling Mac makes me turn round. Immediately the corporal is forgotten and I am kneeling with Webster alongside Mac:

'Mac, Mac, wake up old man, it's me, Jock.'

His eyes open a little. There is a gurgling sound in his throat:

'I'm bleeding freely, I'm bleeding freely.'

Strange words, they come tortuously, but distinctly, followed by a string of curses, stranger still from Mac, which gradually turns into a choking gurgle, then silence, and I feel his body go tense, then limp, in my arms . . .

'If we can only get him to a dressing station they'll patch him up,' I suggest. 'He's bleeding like an ox. Come on, let's carry him. There's a station at brigade headquarters.'

'What about the corp, did you look at him?' Webster enquires.

'No, damn it, I'd forgotten all about him; just a minute.'

The corporal is lying twenty yards away, the upper half of his head missing, and I notice it alongside his helmet five yards further on. We can do nothing for him, so I go through his pockets and relieve him of his field dressing.

To Webster's enquiring glance I give a shrug:

'Mutton, half his head gone. His brains are scattered all over the place. Never thought he had so many.'

Unconsciously I have slipped back to the callous talk of the trenches.

'I've got his pay book and his stock of fags. There's some dough as well,' I add as I slip the lot into my own pockets to go halves with Webster later.

'Oh and here's his dressing. Let's fix it on Mac before we move him. Poor old Mac, it's a hell of a war, Webby,' I blubber as we adjust the last bandage and prepare to move him . . .

Hope and Webster were faced with crossing a mile and a half of ground before they could get Mac to where he might receive some medical attention.

He breathes his last before we have covered half the distance, but still we carry on, telling ourselves we are mistaken, that he still lives and will be all right once the doctor fixes him up. I pray every yard of the way that my pal will live. Dear Mac, how could I face this life without your staunch comradeship and cheery smile? You must live – you can't leave me.

Mac was dead and when Hope and Webster recovered from the initial shock, they would write to his family and let them know what had happened. It would prove a far harder task than either of them expected.

The death of comrades inexorably ground down the resilience of the strongest of men, as did their repeated survival in action when all around had become casualties. In letters home it was not always possible to disguise depression and a resignation to fate that must have sowed great fear into families' hearts. Private Harry James had been serving in France since the first week of September 1915 and had been wounded badly enough to have been sent back to hospital in England. Mended and back out in France, he had been made a Company Bomber, something he freely admitted to his sister meant being a part of the 'Suicide Club', as the men called it. The 'Club' had recently been in action and had been fortunate to survive. 'Our lives,' he confided, 'are all in God's hands so whatever we undertake out here it is His will if we are to come out safely or not . . .'

The tone of his letter may have alarmed his sister more than what he said, almost as if he were preparing his family for the worst.

Well I have managed to come out of some very hot corners and have had any amount of narrow shaves but lately I have got to be prepared for anything to happen as when you manage to come out of all these scrapes you begin to wonder when you will go as everybody around you falls. Still dear Ciss if I am to fall as others have I shall be ready and shall then have the consolation of meeting dear Dad in Heaven. Don't get downhearted at me talking like this, Ciss, as I have dodged the bullets and shells up to now and it is nearly four months since I came out for the second time. I am going to keep on, only it wants some doing at times . . .

Well I must close now as I am going to turn in and try and have a few hours' sleep in my dugout. The worst of it is there is a big shelling going on and the blessed things coming over our heads it makes you duck and cannot get any sleep with the awful din . . .

Don't forget to pray for me dear Ciss. I am longing to come home once again and I should be content if I could only see mum and all of you just once more.

Your loving brother Harry

Harry James, 13th Middlesex Regiment, was killed two months later and his body lost. He is commemorated on the Thiepval Memorial to the Missing. Another who would join him there was Lieutenant Evelyn Southwell, serving with the Rifle Brigade. Like Harry James, he had served on the Somme and while his letters remained reasonably cheerful, there were telltale signs of mental exhaustion; prior to his death in September 1916, the battalion had been in almost constant action. Back in July he had also lost his closest friend, Malcolm White, and in a letter to his mother he could hardly contain his sadness, though he was careful to reassure her of his own situation.

White is dead . . . I have faced the casualty list daily without a tremor for two years now, and now, when I am hard hit myself, I cry out! Mum, he was such a dear; he was so keen on everything, and the most true 'artist', in the full sense, that I have ever known.

This month has opened my eyes to the lot of those who sit and wait, as I have been doing since the push started. For goodness sake, don't let his one case make you think you have any more reason than before to be anxious about my miserable safety – what difference can one example, however near home, make to the probabilities of good or evil fortune in one more among millions? But I can sympathise with you, who are good enough to be anxious about me, better now. Yet do please realize that one friend's death does not increase my risk or chances, any more than it diminishes it; you must not let it make you worry about it. But I cannot be very happy . . . War is a terrible thing, especially lately, as all of us know.

A death in the battalion, even if the individual was not a close friend, left those who survived with a mixture of sadness and a chill, 'a sort of presentiment,' according to Stephen Graham, 'that you yourself would perish before the end and lie thus in trench or battlefield, cold and inanimate, soaked with rain, uncared for, lost to home and dear ones'.

As the war dragged on, the bonds of shared community and experience that had once so tightly held together the volunteers of Kitchener's Army began to fail. And as the proportion of conscripts grew higher, so the feelings of fraternity appeared to decline. Battalions were no longer formed of friends but of drafts of men sent to whichever unit happened to be under strength. The greatest fear among the men was not the fear of death itself but of dying alone and in agony. The thought could easily corrode the morale of anyone and one of those brought closest to despair in 1918 was Private Reginald Kiernan.

There are no heroes here. No one cares. A man is forgotten the next moment. We don't even know each other's names, or our officers' names, and our officers don't know us even by sight. We don't know what we are going to do, or what we are making for when we attack.

We don't know where Jerry is, whether he's three hundred yards or a thousand yards away. We don't know anything at all, and we just go forward – every man for himself. Everything is unknown and unthanked, unpraised, and there is no pity anywhere – not even a 'Poor sod,' as we pass the men who've been killed.

I can't die like that – that is what I fear, I think, more than death itself. But it's Fear, Fear, Fear, all the time when we are not doing anything, and who can describe Fear? He is with you, by your side, round you, over you, in your mind and your body, even when you sleep.

Even a tough regular soldier like Corporal John Lucy found the strains almost too much to bear. He had lost his brother during the fighting of 1914 and a continual drip, drip of mates had been killed or wounded ever since. There was not much of the battalion left with which he had gone overseas. Two more deaths brought him to the point of collapse.

In December [1915] there was a sudden flare-up on our quiet sector. We had asked for it, because every day, from our billets, we had the habit of sending large parties forward with picks and shovels to improve the communication trenches to the front line. The men marched up and back in daylight over open flat country, and worked under sapper officers more in the manner of civilians in peacetime than of troops under enemy observation. One morning the Germans let them have salvo after salvo. The medical officer, called from the mess, left his breakfast and rushed away to tend to the wounded. He was killed. Sergeant Ryan, his orderly, then took his place, tended the wounded, and brought back his officer's body to billets. The working party was then withdrawn for some hours. Ryan laid out his officer on a stretcher in his little dressing-station, and asked me to come and look at him.

Ryan was very much put out, and mourned as if he had lost a dear relation. He cleaned the dead officer's face, combed his hair, and arranged his tie, and then he asked me to kneel with him and say a prayer for the dead. I did so, though my prayers for the dead had lately taken the brief form of a muttered 'Pax vobiscum' or 'Lord have mercy' to any corpse.

'We came away, I comforting Ryan, but he was distressed and fitful in his actions, his face fallen too sadly, and he kept repeating 'O God help us. O God help us. To see him there on his own stretcher. Oh what a shame! I'll have to go back to him,' and back he went, like a dog who will not leave a grave.

Outside, a relief working party was falling in, in bitter weather, and it marched off to repair the blown-in communication trench. Hardly had this party arrived when the Germans shelled again, and up went Ryan to see to the wounded. Ryan was killed by shrapnel almost at once, and his body was brought back and placed on another stretcher beside his medical officer. Each had been killed in the act of binding men's wounds. Ryan's patient had been killed with him.

I went in slowly again to visit the dead Ryan and his officer. I prayed for them both. These devoted men had died directly to save their fellows. There was something Christ-like about them – the young English public-school Protestant and the Dublin Catholic. The red compassionate lips of Ryan were white-grey. His discoloured teeth showed between them. I patted his cheek in farewell. Then I stood up, and I could not move away. The world turned over. My manhood seeped from me. Ryan's death had hammered the congealed nail of grief deeper into my heart, and a long suppressed tide of sorrow rose and flowed about me. I heard strange sobs coming from my lips, and felt my spirit fainting.

In the little dressing-station I missed all my dead friends again.

Utterly shaken, Lucy went back to work. The adjutant noticed his anxiety and sat close to him, giving orders in a manner that was particularly kind, and which Lucy greatly appreciated.

He put his left hand on my right, which I now noticed was trembling, and said, 'Look here, you are beginning to look rocky. Hadn't you better go sick? You have been looking seedy for weeks you know. What's up?' I said, 'I don't know. I have lost Ryan.' He asked: 'You feel that?' and I answered, 'Yes, very much.' I said I did not want to go sick. He then urged me to go home for a spot of leave, and to forget the war for a bit. I gladly accepted.

3

Home and Away

'Our Daddy
Good Night'

6404 Private George Rogers
1st Hampshire Regiment
Killed in action 8 August 1915, aged thirty
Buried Mesnil Communal Cemetery Extension

Home leave was treasured as nothing else. The chance to see family again held a special place in the hearts of men who had wives and children. Here was the opportunity to escape the squalor and fear of trench life, and, though none might say it out loud, the chance to have a break from the all-male family of comrades with whom one lived, slept and ate around the clock. News that leave was imminent, according to Private Frederick Voigt, helped to end 'the long spells of dreary silence interrupted by outbursts of irritability, by grumbling and by violent quarrels. Our talk was all about one subject – not about peace, for we had abandoned all hope of peace and hardly ever thought about it – but of leave.'

Each unit kept a leave roster. This was divided into two columns: one for other ranks and one for officers, with a strict rotation of leave being adhered to. There could be no queue jumpers and even the granting of compassionate leave was extremely rare. Major Rowland Fielding, serving with the Coldstream Guards, remembered applying for such leave for a man in his company whose daughter had been run over and killed, even though Fielding knew his application would probably fail. 'The Higher Authorities are likely to argue that, since the child is dead, the father can do no good by going home; – which is logical, if brutal.'

As the number of soldiers serving overseas grew rapidly from mid-1915, so the number of those receiving leave spiralled. Typically, an allotment of leave would be granted to a unit and men sent home in small batches at a time. From this allocation it was possible to work out when leave might be due by looking at who else was about to go, although this would be a rough guess and soldiers were not officially told until a day or two before a pass was granted, at which time they became intensely nervous.

In October 1917, after a year on the Western Front, Albert Martin wrote that he was 'sweating' on leave very violently, as he estimated his turn was close. 'Leave fever has reduced me to a frightful state of fidgets. Can't keep still for two minutes together.' As leave drew nearer, men became excessively jumpy about any trip towards the trenches and hyper-sensitive to being ordered to any job that was considered perilous. When Lieutenant George Atkinson was ordered to undertake a hazardous job in late 1918, he was not unduly nervous until a corporal brought news of leave.

Instantly the whole affair changed, and I was seized with a blue shivering funk. In six hours I was due to go through the German lines, and there, lying on the table, was a bit of paper waiting to take me to England in the morning. It was the cruellest stroke of all, for I felt certain that I should never return. I went back to my bunk and sweated and shivered with fear. My mind and my body seemed to be completely separated from each other, and I found it quite impossible to stop the quaking of my limbs. I saw Death in a thousand forms.

Broadly speaking, officers could expect leave every sixteen to twenty weeks; other ranks would typically have to wait a year or more. Voigt's first leave, for example, was granted after seventeen months in France. There was a simple administrative reason for this apparent paucity of leave. In response to questions in the House of Commons, it was announced that in August, September and October 1916 some 85,379 men had been awarded leave, or 938 per day. A year later this figure had swollen to 488,865 or 5,372 a day, a monumental number indicative not of a sudden spirit of generosity among the senior command but merely of the rapidly increasing size of the British Army on the Western Front and of the considerable logistics involved in moving daily such a large body of men. The travel arrangements came over and above the normal daily evacuation of wounded and the supply of reinforcements to the line. And for every man going on leave, there was, of course, another returning to his unit.

Home leave: wonderful in the imagination, often difficult in reality. Once men stepped off the leave train at Victoria and dispersed to mingle freely with civilians, there was an inevitable sense of dislocation and unreality. To see people going about their everyday lives, out on seemingly trivial errands, shopping, gossiping, posting a letter, shaking out an umbrella, was hard to comprehend: not one person was in fear of their life. The contrast between the trench life to which men had grown accustomed and the hustle-bustle of a high street was stark.

'London, with its subdued lights, lay all around me. It had not changed since I saw it last, and yet I felt it ought to have changed,' wrote Voigt. 'The reason was that I had changed. And then I began to fear that I had changed beyond the power of recovery. The oppressive sensation that I was in a dream forced itself upon me.'

Every man was different: Lieutenant Hugo Morgan was just glad to be home. He spent his leave enjoying his old countryside pursuits and seeing his family and friends, although he could not help but be struck by the great contrast between home and abroad.

'This morning I could hear the boom of the eighteen-pounders in Belgium, to-night as I lie in bed, the regular tick, tick of a grand-father's clock in the hall is the only sound to be heard, except for the deep chimes of the church clock every quarter of an hour.' The difference was noteworthy but it did not unsettle him at all.

Lots of soldiers revelled in the contrast and set about enjoying their time at home, just as Voigt had intended to do. Charles Carrington, a junior officer in the Royal Warwickshire Regiment, drifted between theatres and restaurants in London with his friends but he was neither clearly happy nor unhappy, but like Voigt simply changed. In all, he had four spells of leave during the war. The first, in April 1916, was characterised as a schoolboy returning home for the holidays, but by the time of his third leave in July 1917 the house that he considered home had been given up and relatives dispersed to war work. Home life had altered but then so, too, had Carrington.

So far as I could see – the old taboos still prevailed. No doubt the social disruption of wartime had encouraged promiscuity, but not in my quiet circle of friends. 'Women who did' were still sharply divided from 'women who didn't'. The change had taken place in me, not in them. I found myself leading a double life. The quiet respectability of my family with its unaltered moral standards could in no way be related to the all-male society of the regiment, with its acceptance of death and bloodshed as commonplace events, and its uninhibited approach to women. If this estrange-ment touched me, who had no experience of love, what must it have meant to happily married men?

Frederick Voigt was disappointed that he was not as cheerful as he had expected to be; he felt a stranger in his own land. The ordi-nariness was disconcerting and he wanted reassurance that civilians knew that a war was going on, so he boarded a bus and sat in a seat where he could eavesdrop on a couple's conversation.

I felt that if they were to talk about the war, the uncanny spell would be broken, the dream would dissolve, and I would be restored to my own fellow-creatures. But they spoke about trivial domestic matters and about a flower-show. If they had only mentioned the word 'war' I would have felt relieved by its familiarity, but they did not mention it once.

After being at the front since August 1914, Corporal John Lucy had received his first bout of leave in April 1915, long before the death of his friend Ryan. Lucy had been involved in one engagement after another and had lost his brother Denis early on. After nine months of fighting, he was still able to return home reasonably cheerful and balanced, although the 'fervent welcomes' of his family reduced him to tears behind closed doors.

I spoke with caution of the fighting, and withheld most of the horrors. Anyway, I wanted to forget them, in this heavenly change to home life, so soft, so easy, so peaceful. Gardens, flowers, regular habits, good food, books, papers, armchairs, talk, and drinks were riches rediscovered. I found I could not stomach the rich dishes provided for me after seven months of army rations, and I secretly slept most snugly on the bedroom floor, because I could not rest in a soft bed.

Lucy visited old friends but found conversation difficult so he escaped into the countryside, picking up on childhood hobbies such as bird-nesting, while enjoying the sensation of uninhibited freedom. Even so, he felt a residual sense of guilt that, while he was safe, his mates were under fire in France.

Was it a similar feeling of unease that bothered William Andrews, a private in the Black Watch? His leave in Scotland was used not to escape the war but to keep the conflict firmly in mind. Andrews was married, and with his wife he spent much of his time visiting the families of his comrades, travelling from Edinburgh to Dundee.

We made a point of going to the homes of men in my company, and passing on messages from the front. I called on many of those whose sons and husbands had been killed, and said what comforting words I could. One woman turned on me with cold anger. 'Yes,' she said when I had finished, 'and when all your fine words in your fine English voice are done, how are they going to help me buy bread?' The poor creature was almost distraught by brooding over her loss, and I am afraid, try as I would, my visit of sympathy merely inflamed resentment.

On being granted leave, other ranks received barely a day's notice. Normally the first thing a family knew was the slamming shut of the wooden gate at the end of the path, the crunch, crunch of boots on gravel and an evening knock at the door. Officers were more fortunate. They usually received notice a week or more ahead of their departure; time enough to tell their families when to expect them and so time enough to prepare, though much harder to contain the excitement.

Marie Leighton, the mother of Lieutenant Roland Leighton, had, like all mothers, fretted constantly about her son overseas. She had buried her face in a pillow and sobbed on the night she heard he was going to France. Nine months had passed since then. He had already been on leave once and gone back, and still he was unwounded. 'It is certainly time he got wounded,' she wrote candidly. 'People are beginning to look surprised when I tell them he has not got a scratch yet. They will soon begin to think he hides all day in his dugout. Yes, he is certain to get wounded soon. But he will not get killed.'

His survival seemed guaranteed for the time being because he was coming home again. Marie Leighton had anticipated the moment her son walked through the door a thousand times after receiving his last letter.

It is between a fortnight and three days since I first had the hope that he might come home on this second leave. The way the sudden hope affected me showed me how little I had expected that he would ever come home again. I had lived through the fearfulness and anguish of his death so many times in the early days when he had just gone out to the Front.

As the hours ticked down to his arrival, she ran over in her mind her memories of her 'Little Yeogh Wough' (LYW) as she called him from his toddler days. He would be home for a full six days' leave, she had been told; her boy, aged just twenty, a lieutenant and the battalion adjutant. Her pride was considerable.

Today? The day is already gone. It must be a quarter to ten by now and I dare not think of what the dinner must be like, or the cook's temper. If she hadn't known him and worshipped him ever since he was little, she would be in an unmanageable rage. I am beginning almost to be a little anxious, because this is his second leave and I am a believer in Compensation. In this world one never gets a good thing twice and the bolts of fate always fall from the bluest skies.

But I will shut these gleams of fear away from me. The room door will be pushed open presently and he will come in with his gay, firm step and his charming smile. His smile has always had something surprising about it, because his eyes are so sad . . .

The initials L.Y.W. are at the foot of this message that I am looking at now, saying that he is coming home. I am getting very hungry, but I will not begin dinner without him. He is bound to come within the next half-hour. I have worked out the trains with the utmost completeness dozens of times today. So has his father. So has his sister. I will get his photograph down from the top of the cabinet and look at it. It will help me to get through the last few minutes – or perhaps half an hour – of waiting.

Harry Lauder's son was on his way home, too, though not as his parents would have wished. The dreaded telegram from the War Office had been received. Their son had been wounded and was in hospital, though as it turned out, mercifully, his injury was slight.

John was ordered home! He was invalided, to be sure, and I warned his mother that she must be prepared for a shock when she saw him. But no matter how ill he was, we would have our lad with us for a space. And for that much British fathers and mothers had learned to be grateful.

I had warned John's mother, but it was I who was shocked when I saw him first on the day he came back to our wee hoose at Dunoon. His cheeks were sunken, his eyes very bright, as a man's are who has a fever. He was weak and thin, and there was no blood in his cheeks. It was a sight to wring one's heart to see the laddie so brought down — him who had looked so braw and strong the last time we had seen him . . .

Living in the countryside, and ever mindful of John's delicate condition, it was possible to protect their son. As he was their only child, there may have been fewer relatives to keep at arm's length. Enquiring neighbours could be politely turned away. Those frustrating rounds of social visits, a typical recollection of soldiers made 'hero sons', could be allayed. The questions that preyed on soldiers' nerves could also be postponed: those well-meaning questions that were as ignorant as they were sometimes unanswerable. 'When would Germany be beaten?' 'Have you seen the enemy?' and then, most annoyingly of all to men who had just arrived home, 'When are you going back?' That knowledge was not forgotten for a moment, the clock in the back of every man's mind that ticked down to the day of return. To escape, some chose to sleep their leave away, others walked for miles in the country-side, but most did accept, albeit reluctantly, the duty-bound rounds of seeing old friends and neighbours.

After his troubled first leave, John Lucy's second homecoming was simply terrible. No longer able to suppress the psychological damage inflicted by fifteen months of war, and most recently the deaths of the battalion Medical Officer and the MO's servant, Ryan, Lucy, this hardened professional soldier, had begun to fall apart.

My leave from the front in the last days of 1915 was a nightmare. My sleep was broken and full of voices and the noises of war. The voices were those of officers and men who were dead. My people at home found me very strange. One morning I was discovered standing up in bed facing a wall ready to repel an imaginary dawn attack. In my nervous condition I took gifts and returned them at once. I did not want their belongings. I wanted nothing. I had a real physical pain in my heart, and there was no lustre in my eyes. I had loved many men and lost them. My womenfolk cherished me, but they stood outside my grief, and their warm sympathy tragically failed to alleviate a pain they had not shared.

A doctor was called and Lucy was diagnosed with 'shell shock' and sent to hospital. It would be eighteen months before he returned to the Western Front.

Just what would Harry Lauder have given to have his son home for that length of time? Like John Lucy, his son was battle weary and troubled and his parents did everything they could to make his stay as comfortable as possible. The only problem for Harry Lauder was his own commitment to the war effort. As a leading light in British entertainment, his appearance on a recruiting platform proved irresistible to would-be soldiers, men who would listen and then act on his appeal for volunteers. For Harry these trips were important but at the same time he yearned to go home.

It grieved me sore not to spend all my time with him but he would not hear of it. He drove me back to my work.

'You must work on, Dad, like every other Briton,' he said.

'Think of the part you're playing. Why you're more use than any of us out there – you're worth a brigade!'

So I left him on the Clyde, and went on about my work. But I went back to Dunoon as often as I could, as I got a day or a night to make the journey. At first there was small change or progress. John would come downstairs about the middle of the day, moving slowly and painfully.

And he was listless; there was no life in him; no resiliency or spring.

'How did you rest, son?' I would ask him.

He always smiled when he answered.

'Oh, fairly well,' he'd tell me. 'I fought three or four battles though, before I dropped off to sleep.'

He had come to the right place to be cured, though, and his mother was the nurse he needed. It was quiet in the hills of the Clyde, and there was rest and healing in the heather about Dunoon. Soon his sleep became better and less troubled by dreams. He could eat more, too, and they saw to it, at home, that he ate all they could stuff into him.

If children noticed their father's exhaustion, the memory of it grew vague. 'That last visit his face was thinner,' recalled Lily Baron, née Jones, of her father, John. 'It really did seem to be thinner, whereas I remember his face being more round, but you didn't dwell on it, you just accepted that he was home, that was all that mattered.'

Donald Overall was five when his father came home on leave. His memory consists of short, intense vignettes of his father's unexpected arrival with his kitbag on his back, then, after the greetings and a chance to relax, there were the games.

He sat me on the instep of his foot and I used to hold his hands and he would rock me up and down. He was in his army uniform and I could smell his khaki and tobacco because he smoked a pipe. I then remember my father carrying me upstairs on his left shoulder, my head was against his face and I can remember seeing his ears and smelling his jacket and his tobacco.

It was the little things that children like Donald remembered: the smell of the tobacco, perhaps the touch of the rough khaki uniform, the sight of the soldier's webbing, the pride in a father's corporal's stripes or his cloth cap, that could be borrowed and worn by a devoted son. The rifle, too, heavy though it seemed, could be examined and re-examined, the trigger squeezed a dozen times as the boy's imagination ran riot. Then there were the puttees; they were always a source of fun.

Madge Maindonald was ten when her brother Edwin came home in 1916.

They used to wear puttees, like a khaki bandage, and they would wind it round and round their legs and it was very tight and my brother would say, 'Come and hold this for me,' so I went across. I was a very obedient child, and I had to hold the puttee against his leg and he began to wind the puttee round and he bound my fingers in the bandage to his leg but pretended not to notice. He then got up and he'd walk across the room dragging me with him and all the time I'm saying, 'I can't get my fingers out,' and he would reply, 'Oh, you still down there?' He did silly things like that but I was his little sister, wasn't I?

Lily Jones remembered her dad balancing her brother Wyndham on one knee and herself on the other, after which he gave each a puttee to play with as he read them a story. As he spoke, each child would slowly roll the puttee into the shape of a cylinder to be let go and rolled up again if the book was not finished. Lily's father had been wounded and had had a spell in Shrewsbury Hospital. His leave was given, as a right, before he rejoined his regiment. As well as his puttees, he had managed to keep hold of a damaged steel helmet that Lily and her brother now played with. There was a hole in the helmet from one side to the other and Lily and Wyndham would look through the torn metal at one another before squeezing their fingers through the aperture and wiggling them. 'I do remember that last time he was home, him saying to Wyndham, "You are the man of the house you know, and so you have to grow up a big boy." And he got hold of me and said, "And you've got to grow up a good girl, won't you?" And I just said yes to him. It stayed in my mind and I'm sure it stayed in Wyndham's.'

Living in the village of Cookleigh, near Kidderminster, was Lucy Neale, a ten-year-old schoolgirl. Her father, Sergeant Harold Neale, had returned on leave to see his family, a time that happily coincided with Lucy's birthday. Now, after a week at home, his time with his family was drawing to a close.

I was in school, and I suppose it was about ten o'clock in the morning, and there was a knock at the door. We couldn't see who was on the other side, as the teacher, Mrs Beeston, went to answer it. I heard her say, 'Oh Mr Neale, how lovely to see you, you're on leave then?' And then she closed the door, much to my annoyance, and I couldn't hear a thing. Then she opened the door and beckoned me and she said, 'Come along, Lucy, you can go home now, you don't want to be in school any longer today.' It was my tenth birthday and we walked to the village, back to where we lived, and I was so proud, he was very handsome for one thing, my dad, and he looked lovely in the khaki uniform. We met one or two folk on the road going home and they shook hands with him and chatted and wished him well and then we went home to mother. I don't remember much about my birthday, really, it was 4 April 1917 and a nice sunny day, and when the other girls came home from school I went out to play with them.

Leave over, soldiers turned their minds to the challenge ahead. Harry Lauder's sympathy for his son was manifest. 'He could live over, and I made no doubt he did, every grim and dreadful thing that was waiting for him out there. He had been through it all, and he was going back.' Wives and parents, if ignorant of the conditions, instinctively appreciated the dangers. They did not need to see it in their loved ones' eyes: the reality was emphasised daily in the press by casualty lists. Even young children with little or no concept of war were swept up by the emotional tide and understood the portentous nature of the parting. With their senses sharpened, they could absorb without being aware the smallest details of those last moments before Daddy walked away, or climbed on to a train. Lucy Neale was typical.

At about six o'clock in the evening, my father called me in and said he'd got to go back to Kidderminster, back to barracks. 'Will you walk with me a little way, just up the hill, will you come with me?' Of course I would. He said goodbye to my mother, who was crying, and we went off down the road and then up this long hill. It was a ten-minute walk, I suppose, but we didn't hurry, we just walked slowly up the hill and I really can't remember what we talked about. I held on to his hand so tight, and when we got to the top, he said, 'I won't take you any further, you must go back now, and I'll stand here and watch you until you're out of sight,' and he put his arms round me and held me so close to him; I remember feeling how rough that khaki uniform was.

'You must go now, wave to me at the bottom, won't you?' I went, I left him standing there and I went down the hill and I kept looking back and waving and he was still there, just standing there. I got to the bottom and then I'd got to turn off to go to where we lived, so I stopped and waved to him and he gestured as much as to say, 'Go on, you must go home now,' ever so gently gestured and then he waved and he was still waving when I went, and that was the last time I ever saw him.

Like Lucy, Lily Jones had just celebrated her birthday when her father left. Lily was living temporarily with an aunt she called 'Auntie Mum', after an accident had left her mother with a broken wrist. The injury had largely healed and the family got together to pose for a photograph just a day before her father returned to his regiment to join a draft going overseas. Later that week Lily saw her father again, when John was part of a squad of men marched down from the Drill Hall, and along the main road through Blackwood to the station.

Wyndham and I were looking hard for Daddy and we spotted him, and Wyndham gave my hand a little squeeze and said, 'Come on,' and we ran and left Mummy and my aunts on the pavement and went down three little steps on to the roadside and next thing we knew an officer picked us both up and plonked us back on to the pavement again, I suppose the marching men would have knocked us over.

We all started walking to the top station, as it was called, and the wives and children were allowed to go on the platforms but no other relatives, so my two aunties had to stand outside at the railings. Daddy and I talked quite a lot; he said to me, 'When I come back you'll come straight back home.' I said, 'I don't know, I'll have to ask Auntie Mum,' so he said, 'You go and ask her then.' I went down the platform, across the rails and up to Auntie Mum to ask her if I would be going home and she said, 'Of course, of course,' so I ran back again to tell Daddy, 'Auntie Mum says of course, of course.' Then he just picked me up and hugged me. Tears were tumbling down his face and my brother was hanging on to his trousers, and then he hugged my mother before the order came to get on the train. Wyndham burst out crying and couldn't say goodbye, he just loved him and hugged him with his arms round his neck. When Daddy got into the carriage Wyndham asked Mummy to lift him up so he could say goodbye. There were a lot of tears on the station amongst the families who were there.

I remember the men in each carriage were on top of one another, their heads sticking out of the window, filling up the whole space. That was the same in all the carriages, the men all with their heads pressed out of the windows trying to wave as the train pulled out. We stood on that platform until we could not see them any more. 'Why did Daddy have to go, why did he go?' Wyndham kept asking. What could Mummy say, other than we wouldn't see Dad for a long time?

Families chose their place to say farewell. A lot of wives and mothers could not bear the highly charged atmosphere of the railway station; it was too public. People would be weeping, some uncontrollably, and it would be difficult not to be swept up in the tide of emotion. The soldiers, too, often found it was easier to say goodbye to their mothers at the gate to the house, leaving fathers to shake their sons by the hand or pat them on the back as they boarded the train with a 'Cheerio, son, look after yourself, I'll be glad to see you back again.' Nerves of steel: that was what both sides required, affirmed one former private of the London Scottish, Hal Kerridge. 'Crying doesn't help him; it doesn't help me. No, you treat it in a man's way . . . I mean our people at home had a duty to do – the same as we had – and their duty was not to make our lives harder than they were already.'

John Lauder made light of his return to France for the sake of his parents. He told them not to fret, that every man had to take his chances out there, 'if he is a man at all'. In turn, his parents remained brave. 'But it was cruelly hard,' wrote Sir Harry. 'We had lost him and found him again, and now he was being taken from us for the second time. It was harder, much harder, to see him go this second time than it had been the first, and it had been hard enough then, and bad enough.'

Staying brave for her son, regardless of her own emotions, typified Marie Leighton's farewell to Roland the first time he returned to France. Back then, they had taken rooms at a London hotel, and in the afternoon of the following day Roland had left. As Marie awaited her son's second homecoming with excitement, she relived the parting of the first.

'Do you still feel you would rather I did not come to Victoria to see you off tomorrow?' I asked him when we said goodnight.

'Yes. I don't feel I could stand it. You know, I've always been like that. I've never wanted people who really mattered to see me off at a station. Other people don't count. They can come in crowds. But not you. It'll be hard enough to go, anyhow.'

'Very well, then, we'll have lunch at Almond's, with that dear Russian friend I want to show you off to, and then you can do the rest of your shopping while I go and keep a business appointment in Farringdon Street. I shall be back here to say goodbye to you at four o'clock.' But the business appointment next day in Farringdon Street kept me longer than I had expected it would do and when I came out I could not get a taxicab easily. Agitated, desperate, I had almost run well on to the Embankment before I picked one up and then I dashed up to the hotel steps to find the boy jumping in and out of his own cab with a harassed look on his face.

'If I stay another minute I shall be too late,' he said.

There was no time for me to explain. One moment's clasp of hands – one quick, yet clinging, kiss – and he was gone!

Gone from me again – back to fight in France!

I stood looking straight before me with an odd feeling as if I were turning to stone. Why had I not thought of getting into the cab and driving to Victoria with him, without going on to the platform?'

The parting over, a sense of gloom and despondency filled the soldiers' train carriage. Men sat wrapped up in their own thoughts, reflecting on the time spent with their families. One man who had every reason to feel depressed was Lance Corporal William Swann of the 12th King's Liverpool Regiment. He was married with two sons, Alfred and Edward. Despite all efforts to the contrary, he felt he had appeared troubled and distant while at home, and it was only on his return to his Regimental Depot that he was able to say what he had truly felt.

Deby, you will please excuse me not being so jolly when I was home on leave, but I kept looking at you and round the house and at our two kiddies (bless em) that it set me wondering if I should ever be able to return home again and see you and so I think you can understand what was going through my mind and why I was so very quiet, but wait till I come out altogether, lovey, that's if I

have the luck, and you will find me entirely different, and I am
sure if any man loved his wife the same as I love you, he would be
the same as me when I was on pass [leave], and so you will excuse
my quietness . . .

'If I have the luck . . .': soldiers such as Lance Corporal Swann
could not help but weigh up their odds of returning, and not a few
were struck with a terrible premonition that they would never see
their family again. One of those men, Gunner Frank Bracey, had
taken the precaution of writing a letter to his wife, just in case his
own worst fears were realised. The letter would not be opened
unless he died; it is accessible today only because he did.

May 5th 1916
Dearest Win
    I am writing just a line Win in case of accidents. Just to let you
know how I have always loved you dear. You are the best little girl
on God's earth . . . I am writing this because I have a feeling that I
shall not come back again . . . You may think I am a bit taped writing this dear but I cannot help it. If I do come back dearest you will
never see this letter but I have a strong feeling today that I shall
never see England again. In case I do pop under the earth I want
you to be happy and look out for a worthier chap than your Humble,
you have been every thing to me Win. I know your love is mine
forever dearest but if I do not come back I wish you the best of
happiness and a good husband. I know you told me what you
would do for yourself if I did not return but Win for the sake of our
love I wish you to be brave, it would be hard for you little girl I
know, but do nothing of the kind. My last wish is that you marry
a good man and to be happy and to think of your Humble now and
then . . . I felt I must write these few lines Win but whatever
happens dear just keep a stout heart and think that your Frank did
his bit for the women of this little isle. I expect you will think your
Humble crazy but I was never saner than I am now . . . Frank

Two months after Frank Bracey died of wounds in August 1916, Lance Corporal Swann was killed on the Somme.

Most soldiers returned to their units in France and Belgium with heavy hearts, all too aware that even if they were to see their families again it was likely to be from a hospital bed. That was all well and good if they had control over the extent of their injuries but bullets and bombs were respecters neither of a man's responsibility nor of his dignity. If a soldier had not written a last letter home, he might do so now; it did not mean that he had a foreboding of death, simply that he understood better the vagaries of war. Lieutenant Andrew Buxton wrote and carried his letter 'only to be posted should I be fatally hit' in his jacket pocket for ten months before he was killed; in fact he lived for longer than he thought he might, and he updated it shortly before he died. Buxton, like many men, wrote his message with no particular expectation that it would ever be opened. Nevertheless, he felt that his family would appreciate a final word. 'Is it stupid to leave this letter?' he asked rhetorically. 'I think not. I think you [mother] would like it.'

The majority of the letters that survive were written by young junior officers, single men, boys even, often ignorant of life but fully cognisant of how they were expected to behave. These were letters that were obviously heartfelt but they were also written as a part of the greater ritual of *duty*: no other word held such a natural resonance for the soldiers of the Great War. Doing one's duty was all-important, and under the umbrella of that word came a procession of others such as 'truth', 'uprightness', 'honesty', 'manliness' and 'justice'. 'We have all been brought up at home, in school, and church, to a creed which places our duty to our country next to our religion, and I should not have been a true son had I stayed at home instead of coming out here,' wrote Lieutenant Francis Potter to his parents shortly before he was killed.

Letters were rarely downcast in tone, in fact many were almost chipper and rattle along: 'My own darling Mother and Father. In

the event of my getting a clean knock-out blow from the Hun . . .'
Lieutenant Stanley Bickersteth wrote, picking up on the idea
fostered during a boy's education that war was an extension of
sport, a higher game. Another officer, Lieutenant Leslie Sanders,
was equally upbeat and matter-of-fact with his father.

> This is a final message for you to read when I am dead. There will
> be little else – just the brief official notification 'The Secretary of
> State for War regrets . . .'; maybe a belated letter or two, speaking
> only of the small happenings of the day; perhaps a tale of a brother
> officer as to how I fell; beyond that nothing. And therefore now,
> beforehand, I say farewell . . .

The notion of war as a higher game was absorbed by boys through
books, school lessons and in the popular Officer Training Corps at
school and at university. In their letters, a number of officers made
reference to their education and many corresponded with their old
schools throughout the war. Such was their affection for those formative years that it was not unusual to leave a final letter for past
masters, presumably to be read out in assembly. It was a homage to
the school and to the noble qualities it had instilled in its Old Boys.
Leslie Sanders died at the age of twenty-three. A former Head Boy,
he left three letters in the event of his death, two to his parents and
one to St Olave's Grammar School in Southwark, south London.

'Some of you will remember me only as a little figure in a blue
gown that called for cheers on Speech Day . . . Some will think of the
few sports I used to take part in – fives after school; paper chases at
Court Farm, swimming for my house . . . Some will remember me at
the Debating Society, always making long-winded, cocksure speeches
on big themes . . .' There was no doubting Sanders' integrity but,
reflecting his youth, his farewell was prone to melodrama: 'I am going
away. Clasp hands once more – the grip that serves when our tongues
are silent . . .' he urged. 'I died content.'

Duty had taught these boys that self-sacrifice in pursuit of a

noble cause was an honour and, for this reason, brave but platitu-
dinous words were used to signify how death meant little or
nothing to them, especially when Christian faith taught the
reality of an afterlife. Bickersteth writes almost blithely that they
(he and his family) would have been dead in forty years in any
case, and that was no time at all when set into the context of
'endless ages'. On this basis there was little point in sorrow.

'Both of you will have to die sooner or later,' he tells his parents.
'If Mother dies first, you Dad will know that I shall be there
waiting at the gate to give her a welcome. And if Dad dies then
you, Mother darling, will know that Dad and I are waiting for
you; isn't that just splendid?'

Meanwhile, Leslie Sanders also instructed his parents not to
grieve, rather, 'I would even bid you rejoice in my death . . .
Rejoice, O Mother o' mine, that your son was privileged to die
for England!' And Andrew Buxton enjoined his mother not to
worry at all, rather, 'Please carry on the same as usual, but more
rest and enjoyment, and less work!' This was the stiff upper lip
taken to seemingly ridiculous extremes but it was one that
served a useful purpose: by making light of the personal loss,
by repeating how content they were in death, and by playing
up the sanctity of the cause, these officer sons plumped up, in
the only way they knew how, the cushion best suited to soften
the blow.

Not only are these letters remarkably formulaic, but they also
leave the distinct impression that an act of personal purification
was being undertaken at the same time. Characteristically, there
was a note of parental appreciation: anything innately good was
derived from them. Then the virtues of the nation's cause were
extolled, and that life or death would be God's will. With that
in mind, there was usually an appeal for forgiveness: 'You know
the faults and failings of my life . . .' And then a rejection of
mere mortal chattels and of all things sullied and impure: 'I
feel one really becomes nearly immortal at such a time as all

earthly things merely disappear.' These letters displayed, if nothing else, a remarkable homogeneity among public school boys, and explains why, with such an ethos, most were able to suppress personal interests and perform their duty under extreme duress.

Such sentiments and the themes they portray rarely changed even when death was faced with rather more immediacy and certainty. However, the tone changed. The news of an imminent offensive whittled down the life expectancy of all, particularly junior officers, and an order to go over the top concentrated the mind. In the days and hours before an attack, the letters written by these young officers were less florid and far more sombre and thoughtful. 'This is not an easy letter to write . . .'; 'This is the most difficult letter I have ever sat down to write . . .'; 'I'm writing this letter the day before the most important moment of my life . . .': the opening lines of just three letters written to parents on the eve of the same battle. These letters were directly preparatory for death. Men talked of having taken Communion: 'I placed my soul and body in God's keeping, and I am going into battle with His name on my lips,' wrote one man; others talk of leaving wills and certain treasured items to specified friends and family; entreaties to parents not to grieve are much more low key.

Officers talk of keeping their nerve, and of 'sticking it'. There is never a hint of shirking responsibility: to do anything cowardly or base would be the worst thing that could happen, and few, if any, expressed a desire to be elsewhere. 'I would not back out for all the money in the world,' wrote one man, despite his anxieties. The greatest fear was not death but critical injury: 'Only one thing do I dread, that is disfigurement – real disfigurement, it would be too awful for my girl,' declared Major Francis Gull of the 13th Rifle Brigade a month before he was killed; another merely confessed: 'The prospect of pain naturally appals me some-what, and I am taking morphia into battle.'

Where there is a change in sentiment, where letters are significantly different, is among men who were fathers. Their sense of duty was as strong as anyone else's, but their duty was hopelessly torn between the national cause and responsibility for their own families. These men had a love of their wives and children that tore at the heartstrings. Theirs was an intensity of emotion that was born of being a parent. Like the young, they professed themselves ready to die for the cause; the difference was that the young espoused those views without responsibility. They were not parents and could not think like parents. Only a child could tell a parent not to grieve and even begin to think that they might not. Twenty-seven-year-old Captain Charles May of the 22nd Manchester Regiment was the father of a baby daughter. On the eve of battle on the Somme, he wrote a last letter to his wife and child.

> I do not want to die. Not that I mind for myself. If it be that I am
> to go, I am ready. But the thought that I may never see you or our
> darling baby again turns my bowels to water. I cannot think of it
> with even the semblance of equanimity. My one consolation is the
> happiness that has been ours. Also my conscience is clear that I
> have always tried to make life a joy for you. I know at least that if
> I go you will not want. This is something. But it is the thought
> that we may be cut off from one another which is so terrible and
> that our babe may grow up without my knowing her and without
> her knowing me. It is difficult to face. And I know your life without
> out me would be a dull blank. You must never let it become
> wholly so. For to you will be left the greatest charge in all the
> world; the upbringing of our baby. God bless that child, she is the
> hope of life to me. My darling *au revoir*. It may well be that you
> will only have to read these lines as ones of passing interest. On
> the other hand, they may well be my last message to you. If they
> are, know through all your life that I loved you and baby with all
> my heart and soul, that you two sweet things were just all the

world to me. I pray God I may do my duty, for I know, whatever that may entail, you would not have it otherwise.

Having had a presentiment that he would not survive the forth-coming attack, Charles May approached his closest friend in the battalion, Captain Francis Earles, and asked him to look after his family if he were killed. The officer was as good as his word, and later married May's widow, Bessie, helping to raise the young daughter, Pauline, as his own.

Charles May died on the first day of the Battle of the Somme, a couple of miles at most from where another father, Private John Scollen, lay dead. Unlike Captain May, his body was never found. Shortly after the attack, his final letter arrived at his home at Seaham, near Newcastle upon Tyne.

My Dear Wife and Children it is with regret I write these last words of farewell to you. We are about to make a charge against these awful Germans. If it is God's Holy will that I should fall I will have done my duty to my King and country and I hope justly in the sight of God. It is hard to part from you but keep a good heart dear Tina and do not grieve for me for God and His Blessed Mother will watch over you and my bonny little chil-dren and I have not the least doubt but that my country will help you for the sake of one of its soldiers that has done his duty. Well Dear Wife Tina, you have been a good wife and mother and looked after my canny bairns and I am sure they will be a credit to both of us . . .

My Joe, Jack, Tina and Aggie not forgetting my bonny twins Nora and Hugh and my last flower baby whom I have only had the great pleasure of seeing once since he came into the world, God bless them. I will try and get to do my duty whilst on this perilous undertaking and if I fall then you will know that I died in God's Holy Grace. Tell all of my friends and yours also that I bid them farewell now. My Dear Wife and children I have not anything

more to say only I wish you all God's Holy Grace and blessing so
GOODBYE GOODBYE and think of me in your prayers. I know
these are hard words to receive but God's will be done.

From your faithful soldier

Husband and father

John Scollen. B Coy. 27th N[orthumberland]. F[usiliers].

Goodbye my loved ones DON'T CRY

*   *   *

After every attack, the wounded lay scattered amidst the shell-
holes and broken trenches. Their chances of survival depended
greatly on whether the attack had been successful. If the enemy
had been pushed back, if the ground taken was now out of sight
of the enemy, it could be scoured for casualties. If he was fortunate, and a relative peace had descended on the battlefield, a
wounded man could call out for help. It might take a while
coming, but help could reasonably be expected to arrive; whether
it came in time to save a life was another matter.

Where the attack had been repulsed, the wounded could be
stuck between the lines and subjected to further artillery fire as
both sides contested the ground. In this case, if the man could not
effect his own escape back to the trenches, he would have to rely
on search parties sent out at night to look for survivors, and
survival in this scenario was extremely problematic. In the interim
the wounded would try to find extra rations in the haversacks of
the dead, and, most importantly, water from the bottles hanging
on the men's equipment; that is, if the bottle had not been punc-
tured by shrapnel or a bullet. Then it was a case of waiting and
hoping, though often in vain.

'I went over a good deal of the ground next day [14 November,
1916],' wrote Lieutenant Colonel Robert Fitzpatrick of the
ground near the Somme village of Beaumont Hamel, 'and saw
many – a great many – dead in no man's land – who had been
there since July 1st, a pathetic sight as obviously a great number

YORK & LANCA[STER]

CAPTAIN
FAULDER H.
CUMMER...
KINGDON A. F.
SMITH S. F.
WORTLEY J. F. M.C.

LIEUTENANT
ALLEN...
BIDWELL...
EDWARDES...

Harold Faulder (1918–2005), born ten weeks after the death of his father in the Ypres Salient, points to his father's name on the Tyne Cot Memorial to the Missing near Ypres. Captain Harold Faulder (*inset*) was killed serving with the 1/4th York and Lancaster Regiment on 26 April 1918. The picture was taken by Captain Faulder's widow Marjorie on a trip to Belgium in the late 1920s.

A fond farewell: a sergeant kisses his young daughter goodbye.

Two men of the 4th Essex Regiment. Such were the numbers enlisting in 1914 that the Government billeted 800,000 volunteers with civilians.

The new Secretary of State for War, Lord Kitchener, addresses a jubilant crowd after the outbreak of war. His appeal for volunteers, while wildly successful, denuded vital wartime industries of labour.

Always thinking of you: a typical postcard of the era. This man, Private William Redley, 1/4th Northamptonshire Regiment, was killed in April 1917.

The note written by Private Thomas Hughes while on board a ship headed for France, September 1914. The note was placed in a bottle and dropped into the sea. Private Hughes was killed two weeks later.

The covering note sent by Private Hughes. The bottle was recovered from the sea in 1999, whereupon Hughes' daughter, then in her eighties, signed for the receipt of the bottle and note.

An officer writes a letter home. By August 1916 some 1.1 million letters were being sent to the Western Front every day.

BLIGHTY

THOUGHTS.

A cartoon drawn by Acting Sergeant Herbert Gibson and sent to his girlfriend in Fenham, Newcastle upon Tyne. The pose captures well the thoughts of soldiers for 'Blighty' and their loved ones.

No 2

When there is nothing
in the mail for you!
SomEwhere in france

Mail When they yell the
is in.
SomEwhere in NO 1

This soldier's sprint underlines the fervour with which men greeted news from home.

The disappointment is clear. Any feelings of isolation could be quickly exacerbated when no mail arrived for one soldier while others received letters and parcels.

Artillery officers distribute festive parcels sent from their loved ones at home in December 1917.

Bedford, 1914: Harry Lauder's son leading his platoon. Harry Lauder describes this charge in his memoirs and was probably looking on when this picture was taken.

Father and son pictured just prior to John Lauder's departure for the Western Front in May 1915. He survived well over a year in France before he was shot by a sniper in December 1916.

The Lauders' house in Scotland where John Lauder spent several months recuperating after being wounded. His parents were shocked by their son's gaunt appearance.

IMPERIAL WAR MUSEUM – Q11281

Harry Lauder talking with Staff Officers at First Army Headquarters at Ranchicourt, 5 September 1918. After his son was killed he spent much of the war on the Western Front singing to troops close to the front line.

DAVID EMPSON

The grave of John Lauder at Ovillers Cemetery, photographed around 1920. Harry Lauder saw the grave in 1917 while entertaining the troops in France.

August 1917: a large crowd of soldiers wave their leave papers at the official photographer in the Belgian town of Poperinge. By mid 1917 over thirty-five thousand men were leaving for Britain every week.

Men in high spirits crowded on deck as the ship leaves Boulogne harbour for England. Ordinary ranks could often wait between a year and eighteen months for leave.

At home on leave and father kisses his baby for the first time. Leave was cherished by the men but often proved emotionally difficult and lasted at most just two weeks.

The isolated grave of Lieutenant W. E. Parke, killed during III Corp's capture of the small hamlet of Outtersteene. Despite severe fighting in the area in April 1918, Parke's grave survived and was taken to the nearby military cemetery established in August 1917.

Graves of Seaforth Highlanders killed on the Somme in 1915. The Somme was a relatively peaceful backwater before the battle and units were able to lavish considerable attention on the graves of the fallen.

Grave markers carefully prepared for five men of the 2nd London Regiment killed in the same incident.

The badge worn by Douglas when mortally wounded and sent home to us by a fellow Officer serving with him

The cap badge worn by an unknown officer and returned to his family after his death, presumably separate from his other possessions. The badge was mounted and framed in remembrance of a dead son or husband.

A somewhat posed image of a wife receiving news of the death of her husband. Children remembered how their mothers visibly trembled as they opened the letter, frequently collapsing on reading the news.

The train drawn for two-year-old George Musgrave by his father shortly before he was mortally wounded. The train represented the bond of love between father and son that has lasted a lifetime. George has built a museum in Eastbourne dedicated to his father's memory.

George Musgrave with his parents, shortly before his father left for France in 1917. While Alfred was lying in hospital, his wife was given permission to visit him in France just days before he died.

Violet Downer, aged about four, standing with her father, Samuel. He was killed on the Somme in October 1916 and is buried in Connaught Cemetery. His wife chose to remarry for the children's sake, but Violet never liked her step-father.

The fraudster Edward Page Gaston paying his respects at the grave of a fallen soldier in 1914. He would later use this image in his publicity, in order to convince families of his integrity.

Gaston apparently cataloguing ephemera belonging to fallen British soldiers. He proposed to return the relics to the families, but his dubious practices cast doubt on whether many, if any, were returned.

A rare postcard distributed around POW camps in Germany in a desperate search for twenty-year-old Private Albert Thompson, missing in action on the Somme while serving with the 1/8th Royal Warwickshire Regiment.

February 1919: a British soldier stands over a German administrator at the POW Camp of Cassel, checking to see that all British prisoners have been indentified prior to returning to Britain. Thousands of British soldiers believed prisoners were never found.

7, Second Aven.
King's Park.
28th Sept. 1916.

My dear Lizzie & Peter,
    We all got a dreadful shock this morning when we read the news of your darling boys death. Words are no use at this time but you know how I feel for you as I am going through the same trial till the end. I would have written sooner but I am so full of grief. Ever since I received your letter I could not keep from thinking

Breach Cover.
Belonging to Peter Miller. Found in trench coincidentally on 27th. September, 1916: about 1000 yds from where he fell. The only possession of his recovered, as far as can be ascertained.

The extraordinary note that came with the breach cover belonging to Peter Miller, which was found by his great friend Raymond Singleton more than two weeks after Peter's death.

After the death of Peter Miller, his parents received dozens of letters of condolence, including this one from Lizzie Miller's sister-in-law, who had only recently lost her son in the same battle.

Peter Miller (*in uniform*) with his parents and siblings. His elder sister Emily wrote to Peter just before he was killed, while another brother, Hector, standing behind her, also went to France and was gassed. Emily lived until she was 108 years old.

The letter sent by Emily to Peter in which she passed on the family gossip and news of the downing of a Zeppelin over Cuffley in Hertfordshire. Peter never received the letter and it was returned to England.

Peter's friend Raymond Singleton, who broke the news of Peter's death to the family days before the official notification arrived from the War Office. Raymond was later commissioned into the Rifle Brigade and survived the war.

Father and son: Major General W. F. Braithwaite and Captain Valentine Braithwaite serving together on Imbros Island in 1915. Captain Braithwaite was later reported missing, believed killed on the Somme. His father would write to the War Office to ask that his son be officially recognised as Killed in Action and not just believed dead.

had died of unattended wounds as many seemed to have tried to make themselves more comfortable by placing things under their head as they lay on their backs.'

What might have passed through the minds of those who lay there, waiting? It was a recurring question asked by those at home, with no hope of answer. It would have meant a lot to know that a father or husband had turned his thoughts to home in those last moments. Human nature suggests it was probable; surviving evidence tells us that they did, as Reverend Arthur Boyce discovered when, in August 1918, he picked up a letter from the battlefield near Rheims. It had been scribbled by a man named only as Fred and it had been left with an instruction to the finder to 'Please Forward'.

> My dear wife, I am dying on the battlefield. With my last strength God bless you and the kiddies. I am glad to give my life for my country. Don't grieve over me – be proud of this fact. Goodbye and God bless you. Fred
>
> When the kiddies get older tell them how I died.

With the dregs of his stamina, Fred wrote a similar note to his mother. It has not been possible to put a full name to this soldier. Not so the next man.

Corporal John Duesbery, of German extraction, had wisely Anglicised his name on enlistment from Duesburg. He had been raised near Bradford and had enlisted in Mansfield soon after the outbreak of war. In September 1916 he was involved in an attack on the Somme. His company, in the 2nd Sherwood Foresters, was sent to attack the Quadrilateral, a strongly held German position. The attack had gone in at dawn and was repulsed, most of the men taking to shell-holes for protection from withering fire. Extremely heavy casualties were suffered, not only from German machine-gun and artillery fire but also from a British barrage ahead of a second, ill-fated, assault later that afternoon, the barrage crossing over the line of shell-holes occupied by survivors of the first attack. The enemy position was not taken, making casualty evacuation extremely difficult.

Dear Mother

I am writing these few lines severely wounded. We have done well our Batt. advanced about 3 quarters of a mile. I am laid in a shell hole with 2 wounds in my hip and through my back. I cannot move or crawl. I have been here for 24 hours and never seen a living soul. I hope you will receive these few lines as I don't expect anyone will come to take me away, but you know I have done my duty out here now for 1 year and 8 months and you will always have the consolation that I died quite happy doing my duty.

Must give my best of love to all the cousins who [have] been so kind to me since I have been out here and the Best of love to Arthur and Harry and all at Swinefleet. xxx

John Duesbery's body must have been found, for his note was retrieved from his pocket book and sent home with his other belongings. His grave would have been marked in a rudimentary way, perhaps with a piece of wood or an upturned rifle, but whatever was placed there it was subsequently destroyed and John's body lost.

Even when a man was rescued there was a harrowing process of evacuation across a shell-pocked battlefield, first on a stretcher, then in an ambulance, either horse-drawn or motorised. This vehicle would have to negotiate terrible ruts and holes in the ground, causing untold pain to the men lying inside. If the man survived to reach a Casualty Clearing Station, perhaps twenty miles behind the line, then surgery was performed to prolong life, before a further journey was undertaken as far back as the coast on a barge or, more commonly, a train. Here, at a Base Hospital, additional operations were undertaken with the possibility that a move to England might be sanctioned.

For the critically wounded, there was a grave risk that taking them by boat would prove fatal, especially if the English Channel was rough. Yet soldiers hankered after a return to Britain, or Blighty as it was known, for just the thought of arriving on home soil was of immense psychological importance to their morale. For men whose injuries were not immediately life-threatening, there was the chance, on warm, sunny days, of being wheeled in their beds on to the cliff tops where, in the distance, the hazy outline of the white cliffs of Dover would both soothe their souls and tantalise their waking thoughts.

Sixteen hospitals and a convalescent depot were based near the French town of Etaples, some seventeen miles south of Boulogne. These hospitals could deal with more than 22,000 cases at any one time, many very seriously wounded and not expected to recover. In May 1915 a cemetery was established close to the hospitals and grew to contain well over 10,700 graves by the end of the war. Most died before there was any chance that a loved one might pay a visit. However, in the same month the cemetery was opened, the Army Council in England gave permission for a small number of relatives to travel abroad to visit their sons or husbands before they died. Only those soldiers deemed terminally ill, but who were likely to live for a few days or longer, were offered the privilege of such a visit.

The first indication that a trip was to be granted came in a War Office telegram, a heart-stopping moment in itself, which stated that the soldier in question was seriously ill and that relatives should reply immediately as to whether or not they wished to travel. Once that wish was confirmed, an official form (Army Form B 104-108) was sent giving details of the trip; a railway warrant would be provided, to be taken to the nearest station at which point a return ticket would be issued at no cost; other expenses would also be met if the individual was too hard up to pay them. The recipient had seven days to undertake the journey, although in practice there was little delay in packing a small suitcase and leaving, once any pressing private arrangements had been dealt with. No passport was necessary: the form, presented to the Embarkation Officer, was enough to guarantee passage.

Families of other ranks were met at the port of arrival by representatives of the YMCA, which provided transport and accommodation for the duration of the visit. For the families of officers, the Red Cross offered a similar service with any one of five designated hostels offering accommodation. In all, almost 3,000 officers' relatives received help in this way.

Staying at the Terminus Hotel, one of the five Red Cross-designated hotels, were Harry and Clara Wakeman. They had received a telegram at 8.30 on Sunday evening, 6 October 1918, informing them that their son, Second Lieutenant Malcolm Wakeman, a pilot in the Royal Air Force, was seriously injured and in hospital. Responding to the invitation to visit him, they were packed within the hour and on their way to a Manchester railway station to catch the 10.30 p.m. train heading south; they paid the third class return fare of £8 12s. 8d. themselves.

On their arrival at the 30th General Hospital, they were met by a doctor who told them that their son was dangerously ill. Malcolm had a bullet wound to the head, received in mid-air combat, and metal was still lodged in his skull; the doctor warned that he had never see anyone recover from such injuries.

Despite the prognosis, Malcolm seemed remarkably well, even describing himself as 'A1 and tophole', and gave a lucid description of the dogfight which had eventually resulted in his crash-landing. His parents remained with him for the next two days until his father returned to England to resume work at his ailing chemical business.

Over the next few days, Malcolm's health fluctuated. He had an operation on his head but doctors were unable to remove the bullet, or fragment of bullet, that could be seen on an X-ray. Each day his mother was picked up by car from the hotel and taken to see her son. On Monday 14 October she wrote to her husband that she was going to see about having her hospital pass renewed for another week, and that Malcolm had seemed a little better the previous day but that his life was still in grave danger.

Wednesday [16th]

My dear Harry

Malcolm had his head dressed again yesterday. The Sister told me he was doing fairly well up to last night but when I went yesterday something had gone into his eye when the dressing was being done. Our dear boy does not know when his head is being dressed. I am going up this afternoon again. I am often there twice a day.

I have just come and had tea with Malcolm. He seems better to day. The Padre was here and wishes me to thank you for your letter to him.

Malcolm never sits up for anything. I am going to walk tonight [from the hotel] so am leaving before dark. Malcolm sends his love to all of you. I remain your affectionate wife. With love Clara Wakeman.

Two days later, Clara received an urgent call from the hospital. Malcolm was dying and she should come right away. She rushed to the hospital but was too late. After seeing her son, she left but returned that afternoon to see him again. Doctors asked if they could examine his body to determine if they could learn anything from the injury for the treatment of future cases and Clara consented. She then telegraphed her husband that their son had died and set about returning home. Malcolm was given a full military funeral three days later with three volleys fired over his grave and the Last Post sounded.

Clara Wakeman arrived home on 20 October and took to her bed. She had, according to her husband, caught a chill. She did not re-emerge for the following three weeks and she was described by Harry as 'confused' and not really able to tell him anything of the events in Calais. Meanwhile, Harry Wakeman began the slow winding up of his son's affairs.

Another wounded soldier who received a visit, in this case from his wife, was Private Alfred Musgrave. He had been wounded in the legs by shrapnel at the end of November 1917 and, although his injuries were serious, they were not at first thought to be life-threatening. He was fortunate to be evacuated quickly to a Dressing Station and then sent down the line to the 12th General Hospital based at Rouen. On 4 December he was well enough to write a brief letter home.

Just a note to let you know that I am still here but getting on as well as can be expected. I expect you have been anxiously waiting for this as it is quite a long time since I wrote. I have not got the least idea how long I shall be here before being sent to Blighty but you have the consolation of knowing that I shall not go to the front again for a long time so keep the home fires burning till I come home.

Please let all know as to my situation and convey my love etc. Will close now with fondest love and kisses to you and the dear boy [George] from your loving husband, Alf.

Shortly after sending this letter, Alf's condition deteriorated. Within two or three days he was critically ill and not expected to survive. His wife Louisa received permission to travel abroad. 'She was given a pass that enabled her to go to Rouen and she told me what a terrible journey it had been,' explained her son George.

It was herself and another woman who went from Newhaven, and they crossed in rough seas. She could hardly talk about what she saw there, going into the hospital, but she told me that the men were crying out seeing an English woman, a civilian, who wasn't staff. I suppose it was a little bit of home, but she found it harrowing.

Dad had gangrene by then and he'd lost fingers as well as having serious problems with his legs. He was still alive when she saw him, and he'd already written a letter home that she received on her return. I don't know if my dad understood the seriousness of his condition.

Exactly one week after writing home, Alf Musgrave died. Louisa had been married barely three years and was left with a two-year-old son with no memory of his father. George, for his part, had only a picture of a train drawn by his father shortly before he was injured. He would treasure it for the rest of his life.

Hastily drawn pictures, scrawled notes of love and affection or long-considered letters: the manner by which contact was made between a soldier overseas and his people at home did not really matter; the act of communication was what was important. Treasured most of all were those last letters, many helping to bridge the gap between the dead and the living through their simple statements of love and adoration. Such letters would give comfort to a widow but also offer a child the lasting reassurance that he or she was special, and a final chance, too, for a father to proffer advice and encouragement which, when set down in words, could continue to give confidence and security from beyond the grave. In April 1916, Sergeant Francis Gautier wrote to his daughter from his hospital bed when he knew he was dying.

To my darling daughter Marie

Dearly loved daughter. This, my letter to you, is written in grief. I had hoped to spend many happy years with you after the War was over and to see you grow up into a good and happy woman. I am writing because I want you in after years to know how dearly I loved you, I know that you are too young now to keep me in your memory. I know your dear mother will grieve, be a comfort to her, remember when you are old enough that she lost her dear brave son, your brother, and me your father within a short

time. Your brother was a dear brave boy, honour his memory for
he loved you, and your brothers [Wilfred and Pierre] dearly and he
died like a brave soldier in defence of his home and Country. May
God guide and keep you safe and that at last we may all meet
together in His eternal rest. I am your loving & affectionate father,

    F H Gautier xxxxxxxxxxxxxxxxxxxxxx

Sergeant Francis Gautier hung on grimly to life but eventually
died of his wounds on 11 June 1916. His son Albert Gautier had
been killed in August the previous year, aged just seventeen.

Marie Leighton had been waiting all evening for her son to arrive
home on leave. As the hours passed she became more fidgety; she
wanted to see her son.

He is certainly very late. It is beginning to look as if he will not
come till tomorrow morning. The weather may be bad in the
Channel. Anyhow, we shall have to go on with dinner. I hear a
noise of the opening and shutting of doors.

    I start to my feet.

    This is he! This must be he!

    But two or three moments pass and he does not come into the
room. And something new and strange and heavy has come into
the air of the house; or so, at least, I fancy.

    My husband comes along. There is something very odd about his
step. And his face looks changed, somehow; sharpened in feature and
greyish white. 'How true it is that electric light sometimes makes
people look a dreadful colour!' I think as he comes nearer to me.

    I ran forward then to meet him.

    'Where is Roland? Isn't he here? I thought I heard him come.'

    And then for the first time I noticed that the boy's father had a
bit of pinkish paper crushed up in his hand.

    'Is that a telegram?' I cried eagerly, putting out my own hand.
'Oh, give it to me! What does it say? Isn't he coming to-night?'

One of my husband's arms was put quietly around me.

'No. It's no good our waiting for him any longer. He'll never come any more. He's dead. He was badly wounded on Wednesday at midnight, and he died on Thursday.'

'For minutes that were like years the world became to me a shapeless horror of greyness in which there was no beginning and no end, no light and no sound. I did not know anything except that I had to put out my hand and catch at something, with an animal instinct to steady myself so that I might not fall. And then, through the rolling, blinding waves of mist, there came to me suddenly the old childish cry:

'Come and see me in bed, mother!'

And I heard myself answering aloud:

'Yes, boy of my heart, I will come. As soon as the war is over I will come and see you in bed – in your bed under French grass. And I will say good-night to you – there – kneeling by your side – as I've always done.'

4

Finders, Losers, Weepers

'No No No, Oh God
Not For Nought'

2nd Lieutenant Harold Linzell MC
7th Border Regiment
Killed in action 3 July 1916, aged twenty-one
Buried Dantzig Alley British Cemetery

In the first days of June 1916, just weeks before the launch of the Somme offensive, twenty-year-old Lance Corporal Arnold Ridley was walking through the streets of Plymouth when he heard news of a major battle. It was not this time on land, but, rather, at sea. The Royal Navy's Grand Fleet had engaged the Imperial German High Seas Fleet at Jutland and news of the encounter was just beginning to filter home.

> Not only did the first reports suggest a major defeat [for the navy] but most of the sunken ships were Devonport-commissioned. Union Street seemed full of women – some hysterical, some crying quietly and others grey-faced with staring unseeing eyes and leading small children by the hand. They had no illusions, these women – they knew only too well that, when large ships were sunk in battle in the North Sea, there could be but few survivors.

Arnold Ridley, later to find fame as an actor, perhaps most memorably as Private Godfrey in *Dad's Army*, had witnessed what could happen when a tight-knit community sustained severe casualties in one single shattering event. Less than a month later, precisely the same scenes of hysteria and fear were repeated in towns and cities up and down the country, from Glasgow to Grimsby, from Newcastle upon Tyne to Nottingham and from Carlisle to Cambridge. Kitchener's New Armies had gone into action, fully trained and committed, but they had suffered heinous casualties. Entire battalions drawn overwhelmingly from their local communities had, in some cases, almost ceased to exist.

Back in Britain, precise details of their endeavours remained unclear for several days although early rumours excited frantic speculation. In Barnsley and the surrounding villages, the fortunes of its two Pals Battalions were still hazy after a week, the *Barnsley Chronicle* printing a notice in an effort to calm emotions. After maintaining the official view that the British were continuing their 'gloriously successful push in France', it added on 8 July:

> All sorts of wild rumours were yesterday current locally concerning the Barnsley Battalions, and whilst we are not in a position to give them the lie direct, we can authoritatively say that no official news has come through which would in any way corroborate the startling tales afloat regarding the fate of our lads . . . During the next week – should any news come through regarding the Barnsley Battalions – we shall post the messages on the front window of the *Chronicle* buildings. In the event of no message being posted it must, therefore, be taken for granted that nothing of outstanding importance has happened.

It would be another seven days before the truth emerged in the newspaper after letters confirming fatalities had reached frantic wives and parents: 210 killed or died of wounds and perhaps twice as many wounded.

The widespread speculation may have been due to other newspapers listing the names of casualties on the same day the *Barnsley Chronicle* published its call for calm. The *Yorkshire Evening Post* had been more proactive and collated the reports of local officers serving in the Leeds Pals who had been killed, information that arrived swiftly by telegram. The paper had also drawn up lists of wounded from among those men from Leeds and the surrounding area who had managed through hastily scribbled notes from hospital to make private contact with home. Dozens of men were reporting to their families that they were injured but safe; one man, already in hospital in Manchester, wrote home that 'we suffered heavily'. It is not hard to imagine how such small but significant details would travel around a community. Barnsley and Leeds were just twenty miles apart and their Pals Battalions served in neighbouring brigades in the same division. They had, in fact, been fighting from neighbouring trenches; Barnsley's anxiety was by no means misplaced.

Maud Cox, born in 1910, was a young girl from the small east coast mining village of Methil in Fife. The daughter of a grocer, she watched as her mother pasted up the latest lists of casualties in the shop window. The reaction to those lists suggests that this was the first some people knew about fatalities within their own families.

When the villagers heard the train come in, I mean the train was practically in the high street as it was just a little village, well, then they'd know that news was arriving and they'd start to gather. The lorry came from the station and dumped the bills and my mother went out with a bucket full of paste and a big white wash brush, and by that time there was a crowd waiting for her. The lists were always in alphabetical order and as people read them they shouted out to friends, who were too far away to see, 'You're all right, your lad's not on it.' Then you'd hear somebody start to cry. I remember one time going outside and there was a woman and she was rolling on the pavement and screaming her head off and my mother just grabbed me and brought me in. She said, 'What are you doing out there?' And Jessie, a girl who worked for Mum in the shop, said, 'I'm so sorry for Mrs Greer. She's lost her man and she's left with six steps and stairs.' I couldna think why anybody was getting excited about steps and stairs, I didn't realize at the time that it meant six children with only about a year between them all.

The press should not have been in a position to publish lists of casualties before families learned the news for themselves. Since early September 1914, *The Times* had printed lists of the dead, wounded and missing, in its Roll of Honour, the columns scoured daily by civilians looking for recognisable names. If the War Office had the information to release a name to the press, then a telegram or letter should already have been sent to the immediate family and it was therefore more than a little unfortunate if publication preceded private disclosure. In November 1914, Herbert Vacher had cause to write to the War Office when his son's name appeared in *The Times* amongst 'The following casualties to officers in the Expeditionary Force are reported from General Headquarters under date November 11.' Vacher's name is ninth in the list of 'Killed'.

Sir, amongst the returns of killed published in the papers yesterday, I find the name of my son G[eorge] M Vacher, 2nd Lt, Royal Warwickshire Regiment. As that is the first intimation I have received of his fatality, may I ask for an official notification as confirmation thereof. Yours faithfully, HP Vacher.

The letter is remarkably controlled, considering that the shock of seeing his son's name must have been severe.

Often a family's first source of definite news about a death was from an intimate friend of the casualty. The likelihood of this arose during major offensives when pressure on the army's administration was severe and it might take a couple of weeks or longer before official confirmation of death reached home.

Peter Miller, the younger brother of Emily, had been killed

shortly after going over the top at High Wood. The letter of homely gossip Emily had written to him on 4 September had not reached him before his death on the 9th, although his father did not receive the War Office confirmation until the 29th. On receiving the news, he wrote in his diary: 'It is awful to think of it! And how many thousands of homes are the same.' He was, however, already grieving because he already knew.

The family had been on tenterhooks throughout the second half of that month. They had heard nothing from their son for far too long and Peter had always been a regular correspondent. Then, on the 26th, three days *before* official notification, a letter came from their son's closest friend, Raymond Singleton. He, along with Peter and another man, Howard Proctor, had been inseparable mates since training together in England.

Dear Sir

On Saturday, the 9th inst, after being in the trenches for a couple of days, we took part in a charge. Proctor and I had just returned from a ration fatigue; and were told to prepare to 'go over the top'. Peter was therefore not with us at the time. About a dozen of us, with a young officer, lost touch with the remainder of the company. About six o'clock in the evening we at last were ordered by the officer to advance. After going quite safely for some distance we jumped into a trench for a short rest. There, to my surprise, I found Peter next to me. He greeted me in his usual cheery manner, and even when I shook hands with him, he did not seem to realise the danger of the situation. If he did, it made no difference to him. He was even cool enough to change his empty water bottle for one with more water in it. From this trench we ran for some shell-holes about a hundred yards ahead, which we thought formed our destination. The three of us were now in different holes. I crawled over into the one in which Proctor had taken shelter; whilst doing so, a bullet went through the rim of my steel helmet.

Singleton and Proctor waited in their shell-hole until ordered back at dusk. They did not know that Peter had been killed but later discovered that their friend had been beckoned to another shell-hole by a sergeant and, as he made his way across, he was shot by a sniper and died almost immediately.

I am not an expert in expressing sympathy; forgive me if I have caused you any unnecessary pain in the mention of these events. I know that I have lost a sincere friend, who was much attached to me: that you have lost a faithful and good son: and the world a devout and thorough Christian . . .

I have written to you rather than to his mother, partly because he seemed to have more letters from you; but more because I thought you could stand the blow better, and so break it to the other members of the family. Maybe, when this war has reached its conclusion, we shall be able, calmly, to personally discuss present events, and to look back upon the life of him who will be so well remembered by you as a dear son, and by us as a good friend.

Yours truly

R Singleton

A few years before, the Millers had lost a young son in a tragic domestic accident, and now a second had gone. 'Our hearts are broken today,' wrote Peter's father in his diary. 'Received a letter from one of Peter's friends, telling us that he was killed on the 9th shot by a sniper. I can hardly believe it. There must be a mistake somewhere! It is over a fortnight since we heard from him. It is terrible I cannot write about it.'

In Emily's letter to her brother she had told Peter of the move the family were about to make to another parish. Emily's father had taken his last service in Hornchurch and the family were packed to go, as her father confirmed in his diary.

Last night we had our farewell meeting; and now I have to go and begin my new work, God help me, I don't know how I will manage. Oh my dear boy; no one knows how dear he was to me, nor how proud I was of him. If ever there was a true Christian boy it was he! He was far too good for this world! May God uphold and support my darling wife, the blow is harder for her, perhaps than for me. I don't know how I can go and leave her. I pray for guidance. I believe it shall be given.

30th Sept. 1916

Left Hornchurch, with a sad heart, today. I don't seem to care for anything, if I only knew my boy was alive how different it would be! I don't know however I shall manage to get through tomorrow.

Perhaps Peter had agreed with Raymond Singleton that one of them would write should the worst happen to the other. It was very common for such pacts to be made among friends. Private William Brown serving with the 1/4th Oxfordshire and Buckinghamshire Light Infantry made just such an agreement before one attack with three of his 'best chums' as he called them. 'It was my sad duty to write a letter to the parents of each of the three,' he dolefully wrote.

Len Whitehead's brother George had gone to France on the last day of May 1915. It was a year since he had strutted about his mother's bedroom, cane under his arm, full of patriotic fervour and intent on enlisting. Now his army pal wrote to Len's mother, Jane, after her son had fallen in action at the Battle of Loos, not four months since he had sailed.

'There was no gentle breaking of news,' acknowledged Len. '"Dear Mrs Whitehead," he wrote, "I am writing to tell you your son George has been killed."'

I remember my mother had a terrible headache that morning and so my brother had read her the message and she had immediately started sobbing. After a time she calmed down a little and she said to me, 'Go and tell your father.' My father was ploughing in a field near the farmhouse.

I waited for him to finish a turn with his plough and two horses. 'George has been killed,' I told him. He stood for a moment. He didn't answer, didn't say a word, but left his horses all steaming in the early November weather and together we walked back in silence to the house. When we got home my father went to the bottom of the stairs and called up, 'That's right, ain't it?' He made no attempt to go up and to comfort my mother but went into the kitchen, sat in his wooden armchair and put his arms on the table and his head on his arms for a little while – wept for a few moments, I think. No, that sticks in my memory, that he didn't go upstairs to comfort my mother. I suppose his boots were all muddy and he'd been ploughing in wet weather. You would have thought he would have taken his shoes off and gone upstairs, but he didn't.

There was nothing much to be done, you see, there was no funeral arrangements to be made, or the bringing home of a body. So he went back to his ploughing. My eldest brother was then sent to Great Saling Post Office to send two telegrams, to each of my two sisters in service in London. 'George killed – come if you can, Mother.' By mid-day the next day they were both home.

A letter from a soldier's pal might be detailed or it might be short: it might be a simple statement of fact or something more prosaic. Lieutenant Robert Verende, himself destined to die in the war, censored one such letter to the mother of a man killed in his company. The letter had been fairly typical in its opening senti-ments but had then gone on to elaborate in a way that impressed Verende. 'It really was one of the nicest I've seen,' he wrote to his own wife.

He said – 'We found your son in the ruins of the dug-out, where death must have been instantaneous. His head drooped forward a little, and there was a very peaceful expression on his face as I took him by the hand for the last time.' The man enclosed some snow-drops 'picked just behind the lines'.

Not everyone was so sensitive. George Whitehead's pal had been fairly forthright but one hopes few were as gauche as one Private Ernest Cole, who took it upon himself to write to the parents of Private Arthur Gardner. Gardner had been killed in 1917 while serving with the 1st/1st Herefordshire Regiment against the Turks in the Middle East.

It is with great sorrow that I have to tell you the sad news that your son Arthur has been killed in action on November 6th, about 4 o'clock in the morning. He was shot through the chest twice close to the heart and then bayoneted. He was buried two days after he was killed. He was buried decently and some stones put on his grave. The Turks had taken the silver ring off his finger which you gave him and also the boots off his feet and the cross he had round his neck . . . We were all sorry to lose him.

Or, in other words: your son may or may not have been killed by the bullets that missed his heart, but if he was still alive then he was finished off with the bayonet. He then lay bloating in the arid desert heat for two days before burial, though not before he was robbed of everything that was precious to him and probably to you.

Quite how George and Mary Gardner responded to such news is not known, though not hard to imagine, nor is it known if they ever wrote back thanking Private Cole for his 'kindness' in writing; it is doubtful they would have asked for more details. Finally, the local newspaper in the Gardners' home town of Leominster ran the news of their son's death under the indelicate heading 'Wounded man bayoneted'. Not a nice thought for the Gardner family nor for anyone else in the town who had a son or husband at the front.

In due course another letter would arrive from the battalion, this time written by the dead soldier's platoon officer who was expected to offer his sympathy. This letter would almost always be short and normally formulaic. The tradition was to write a letter in which the victim had suffered no pain. 'Shot through the head' or 'heart' was typical; 'he did not say a word, nor did he suffer'; then came the epitaph: 'He was one of my most reliable and trustworthy men and he will be very much missed by all officers and NCOs alike . . .'

Illustrative of such letters was that sent to the mother of Sergeant Thomas Buckle, killed in August 1916. It was written in this case by his Company Commander.

It is with the greatest regret that I have to inform you of the death of your son, Sergt. Thomas Buckle. He was killed in action whilst gallantly advancing with his platoon under severe shell and machine gun fire. He was one of my most valued sergeants and I shall miss him sorely. I feel the deepest sympathy with you in your great loss. You have, at least, the satisfaction of knowing that he died a noble death whilst taking part in a most glorious deed.

His death has caused me great pain, as I looked upon him as one of my best N.C.O.s, and whilst he was serving with the M.G. section I found it a very hard job to fill his vacancy. In the trenches he was not only brave and courageous, but was quite extraordinarily efficient as a soldier. I know that I could rely on him for anything. The men in his platoon simply worshipped him. His death is a real loss to his company.

The letter ticked all the boxes and could have been used as a blueprint on how to address recommended points of inclusion such as references to patriotism and gallantry.

During prolonged and heavy fighting, large drafts of men

would be sent out to battalions that had suffered severe losses, and many would themselves become casualties within weeks, days and sometimes hours. In such circumstances, a junior officer, who might well be new himself, was overwhelmed with writing letters of sympathy and was hard-pressed even to visualise the man in question, let alone remember anything worthwhile to say about him.

One of the abiding images of the Great War is that of the telegram boy whose appearance in a street struck fear into the hearts of all those with close relatives at the front. This memory is largely confined to middle- and upper-class districts, for notification for officers' families came in a War Office telegram, but for other ranks as a standard letter in a buff-coloured envelope. As the ratio between officers and other ranks remained at roughly 1:40 in the infantry, it stood to reason that in the vast majority of cases it was the postman not the telegram boy who delivered the hateful news of death. While the latter was rightly associated with important news, 'important news' did not normally mean casualties. Even so, the popular memory of the fear created by a telegram delivery has become folklore.

It was the fateful knock at the door that people remembered all their lives, normally at breakfast, before school: the postman's knock. Donald Overall was at home with his mother when the news came.

I remember the day we heard very distinctly. We lived just off the Old Kent Road in Flinton Street, which was a row of terraced houses, each divided into three flats; we rented the middle flat. Mother and I were downstairs in the main hall when the doorbell rang. I was hiding behind her as she was handed an envelope. I remember she opened the letter immediately. I didn't know what it said, but she screamed and collapsed on the floor in a dead faint. I tried to wake her up; I didn't know what was wrong. I was holding on to her skirts and called out for help and an elderly couple who lived in a lower flat came out and comforted both of us.

Mother came round slowly and they eventually got her upstairs into the bedroom. She was there for about ten days and it was while she was getting better, that she turned onto her side and said to me, 'Your father's dead, he won't come back. Now you are the man of the house, you must do things as best you can.' And I said, 'Me, Mum?' I was five years old. That changed my life; it had to. I had to stand up and be counted, and I did stand up straight and I've always stood up to be counted.

That knock at the door is recounted by many children, as is the collapse, for such was the strain that wives were under, so powerful a punch did the news deliver. Dennis Gilfeather recalled it was on a Saturday morning that their letter came. Even after so many years he could still hear the hammering at the door and see his mother's slight annoyance at the disruption. He saw her rip open the letter; remembered the nervousness of her hands, the shaking, and then her fall.

John, the eldest boy, told me to go to Mrs Lawson's, a neighbour of ours. So I went and knocked at her door. 'Would you come please, my mum doesn't seem well,' the news hadn't penetrated to me what had actually happened. Mrs Lawson came round and attended to my mother, washing her face and giving her a cup of tea and then we were told that Dad was not coming home. It hit me, I suppose it hit my brother too, but there was a sickness in your stomach; you did not absorb the news very well but the nerves in your stomach are tumbling and you shudder, and all the time you're thinking what's going to happen to us?

'I was in the bathroom at about 8am when my sister Lulu came up the stairs to speak to me,' recalls Joyce Sherington, younger sister of Arthur, serving with the 1/5th London Regiment in France.

She put her arm round me, and I remember her words to this day, 'Don't say anything about Arthur, Mother has had terribly bad news, but she's had a lovely letter from his Captain.' I thought, 'Gosh, news like that and you can still note the quality of the letter.' I went to speak to my other sister, nicknamed Bill, to tell her what had happened; we wouldn't have spoken much, then I went downstairs and found Mum looking terrible but still managing to do the washing up. I gave Mum a hug, there were no tears and I simply said, 'Shall I take Daddy's breakfast up on a tray?'

Our letter said 'Missing presumed killed' and that was the awfulness, not knowing. It was bad for all of us, but for my mother it was purgatory. That glimmer of hope affected her tremendously. Dad was very ill and in bed. He had been ill for four years with neuritis, desperately painful. On hearing the news he said, 'Right I must get up,' and he immediately went up to town trying to make contact with anybody amongst his many friends and contacts in journalism who might have news. He did that each day, but this was happening to everybody and my brother was just an ordinary Rifleman.

You felt you were letting your brother down if you doubted he was alive, because there was always hope, however small. Equally you didn't pretend that he was alive either, you carried on as usual because there was that feeling that everyone must be brave about this until we heard more.

The shock of losing someone could induce hysteria in some, stony silence in others. Len Whitehead's father, Frederick, had shown almost no emotion, nor had Letitia Sherington. Lucy Neale's grandmother showed none whatsoever when news arrived that her boy, Sergeant Harold Neale, had died of dysentery after being wounded. She had lived for two years with the terrible anxiety of having all four of her sons serving abroad.

It was six months since Lucy had walked with her father as he made his way back to his barracks after ten days' leave. Now Lucy was given the responsibility of taking the War Office letter to her grandmother's house as there had been friction between Lucy's mother and grandmother and they were not on good terms. Lucy walked up the road numbed by the news. When she arrived she found her aunt Jess was staying. Lucy handed the letter over.

I put the letter on the table and Gran said, 'You open it Jess,' and she opened it and said, 'Oh no, he's dead, Harry's dead.' My poor Gran, she could only say, 'Oh, not another one,' because she had already lost two sons in the war. Gran didn't cry, she sat there like someone made of stone, she didn't say anything, but Auntie Jess began to cry terribly. I seem to remember my aunt making a pot of tea and then I said something like, 'I'd better go back home now,' and left. I don't remember crying. I was so stunned, I couldn't believe it – I'd never see him again. It is hard to realize tragedies when you're only ten years old.

Unlike letters, telegrams could arrive at any time, day or night. Sir Harry Lauder had returned from a small gathering of friends to his hotel where he was staying for an extended period while performing at a nearby theatre. It was New Year's Day 1917, and although he went to bed he could not sleep and he lay there thinking about his son, Captain John Lauder, and wondering what the year would bring him. He had hardly closed his eyes when there was a pounding at the door long enough 'to rouse the heaviest sleep there ever was,' Lauder wrote.

My heart almost stopped. There must be something serious indeed for them to be rousing me so early. I rushed to the door, and there was a porter, holding out a telegram, I took it and tore it open. And I knew why I had felt as I had the day before. I shall never forget what I read:

'Captain John Lauder killed in action, December 28. Official. War Office.'

It had gone to Mrs Lauder at Dunoon first, and she had sent it on to me. That was all it said. I knew nothing of how my boy had died, or where – save that it was for his country.

Realization came to me slowly. I sat and stared at that slip of paper that had come to me like the breath of doom. Dead! Dead these four days! I was never to see the light of his eyes again. I was never to hear that laugh of his. I had looked on my boy for the last time. Could it be true? Ah, I knew it was! And it was for this moment that I had been waiting, that we had all been waiting, ever since we had sent John away to fight for his country and do his part. I think we had all felt that it must come. We had all known that it was too much to hope that he should be one of those to be spared.

The black despair that had been hovering over me for hours closed down now and enveloped all my senses. Everything was unreal. For a time I was quite numb. But then, as I began to realize and to visualize what it was to mean in my life that my boy was dead there came a great pain. The iron of realization slowly seared every word of that curt telegram upon my heart. I said it to myself, over and over again. And I whispered to myself, as my thoughts took form, over and over, the one terrible word: 'Dead!' . . .

I fell at once to remembering him. I clutched at every memory, as if I must grasp them and make sure of them, lest they be taken from me as well as the hope of seeing him again that the telegram had forever snatched away. I would have been destitute indeed then. It was as if I must fix in my mind the way he had been wont to look, and recall to my ears every tone of his voice, every trick of his speech. There was something left of him that I must keep, I knew, even then, at all costs, if I was to be able to bear his loss at all.

Sir Harry had a vision of his son going forward to death, then there was an image of him lying dead, 'stark and cold', mud on his uniform, and for a few minutes he was consumed with rage. He cursed war and the men who had caused the war and the Germans who had killed his son and he was overtaken with a savage hatred. He was incapable of rational thought until he calmed slightly and thought of his dear wife at home in Scotland.

The thought of her, bereft even as I was, sorrowing, even as I was, and lost in her frightful loneliness, was pitiful, so that I had but the one desire and wish – to go to her, and join my tears with hers, that we who were left alone to bear our grief, might bear it together and give one to the other such comfort as there might be in life for us. And so I fell upon my knees and prayed, there in my lonely room in the hotel. I prayed to God that he might give us both, John's mother and myself, strength to bear the blow that had been dealt us and to endure the sacrifice that He and our country had demanded of us.

As news of a soldier's death seeped out to relatives and then into the wider community, letters of sympathy and help arrived. Peter Miller's family was well known and well respected, and letters and mourning cards edged in black arrived with almost every post, addressed to his parents, Eliza (Lizzie) and Peter. Two letters in particular brought home the desperate tragedies being played out in families across the country. The first was written by Mary Keeling, who was married to Lizzie's elder brother, Thomas. Their twenty-one-year-old son Henry (Harry) had been killed two months before, serving with 219th Field Company, Royal Engineers, on 14 July 1916 and was buried in Aveluy Communal Cemetery Extension.

28th Sept. 1916
My dear Lizzie and Peter
    We all got a dreadful shock this morning when we read the news of your darling boy's death. Words are no use at this time but you know how I feel for you as I am going through the same and will till the end. I would have written sooner but I am so full of grief. Ever since I received your letter I could not keep from thinking about Peter. I would have loved to have seen him as he had grown up such a lovely boy . . . Oh Lizzie, I often think my grief is greater than I can bear and so will you as time goes on. Harry was a lovely boy. He was so manly and good.
    I wish we were leaving this house as I see his bedroom and

ever so many little things he did, such as planting trees. I think you will be better to get away from your house as soon as you can.

I trust God will give you strength to bear up for the sake of those you have left as they require a mother's care for a long time yet . . . I am not able to write more as my eyes are full of tears. I have cried ever since we received Peter's letter this morning.

I remain your affectionate sister [-in-law], Mary.'

The second letter came from Corporal George Maidment, a thirty-nine-year-old sorter with the General Post Office. He had become good friends with the Millers through the church and had visited them during his embarkation leave in mid-September. He set sail for France the day news arrived of Peter's death.

21.10.16
Dear Mr Miller

I received your letter last night. I am very sorry indeed to hear of the death of your son Peter, it must be a shock to you all, no wonder you cannot settle down. You were waiting to hear from him the evening I saw you when I was home on [embarkation] leave, God alone knows whether I shall ever see my home and dear old Hornchurch again. It is nearly nine and a half years since I first went to Hornchurch and I look back on the happy days I spent at the chapel and the C.S. Society and wish I could live them over again. I trust that if it is His Will I may be spared to go back to my loved ones again if not I bow to the Divine Will and say Thy will be done. Knowing that all things work together for good to them that love God . . . I have not much news to tell you, we cannot say where we are, I have left Havre and your letter was redirected on from there. I shall be pleased to hear from you again, address letters No. 6544 Cpl G Maidment 10 Platoon, C Coy, 1st Kings Royal Rifle Corps, BEF France.

Now please excuse short letter and accept my condolence and

convey the same to Mrs Miller & family at the loss of your dear son. Now goodbye, God bless and keep you all. Looking forward to the time when we shall meet again, if not on earth, in the Father's House on High where all is joy and peace and all tears are wiped away. From your sincere friend

G Maidment.

George Maidment was killed just three weeks later on 13 November. He was married with three children.

After hearing the news of John's death, Sir Harry Lauder went home to his wife. Taking a train from London to Glasgow, he arrived at his house the following day, 'a sad, lonely wee hoose it had become now!' he accepted.

It was the place for me. It was there that I wanted to be, and it was with her, who must hereafter be all the world to me. And I was eager to be with her, too, who had given John to me. Sore as my grief was, stricken as I was, I could comfort her as no one else could hope to do, and she could do as much for me. We belonged together . . .'

* * *

After the death of Arthur Sherington, Joyce's mother was protected by the rest of the family; whatever she wanted was accepted, and in their case it meant that Arthur was never spoken of again in the house, or at least not in their mother's presence. There would be no outward signs of grieving, no wearing of black.

We children understood that we must support Mother in every way that we could. If there was a job to be done by one of us, it was done and done to the best of our ability. We wanted to be a happy family and there would be no quarrelling. Life had to carry on.

With no funeral arrangements life could just 'go on'. Len Whitehead's father had returned to his ploughing and Letitia

Sherington could continue washing up and preparing her
husband's breakfast; it suited some people to focus on even the
most menial tasks in order to hold themselves together. In time,
Joyce's mother would throw herself into a job that required all her
powers of concentration and energy, in part to earn money for the
home, in part to keep her sanity.

> No one wanted to talk about Arthur; it was an unspoken under-
> standing. I am not sure I was even really conscious about it at the
> time; it was an atmosphere. I think we all felt that Mother would
> want us to carry on as normal. My eldest sister had a boyfriend
> called Arthur Jupp and so we called him Jimmy, we couldn't use
> the name Arthur so he was Jimmy Jupp. Arthur was never
> mentioned again as far as Mother was concerned. There were also
> no visible pictures of him; pictures from his training days on
> Salisbury Plain and a professional portrait of him were not brought
> out again until after my mother died in 1949.

Although Arthur's presence in the house was stifled, his memory
created in Letitia an inner turmoil that could barely be contained.
She could not relax or stay still for any length of time, and sleep
proved difficult.

> She would often go out in the evening with one of my sisters and
> they would just walk around the streets of Hornsey. I was conscious
> of hearing the front door shut night after night, and because Mum
> bottled her emotions up it made the pain much worse. I would
> listen for the front door opening because I felt that it was my
> responsibility to get downstairs and get the kettle on for a cup of
> tea. This would be about 10 at night.

Letitia's continual restlessness would have been well recognised
by Florence Billington. Her boyfriend, Ted Felton, had gone to
war convinced he was not going to come back and no comforting

words from Florence could settle his mind. In May 1915 he was killed and Florence's letters were found on his body and returned to his distraught girlfriend. Florence was working as a housemaid in a hotel in Buxton and, although she confided in the other girls, she did not receive support as she might have done from her family.

> My life increasingly became a roller-coaster after Ted's death. I wasn't sure what I wanted to do, I was always chopping and changing. I would get a job, then I would want to go home. I'd get homesick and I would go back and my parents thought, that's Flo, yeah, couldn't settle down. But I was thinking of him, that's what it was.

Young children, those aged ten or under, often remarked that they could not truly register the death, and that their immediate concern was far more for their surviving mother. In large families the difference in age could also be a factor. Len Whitehead was eight when his eldest brother George died aged twenty-five. Although most of the sons still lived on the farm run by his father, Len was not especially close to a brother eighteen years his senior.

> I was sad that we wouldn't see him again but I was only a boy and it didn't sink in to the same extent that it does when you're an adult. He wasn't my favourite brother; he was inclined to tease us, and he didn't look after us kids like another brother, Jack; it would have been worse if it had been him.

Very often the passage of time, with the extended absence of the father, led to a natural sense of disconnection. This situation was compounded by the unreality of death. In the past, the elaborate funeral rituals demanded by society had included the active participation of children; they were often taken to see the dead and kissed their hands, but now there were no funerals.

Nine-year-old Ellen Elston 'nearly forgot' that she had a dad, having seen him only once between the time he left with his regiment for France and the time of his death in 1917, perhaps the best part of two years. Granted there was a gold-framed portrait of him hanging on the dining-room wall, but what was always there was also easy to overlook. Now Ellen's attention was drawn to it only because her mother had turned it to face the wall, so incapable was she of seeing his image without crying.

'It may sound funny,' she recalled, 'but my father's death meant a new dress to me.' Ellen's mother quickly made her daughters black-and-white check dresses with a black belt to wear while outside; Ellen was aware of the sympathetic looks she received from local people for a man well known in the area, but 'I don't think Dad's death registered, somehow, because he was buried out there'.

> You are upset for your mother, really, you are upset because your mother is upset. I could hear her wandering around the house crying, although she tried to put a brave face on it in front of the children. Yes, I can remember crying and crying – for my mother – not because my father was killed.

Children were rarely kept out of school longer than a day. There was no reason to keep them at home and it was generally felt that the quicker life returned to normal, the less children would be affected. In so many ways nothing obviously altered: Dad would still have been away whether alive or dead, and a peculiar reality existed in which it was entirely possible to pretend nothing untoward had happened at all. After Mabel Hunter's father was killed in 1916 she went back to school and her mother soon went back to work. Her father's death felt entirely remote. She had become used to morning prayers in which other children's fathers or brothers had been remembered and the child's name read out, but the names and what they meant did not impinge on Mabel's consciousness.

I remember being lined up at the back of the school hall, looking out of the low windows and wasn't taking much notice of what was going on inside, when I suddenly heard my father's name Corporal Ernest Hunter and my name and that I had lost my father and that hit me really hard, that's my dad that's gone down. Hearing my father's name called out to all these children and teachers, the shock was such that I blacked out I just sunk to the floor until someone brought me round and gave me a drink of water and that was my first real realization that I had not got a dad any more. I remember the teachers getting my brother from the other school to take me home to look after me as Mum was out working and only Gran was there. My dad wasn't coming home from the war and I wondered how things would turn out.

Lucy Neale was older than Mabel. Now aged ten, she was fully aware that her dad had died; she had had to carry the news to her grandmother's house herself, and she'd seen the reaction. Yet even Lucy was partly in denial.

School started, and because we said prayers, all three classes came together in one room. Mrs Bywater, the headmistress, said, 'Before we have our prayers, I just want to tell you that Lucy has lost her father, so I think we ought to pray this morning for Lucy and her mother,' but I couldn't take it in, I was in a dream. The Lord's Prayer was said, and the usual prayers and a little hymn we used to sing, but I couldn't, or I wouldn't, perhaps, face the fact that I would never see him again. That day, that was the worst day, and then a day or two later another girl, she lost her father, and we said prayers again for her.

There was a natural tendency for the bereaved, and friends of the bereaved, to believe that it was God's will that this or that soldier had not survived. Letters of sympathy are full of such well-meant comforts: that God had designed another higher purpose for the dead. Soldiers believed it, too. Corporal George Maidment wrote as much when he offered his condolences to the Millers. George himself bowed to Divine providence; as he said, 'If it is His Will I may be spared . . .'

The problem was that people chose either to accept or rail against that will. When Ellen Elston's father died near Ypres, his brother, a monk, came round to visit. He was given short shrift. 'My mother ordered him out of the house. I can remember that quite plainly. She said, "Please don't come telling me there's a God because I don't believe in him any more."'

Letitia Sherington found herself gradually alienated from the Church. She continued to go for a while but she eventually became indifferent to the service.

> The words conveyed no meaning whatsoever. That is really why I gave up going to church. I could hear the words, I could even give the meaning of each one and yet they conveyed nothing. I could feel, as it were, the wheels going round and round in my mind and not gripping anything. It was terrifying.

The idea of God's will at work was broadly uncontested, especially when most Britons believed that they were involved in a righteous struggle with the enemy. One who did question the whole notion that God would take sides was the father of Ronald Poulton Palmer. Sir Edward Poulton in his memoirs recalled a letter to his son from Walter Carey, the former England rugby forward and Anglican chaplain.

> It is God's will, is another thought often offered in kindly sympathy. I find no comfort in it and do not believe it to be true. On the contrary I entirely agree with what Walter Carey said in his letter to Ronald that God regards the War with horror and aversion and that it is so clearly the result not of His will but of human crime and human folly.

Sir Harry Lauder was equally sure that the war was not being fought on God's direction. He believed it to be a wicked war of 'wanton cruelty and slaughter', but a war, that, nonetheless, had to be fought and won. His faith led him to believe that while his son's death was no one's will other than that of the enemy, John would be with God and he [Sir Harry] and his wife would one day be reunited with their son.

Almighty God, to whom we prayed, was kind, and He was pitiful and merciful. For presently He brought us both a sort of sad composure. Presently He assuaged our grief a little, and gave us the strength that we must have to meet the needs of life and the thought of going on in a world that was darkened by the loss of the boy in whom all our thoughts and all our hopes had been centred. I thanked God then, and I thank God now, that I have never denied Him nor taken His name in vain.

There were those for whom the news of a family death had the greatest resonance of all because both father and son were present on the battlefield. A number of senior officers lost sons in France and Belgium, and there were as many sons who lost their fathers.

Lieutenant General Sir Walter Congreve and Major William 'Billy' Congreve were both highly regarded and highly decorated officers. Lieutenant General Congreve had won the Victoria Cross in South Africa in 1899 and by 1916 his twenty-five-year-old son had already been awarded the DSO and MC. He was about to be awarded the Victoria Cross, too, albeit posthumously, for his outstanding work in the field over a period of two weeks prior to his death.

Lieutenant General Congreve commanded XIII Corps on the Somme where his son was serving as a brigade major to the 3rd Division. Lieutenant General Congreve would have known more than anyone the perilous nature of his son's work and the very imminent danger he was under while fighting in an offensive. It was his father's duty to fulfil his own responsibilities to the best of his ability without outside distractions or the influence of private concerns.

During the second half of July, he was at his headquarters when the telephone rang. His son had been shot and killed by a sniper that morning. Brigadier General W. H. Greenly, a staff officer, had to relay the news at a critical point in the operations and when the Corps Commander's direction was of crucial importance.

When I told him what had happened he was absolutely calm to all outward appearance and, after a few seconds of silence, said quite calmly, 'He was a good soldier.' That is all that he allowed to appear, and he continued dealing with everything as it came along in the same imperturbable and quietly decisive way as usual.

I shall never forget the incident or lose the admiration I felt for the marvellous self-suppression of the 'man' in the capacity of the commander.

Major Billy Congreve was immensely popular among the men under his command. Later that day his body was brought back to Corbie, where his father proceeded after attending a Fourth Army Conference.

I saw him in the mortuary, and was struck by his beauty and strength of face . . . I felt inspired by his look and know that he is 'helping' me, as he used to say, and that he always will do so. I never felt so proud of him as I did when I said goodbye.

A lot of flowers were sent by kind people, amongst them wild mallows from the fighting line by some of the men. These, I had put into the grave; and a huge wreath tied with the tricolour riband from General Balfourier. I myself put in his hand a posy of poppies, cornflowers and daisies . . . and with a kiss I left him.

Major Billy Congreve's Victoria Cross was awarded three months later. His widow, Pamela, who was expecting his child, received the medal from the King at Buckingham Palace. Billy Congreve was the first man in the war to be awarded all three gallantry awards available to an infantry officer, the MC, DSO and VC. In December 1919, Congreve's great friend and best man at his wedding, Major William Fraser, married Pamela, helping to raise Billy's daughter Gloria, born in early 1917. The notion that the army was and remained part of an extended family proved apt in this further example of a fellow officer marrying the wife of a fallen comrade.

Lieutenant General Congreve had been fortunate to be able to say goodbye to his son. For the vast majority there was no opportunity to see the bodies although some might have the chance to visit a grave. Army padres had perhaps the greatest freedom of movement. Wyn Griffith, an officer serving with the Royal Welsh Fusiliers, found himself in conversation with a signalling officer named Taylor. Taylor was highly experienced and respected; he was also exhausted from many hours of continuous work keeping the telephone lines open between the front line and Brigade Headquarters. Griffith sat down beside him. Taylor asked, 'You know old Evans the padre?' Griffith replied that he did.

I met him this morning, half an hour ago, just as it was getting light. He was going to do a bit of burying. I thought he looked queer . . . he was talking to himself, praying, maybe, when I walked along with him. It was in North Wales Welsh, and I couldn't make much of it. I got talking to him, and I asked him why he was up so early. He said he hadn't been to bed. He went towards Fricourt yesterday evening looking for a grave. Someone you knew, said I . . . Yes, my own boy's grave, said he.

'Good God, I knew young Evans well – he was in the ranks with me,' I answered.

Well, Evans, poor chap, had heard yesterday evening that his boy was killed near Fricourt the day before, so he went off at once to try to find his grave. He walked about for hours, but couldn't find anyone who knew where it was, nor could he find the padre who buried him. He walked till he could walk no more, got a cup of tea from some gunners, and had a rest, and then walked back here. And now he's out again. Going to bury other people's boys, he said, since he couldn't find his own boy's grave to pray over . . . What could you say?

The chances of finding a grave would have seemed slim in the morass around the Somme village of Fricourt. The area had been heavily bombarded and then attacked on 1 July, causing terrible casualties among assaulting battalions. The Germans subsequently evacuated the village but the area was still heavily shelled, this time by the enemy, and further casualties were frequent, including lads like Evans. 'My Welsh isn't very good, as you know,' continued the Signalling Officer to Griffith, 'but I managed to say to him,

'I'm not a soldier now, padre; I'm taking off my hat to you.' And so I did, I took off my tin helmet. You couldn't talk English to a man who had lost his boy.
'No . . . not to a Welshman,' I replied.
'But there's a man for you, Griff . . . off to bury other men's boys at five in the morning, and maybe his own son not buried yet, a couple of miles away. There was some shrapnel overhead, but I saw him going up the slope as if he were alone in the world.'

Canon Frederick Scott, another army padre, had only a slightly better chance of finding his son when he set out for the village of Courcelette. He did at least have a map, roughly drawn by an officer who had watched the burial of Scott's son and so was able to mark the approximate position of the temporary grave. Captain Henry Scott was serving with the Canadian Infantry on the Somme when he was killed in late October 1916 as he prepared to lead his men forward into an attack. He had been hit by a burst of machine-gun fire and killed instantly.

Captain Scott's father had been in billets behind the lines when the incident occurred. He had on many occasions gone forward to the front line to celebrate Holy Communion with the men; indeed, it was not long before that he had given Communion to the men of his son's own battalion, the 87th Canadian Expeditionary Force, when he was billeted in the town of Albert. From his upstairs window he had been able to watch his son's battalion camped on high ground just east of the town, close enough to see clearly the officers and men walking around their lines.

Now the owner of the padre's present billet delivered the news of the captain's death, handing over the envelope and simultaneously taking Scott's hand to utter the words, 'Have courage, my brother.' It did not take a second to understand what the Frenchman meant, and not much longer for him to resolve to find the spot where his son lay. Later that afternoon the necessary arrangements were made: he would leave the next day and arrive at a gun battery in the dark from where he would set out on his search.

The Brigade Major of course tried to dissuade me, but I told him that I was going in any case, that he was not responsible for my actions, but that if he liked to make things easier for me, he could. He quite understood the point, and telephoned to the 11th Battery.

About half-past one, I started up the street which led to the Bapaume Road. The moon was shining, and I could see every object distinctly. Near our old headquarters I got a lift in a lorry, which took me almost to Pozières. There I got out and proceeded on my way alone. I entered the Y.M.C.A. hut and had a good strong cup of coffee, and started off afresh. That lonely region in the moonlight with the ruined village to one side and the fields stretching far away on either hand gave me an eerie feeling . . . Not a living soul could I see in the long white road. I walked on till I came to what was known as Centre Way, a wooden path which led across the fields down to the battery positions in the valley. Huge shell-holes, half filled with water, pitted the fields in every direction, and on the slippery wood I had great difficulty to keep from sliding into those which were skirted by the path. Far off beyond Courcelette I saw the German flare-lights and the bursting of shells. It was a scene of vast desolation, weird beyond description.

Canon Scott was taken the rest of the way by at least two men from his son's battalion. They were willing to locate the shell-hole in which Captain Scott was buried and then, if Canon Scott wished, they would exhume his body. The hastily drawn map led them down a communication trench and into the front line although the mud was so glutinous it was nigh impossible to pass.

The previous night a cross had been placed there [on the grave] by a corporal of the battalion before it left the front line. No one I spoke to, however, could tell me the exact map location of the place where it stood. I looked over the trenches, and on all sides spread a waste of brown mud, made more desolate by the morning mist which clung over everything. I was determined, however, not to be baffled in my search.

Suddenly the runner, who was looking over the top, pointed far away to a lonely white cross that stood at a point where the ground sloped down through the mist towards Regina Trench. At once we climbed out of the trench and made our way over the slippery ground and past the deep shell holes to where the white cross stood out in the solitude. We passed many bodies which were still unburied, and here and there were bits of accoutrement that had been lost in the advance. When we came up to the cross I read my son's name upon it, and knew that I had reached the object I had in view.

As the corporal who had placed the cross there had not been quite sure that it was actually on the place of burial, I got the runner to dig the ground in front of it. He did so, but we discovered nothing but a large piece of shell. Then I got him to try in another place, and still we could find nothing. I tried once again, and after he had dug a little while we came upon something white. It was my son's left hand, with his signet ring upon it. They had removed his identification disc, revolver and pocket book, so the signet ring was the only thing which could have led to his identification. It was really quite miraculous that we should have made the discovery.

Sergeant Alex McClintock was one of those who accompanied Canon Scott to find the grave. In his memoirs he evoked the quiet dignity of the padre despite the very evident and continued dangers from shellfire.

We managed to find the spot, and, at the chaplain's request, we exhumed the body. Some of us suggested to him that he give us the identification marks and retire out of range of the shells which were bursting all around us. We argued that it was unwise for him to remain unnecessarily in danger, but what we really intended was that he should be saved the horror of seeing the pitiful thing which our spades were about to uncover.

'I shall remain,' was all he said. 'He was my boy.'

It proved that we had found the right body. One of our men tried to clear the features with his handkerchief, but ended by spreading the handkerchief over the face. The old chaplain stood beside the body and removed his trench helmet, baring his gray locks to the drizzle that was falling. Then, while we stood by with bowed heads, his voice rose amid the noise of bursting shells, repeating the burial service of the Church of England. I have never been so impressed by anything in my life as by that scene.

'The mist was lifting now,' recalled Canon Scott.

We heard the crack of bullets, for the Germans were sniping us. I made the runner go down into a shell hole, while I read the burial service, and then took off the ring. I looked over the ground where the charge had been made. There lay Regina Trench, and far beyond it, standing out against the morning light, I saw the villages of Pys and Miraumont. It was a strange scene of desolation, for the rains had made the battlefields a dreary, sodden waste.

There was nothing more to be done but continue his ministry in France. To people like Canon Scott, carrying on was the greatest tribute they could pay to their loved ones: to resist being crushed by loss and instead find a way to forge a new life that was worthy of the sacrifices made.

Harry Lauder could easily afford to walk away from public life and never to work again.

What! Go out before an audience and seek to make it laugh? Sing my songs when my heart was broken? I did not decide not to do it. I did not so much as think of it as a thing I had to decide about.

The letters he received changed his mind. They came from the families of the fallen, the very people who in their grief desired something to make them laugh again. Harry Lauder, the consummate music-hall artist, was needed. 'Don't desert us now, Harry!' It was so that they put it, one after another, in those letters. 'Ah Harry – there is so much woe and grief and pain in the world that you, who can, must do all that is in your power to make them easier to bear!' Sir Harry returned to entertainment, although much of his work was spent in hospitals with the wounded before he made the decision to go to the Western Front and entertain the troops there.

It was the real front I was eager to reach. I wanted to be where my boy had been, and to see his grave. I wanted to sing for the laddies who were bearing the brunt of the big job over there – while they were bearing it . . .

Sir Harry left for France in early June 1917. He took no changes of costumes, no theatrical props, and most of the time he would be well away from the specially built theatres constructed for soldiers' entertainment. He had nothing except a small piano that was transported around in one of two army cars provided for his 'tour'. He had no official accompanist but found pianists from among the wounded or the fighting fit. Sir Harry sang everywhere he was booked: in hospitals, YMCA huts and rest billets. He met soldiers while under fire on shell-blasted Vimy Ridge, sang by the roadside to men going up the line at Ypres, and to Highlanders in the trenches near Arras, always handing out thousands of free cigarettes as he went.

He appeared in his element among the men with whom his son had fought. Yet the grief was never far from the surface. When under fire, he had expected to be nervous. On Vimy Ridge he listened to the constant drone of shells flying overhead, and the 'powdery squirts of smoke' as rounds hit the German lines.

That day one overpowering emotion mastered every other. It was a desire for vengeance! Yon were the Huns – the men who had killed my boy. They were almost within my reach. And as I looked at them there in their lines a savage desire possessed me, almost overwhelmed me, indeed, that made me want to rush to those guns and turn them to my own mad purpose of vengeance.

It was all I could do, I tell you, to restrain myself – to check that wild, almost ungovernable impulse to rush to the guns and grapple with them myself – myself fire them at the men who had killed my boy. I wanted to fight! I wanted to fight with my two hands – to tear and rend . . .

But that was not to be. I knew it, and I grew calmer, presently.

Grief drove Sir Harry to do all he could for soldiers facing just the same difficulties and predicaments as his son. His tour would last as long as it needed to, out on the Western Front, but always in the back of his mind was his son and the grave that he would visit when the opportunity came.

Towards the end of November 1916, Canon Scott received news that his boy's body had been brought back from its temporary grave in a shell-hole. He at once motored to Albert and from there to the graveside on the same hill that he had watched from his billet windows and seen his son and the men from 87th Battalion milling about their camp. The little cemetery in which Captain Scott would find his final resting place already held the bodies of several other men from the battalion, and his father was grateful that his son would lie somewhere where he could always be visited. At Bapaume Post Military Cemetery, Canon Scott conducted the burial service for his own son.

The gentle hill on which his son was laid to rest overlooked a shallow valley. If Canon Scott had chosen to walk up to the top of that rise, he would have seen a larger British cemetery in the middle distance: Captain John Lauder lay buried there.

5

As Next of Kin . . .

'When days are long
And friends are few
Dear son
How I long for you'

8163 Private John Clifford
1/14th London Regiment (The London Scottish)
Killed in action 30 September 1916, aged twenty
Buried Grove Town Cemetery

In August 1915, Alexander Gillespie, a young subaltern serving with the 2nd Argyll and Sutherland Highlanders, was taking a working party to dig a communication trench in daylight. It was unusual to commence such a job during the day, as the risk of enemy fire was significantly greater than at night. Nevertheless, orders were orders. Rather than standing idle while the men dug, Gillespie decided to take the opportunity to look around.

I suddenly came upon young Gladstone's grave, in the corner of an orchard railed off, where he lies with about fifty men of different regiments; it's curious to think of him there and his grandfather in Westminster Abbey; but they are both in honourable company.

No name in Britain was held in higher regard than that of William Ewart Gladstone, the former three-times Prime Minister. His grandson, whose grave Gillespie had found, had been Liberal

MP for Kilmarnock Burghs, but enlisted in August 1914 to serve with the Royal Welsh Fusiliers. Lieutenant William Gladstone, twenty-nine years old, was killed on 13 April 1915, just three weeks after arriving in France, and buried in a burgeoning British cemetery near the French town of Levantie.

Despite the appearance of a grave with, presumably, an identifying wooden marker, William Gladstone's body was not actually there. Less than a week after being shot by a sniper and his body buried, William had been disinterred and returned to Wales and the family estate at Hawarden. In a memoir of his nephew, published in 1918, Viscount Herbert Gladstone recollected: 'It was the earnest wish of his mother that the body should be brought home, and Henry [Gladstone, another uncle] took prompt and effective action. He communicated with the Prime Minister, and by the permission of the King, the War Office gave the necessary instructions for "the King's Lieutenant" to be brought home.' Henry Gladstone was authorised to go to the front to make the necessary arrangements. Just nine days after he was killed, Lieutenant Gladstone's body arrived at Hawarden where it was placed in the Temple of Peace. The funeral the following day showed how deeply and widely William's loss was felt.

Local people turned out to throng the streets while close personal friends arrived from across the country. There were representatives from the various associations with which William had been connected and officers from the Royal Welsh Fusiliers attended to pay their own respects. William Gladstone was laid to rest with full military honours.

Lieutenant Gladstone was not the first dead officer to be brought back across the Channel from the Western Front, but his body was to be the last, at least officially. The bodies of around a couple of dozen officers had already made the journey, most of whom had died of their wounds at Base hospitals. These men had been brought home with the cost being met by the wealthy families from which they came, although that was hardly a justification. No one else could have their son back – there is not a single known case of the body of an ordinary rank being repatriated during the war – and public disquiet at the apparently superior rights given to these wealthy individuals was cause for concern in Parliament. The army, too, grew mindful of the negative impression such exhumations might create among the rank and file. It was undoubtedly prudent that the full details of this exhumation were not publicised, for it had been carried out by British soldiers under fire: fortunately none of them needed the vacated grave.

After the return of Gladstone's body, the implicit decision to allow repatriation was abruptly overturned by the army. All the dead would remain overseas, a decision that would in time prove a hammer blow to the many families who wished to see their loved ones brought back to Britain. The symbolic exception would be the body of the Unknown Warrior brought home in 1920.

What was significant about Gladstone's case was not just that a few influential families could organise the return of their fallen to Britain in wartime, but that 'ownership' rights to the body might be waived or revert to the family, usurping the traditional privilege claimed by the regiment.

It had originally been the men of Gladstone's own battalion who had been charged with burying their officer. This was not seen as an inevitable chore given to men who were on the scene at the time, but rather an honourable task expected by the army of all its regiments. The dead of the regiment belonged to the regiment and tradition ensured that burial would be conducted by those serving with it whenever practically possible. The army authorities had noted the feeling that regimental comrades had proprietorial rights and, when it came to burial, the resentment of intrusion by other units. This feeling certainly forestalled the setting up of any permanent force to deal with the dead.

It was remarkable to what lengths a battalion might go to recover its own dead from no man's land, although risks were always calculated and few colonels would choose to endanger excessively the lives of more men. Even so, every effort had to be seen to be made.

In June 1918, Lieutenant Colonel C. E. Thompson of the 1/5th
South Lancashire Regiment was severely taken to task by his Brigade
Commander after a trench raid had gone awry. The Brigade Commander's wrath was in part directed at his hapless subordinate for the
failure to take a roll call after the attack, an inexcusable error which
had seen an initial report of twelve casualties later increased to twenty,
including not one missing, as first reported, but four. However, he
also made it abundantly clear that his hackles had been raised because
men who in all likelihood had been killed were also abandoned.

'I have ordered the Officer Commanding the Battalion to make
every endeavour to recover the bodies, and so remove what must, if
they are left in No Man's Land, remain a slur on the good name of his
Battalion.' A search party comprising one sergeant and three men was
sent out the next night. The area they had to search, estimated at
7,000 square yards, contained several old trenches, as well as ditches
and shell-holes. It was also covered with long grass. Not surprisingly,
no missing men were found. The battalion's CO later filed a report in
which he acknowledged that 'no credit can ever be attached to a Unit
which leaves its dead or wounded behind in a minor enterprise',
although he then went on to give reasons why certain extenuating
circumstances might ameliorate, in part, the stiff criticism.

Even if a body were found and identified, it might take a great
effort of will to remove it from the front for burial. Private Stephen
Graham recorded the energy expended in carrying back one officer,
Lieutenant Evan Balfour, 'a fine tall fellow and a great dead
weight'. The men were already extremely tired from their night's
work but as a guide had been found to lead the way and a stretcher
was available, the men set to work to take back their officer.

We shouldered the dead body and began our slow journey to the
limber. We changed hands and positions at least a dozen times
whilst carrying it, and as German shells burst near us there was
danger of the stretcher capsizing, for one of us was very nervous
and wished to fall flat to earth every time the menacing buzz of a

projectile assailed his ears. So the heavy, ill-balanced body swayed and lurched, registering the nervous tension and fatigue of those who bore it. We perspired and gasped . . .

Eventually the body was transferred to a limber and taken back to the battalion's encampment. The journey had taken four hours. Next day it was carried further still to the village of Berles-au-Bois and the cemetery where he was buried near a number of others from the regiment.

Keeping casualties from the same regiment together mattered to their surviving friends, and was comforting to relatives who wished to know where their loved ones lay. Early on in the war, especially where a battalion occupied a district for any length of time, a battalion cemetery was frequently formed. If the sector was relatively quiet, considerable attention would be given to the appearance of the graves. In the months before the Somme offensive, there were many examples of graves decoratively edged with chalk and sown with flowers. Often, at the head of each, stood a durable and well-made cross. All such graves would be well maintained while comrades remained nearby, and, even when the battalion did move on, graves could still be cared for. The father of Ronald Poulton Palmer was delighted to record that his son's wooden cross was replaced twice during the war, once after it was damaged by shellfire.

In August 1916, Captain Samuel Whitnall, a pre-war friend of Ronald's, was riding a bicycle when he and a friend passed a small cemetery on the edge of Ploegsteert Wood. 'At the very moment of passing,' he wrote to Ronald's father,

I turned my head at seeing two men replacing one simple cross by another as simple but painted white, and caught the name. An officer of the 3rd Hussars with me exclaimed 'Why, that's the name of a fellow I was with at Rugby!' and so we helped [replace the cross].

One of the soldiers digging said, 'The boys were very fond of him, sir, by the way his grave has been looked after.'

The cemetery to which Captain Whitnall referred was begun by Poulton Palmer's battalion in April 1915 and carries the regimental name to this day.

At the start of the war, each soldier wore just one identity disc. This was taken along with the man's pay book and handed in as proof of death. The identification of those who had died was to do with army accounting not, as would be acknowledged, directly concerned with preserving details of the dead. In past conflicts, battles had ended or moved on with bodies collected, identified and buried on the spot. The Great War abruptly departed from this tradition for suddenly fighting was largely static with the same ground being fought over time and again. It might be possible to remove an identity disc in the dark to enable the army's administrative process to begin, but not to bury a man and, furthermore, maintain a known grave. This problem was recognised and rectified with an Army Council Instruction of September 1916 whereby soldiers were instead issued with two identity discs, the existing red one and an additional one that was green and eight-sided. The red disc would be removed on death, as before; the green disc would remain with the body.

Both discs were marked with the soldier's surname and initials, his regiment, number and his religion, typically the denomination of the individual, such as CE for Church of England or METH for Methodist. The tags were worn together and were made of a fibre that was, regrettably, biodegradable, a curious oversight when it came to identifying bodies that were not picked up soon after death. For this reason many men also wore a metal bracelet, characteristically a disc with the same personal details as on their army-issue tags. It was one of these discs that Roland Leighton had requested from his mother, Marie, and which caused her such pain.

In dealing with the dead, almost all identifying and personal possessions were removed from the body (including the red disc). However, if no proof of identity was found then other details were noted, such as regimental badges and a description of the body.

Commanding Officers were responsible for making sure that all personal effects, including those of a 'sentimental value', were forwarded to the officer commanding the unit to which the dead man belonged. From there the items were directed to the Deputy Adjutant General at General Headquarters with the least delay.

In September 1915, Captain Henry Kaye, serving with the 43rd Field Ambulance, 14th Division, recalled the operation to remove personal effects. The preliminary rites, including the collection of pay book, letters and identity disc, had been concluded when the subaltern in charge remarked of the next of kin:

'I wonder if they would like a button' – 'Yes, sir, a large one,' chipped in a young soldier. 'No, sir,' said the experienced older soldier, also of the party, 'one large and two small, then they make a brooch of 'em.' These three were then gravely cut off his tunic and tied up with the rest of his possessions, rather a nice piece of thoughtfulness for the unknown man's people when you picture the circumstance (which *you* can't do).'

Battlefield burials were divided into two classes. The first was under normal conditions when a battalion was holding a prepared line, and the second during heavy fighting when advances were anticipated.

As well as being responsible for the burial of their own dead, COs were expected to inter any other extraneous dead lying within the 'area' under their control. As far as possible, bodies were buried in plots according to their known nationality, while enemy dead were to be registered and recorded in the same way as British and Allied troops but were not to be buried in cemeteries.

Under normal conditions, bodies were to be taken to designated cemeteries only, with graves five feet deep, two feet wide, six foot six inches long and not more than a foot apart. A path of no more than three feet between rows was to be left. Each grave was to be marked with either a wooden peg with a grave registration label filled out and attached or, preferably, a label placed in a bottle with the neck turned into the earth. Pegs were left in boxes in the cemetery. Commanding Officers were responsible for seeing that labels were written in block capitals and in hard black pencil.

During a rolling campaign, where it was not possible to remove bodies to a designated cemetery, the army directed that the dead should be collected and buried in an appropriate spot, making sure that any burials were at least 100 metres from the nearest housing and 'NOT near a well'. Where bodies were interred in trenches, the rule was that officers would be buried with men except officers of the rank of general or above. If it was not possible to note the identification of bodies, each would be given a serial number and the trench marked by burial discs and rods with a note of the divisional sign.

This was the idea in theory, but war was never so precise or so clean and tidy. In a small number of cases, it was later discovered that the identity of bodies in graves had been incorrectly attributed to men found to be very much alive in Britain or held as prisoners of war in Germany. Men such as 8822 Lance Corporal James Harris, 2nd Border Regiment, and 9544 Private Frederick Pocock, London Rifle Brigade, might have been amused to know that reports of their deaths had been greatly exaggerated. In each case the cross was removed, and an unpleasant examination of the grave undertaken to try to determine just who was there.

Whether it was possible to bury a body with due ceremony was in the lap of the gods, although the proximity of a cemetery to the enemy and the attitude of the individual officiating also made a difference. If time permitted, bodies would be wrapped in army-issue blankets, but where men had been blown apart sometimes a sandbag would do. Normally a man would be buried in his uniform, with the webbing and boots removed (salvaging reusable government property was an absolute necessity in time of war).

After one attack, Roland Fielding oversaw the burial of a number of men of the Civil Service Rifles killed several days before.

There was no time for anything elaborate, so the poor bodies with their blackened faces were just lifted into shell-holes or into a trench, one or two or three or four together, and earth was put over them. Then a rifle, with bayonet fixed, was stuck into the ground, butt uppermost, to mark each grave – with the names on a bit of paper attached to the trigger-guard.

A service was conducted by a padre but once again only when this was feasible; otherwise, an officer would preside, reading some appropriate words, followed by a short prayer; failing him, anyone would do.

Catholic priest and army chaplain Father Benedict Williamson went to bury six men of the 47th Division to which he was attached.

I have rarely seen anything quite so pathetic: the grave, dug in Flanders mud, was already filling with water; the poor bodies in their uniform as they had fallen, the utter desolation of everything all round, made up a scene not easily forgotten. The adjutant and the burial party stood by; I had only just begun the burial service when a shell burst close by. 'Don't make the service too long, Father,' whispered my servant over my shoulder. Two or three more came over ere the ceremony was complete, and the burial party began hastily filling in the grave.

Further back, even when time and opportunity allowed for a proper burial, there might be so many dead to bury that the ceremony remained perfunctory. Captain Alan Thomas was shocked by the Divisional General's attitude at the burial of six officers who had been under his command. This senior officer could be jovial and good-natured but he could also be extremely hot-tempered. At 7.30 a.m. a small group of officers had attended the funeral, standing around the padre who read the service. The padre, Thomas recalled, was nervous and had a voice that naturally irritated. This, coupled with the fact that the officers present wanted their breakfast and preferred food to standing in the rain, led to an incident that was regrettable but said something, too, about the attitude to life and death at the time.

'Ashes to ashes, dust to dust,' quoth the Padre, taking up a handful of earth and scattering it upon the first body.

'Ashes to ashes, dust to dust,' he repeated, taking up another handful of earth and scattering it upon the second body.

The General shifted from one foot to the other and heaved a very audible sigh.

'Ashes to ashes, dust to dust,' began the Padre, stooping for yet another handful of earth.

The General exploded.

'That's the third time you've said that!' he exclaimed. 'Why must you keep repeating yourself?'

Even the tough ones among us were shocked at this interruption of the funeral service. We took deep breaths and looked down our noses.

The Padre made a feeble attempt to stand his ground.

'The Church ordains, sir,' he said, 'that those words shall be spoken over each body.'

The General shrugged his shoulders.

'Get on with it,' was all he said.

To his shame the Padre funked the rest. Forsaking the ordinances of the Church he scattered his last handful of earth upon the three remaining bodies, hurrying through the words as best he might. In another two minutes the service was over.

Sadly, burial could be even more perfunctory when the bodies were unknown to those present. Captain J. C. Procter, serving with the 13th Gloucestershire Regiment, watched the miserable overture to one burial service. In the end he did not wait to see the interment, having witnessed too many of their ilk before.

At dusk I passed one of the numerous roadside cemeteries, with its neat row of graves and wooden crosses. On the roadside outside were numerous stretchers and carrying parties, and on the stretchers lay the mummy-like figures of some of these poor little fellows, tightly and neatly stitched up in blankets, waiting till it was dark enough for the parson to come and do his job. The sight was sufficiently depressing . . . I hurried on. I'd no wish to see the last act, the hasty words of the burial service, the one sordid Union Jack snatched hastily from a body 'finished with' and flung over the next, while the bearers smoked in the road outside.

Afterwards, a burial return would be made either by the officer conducting the interment or by the chaplain. The return included all the soldier's particulars, the name of the cemetery and a location taken from the 1/40,000 map or, failing this, a description making note of local features such as houses, woods and crossroads. In November 1915, six weeks after the death of his son Raymond, Sir Oliver Lodge, the famous scientist, was sent the detailed location of his son's grave, given as 'Ref. Map Belgium, Sheet 28. Scale 1/40,000. Square 1. 16. B. 2. Near Ypres'. This was noted as a position 1,000 yards north of Zillebeke village to the south-east of Ypres, a setting where there were two tiny cemeteries known as Union Street Graveyards, no. 1 and no. 2.

Touching letters of sympathy from close friends and commanding officers took no more than a few days to reach home. And, almost inevitably with any batch of letters sent, there were likely to be responses that might require a further round of replies. Letters from home usually thanked the officer for his kindness, and perhaps wished him better luck than had befallen the correspondent's own son or husband. They might offer continued prayers for the pals of the fallen man and a few, such as the one written by Sergeant Thomas Buckle's brother-in-law, Mr Dunville, asked for more details of the death.

I shall be thankful if you will give me full particulars of poor Tommy's death. Will you tell me all, and how his last moments were spent. For I feel sure that his thoughts would be of home and his loved ones, for you know he was always so kind and considerate to everybody. Did he leave any message for us?

Grieving relatives would not have wished to add to the officer's burden, but they could not understand the pressures heaped upon the shoulders of company officers any more than they could the conditions on the Western Front.

Requests for more information could put the recipients on edge, uncertain how to respond. After Private Thomas Hope's close friend Mac was killed, he dutifully wrote to the family, though he does not appear to have included all the usual blandishments, for Mac's sister replied asking whether her brother had 'died peacefully or in pain'. It 'seems a strange request,' she wrote, 'but what a relief it would be to us all at home, especially Mother, just to know that even though he died far from home, he had a friend near him at the end who may have heard his last words . . .'

It might be that a request to be told 'all', as the Buckle family asked, was really nothing of the sort. Perhaps it was really a search for comfort, hence leading questions such as Mr Dunville's 'hopes' that Sergeant Buckle's last thoughts were for his family, and Mac's sister's hint that it would be a 'relief' to know her brother was with a friend when he died, one who had heard his last words. Wondering how he might reply, Thomas Hope sat down with a stub of pencil and a piece of paper. His great friend Webster looked on as Hope began to write.

'Dear Miss McDonald,' and there I stick.

Webster takes the letter and reads it over again and then puts it down in disgust:

'No, this aint in my line, I give it up. 'Arf a mo' though. I'll tell you what we could do. How about spinning a yarn? We could say we were attacking. All the officers had gone west and Mac led us on but was killed by a shell just when we had captured the trench – you know the style of thing.'

'That's useless,' I answer irritably. 'What if his folks should find out the truth afterwards? Besides, we don't know what the captain has told them.'

'Oh, he won't have said much, just the usual. I know it off by heart: "Your son was one of the most cheerful and reliable soldiers in my company, a gentleman in every sense. He will be greatly missed by all."'

'That's all very well, but we can't be sure. Besides, Mac wouldn't want us to spin the tale to his old folks. No, we'll just have to tell them the truth for once, Webby.'

'Oh well, carry on, you're writing it.'

Hope concocted a story that was broadly truthful and which picked up on the tendered hints. After careful deliberation, he wrote that they had managed to stop Mac bleeding, and had endeavoured to get him to a Dressing Station. 'He was unconscious and, I am sure, felt no pain.' Then Hope added the embellishment the family no doubt hoped to hear. Mac had briefly regained consciousness, and had evidently tried to talk:

. . . but the only words I could catch were Mother and Sis. He died with his hand in mine.

'Amen,' Webster finishes, 'and that's that.'

'Will it do?' I enquire.

'It sounds all right, better than I could have done. All the same I'd have liked to have given him a better show than that.'

'How can we? We haven't kept to the facts as it is; that would hurt too much; but if you have any decent suggestions.'

'Suggestions be damned, give the bloody thing to the Post Corporal and get done with it. What the hell folk want to send letters like that to us for, I don't know.'

Agnes Cottrell would have liked to have asked more questions of the friends of her son, Second Lieutenant Harold Cottrell of the South Lancashire Regiment. Two officers had written to her sympathising with her loss but, as she pointed out in a letter to the War Office, both of them had themselves been killed shortly afterwards.

Agnes also wished to know 'all', but in her case she wanted the truth about Harold's death, and not the usual 'platitudes', as she called them. Agnes was furious that her son had been sent up the front line just a matter of days after he had landed in France. She blamed the Commanding Officer of her son's battalion, Colonel Hugh Craigie-Halkett, for putting Harold so quickly in harm's way, and she blamed the government for allowing her son to embark for France in the first place. He had died shortly after his eighteenth birthday, and, according to statements made in the House of Commons and reported in the press, he should not have been sent overseas until he was nineteen. This was correct, but no Army Council Instruction had yet been released which authorised the change of policy that brought the age of overseas service for officers in line with that of other ranks.

With the death of Harold, Agnes had lost her second and sole remaining child. She wrote continually to the War Office asking for explanations. The problem was that no answer was going to assuage her grief, and the answers that were given only maddened her further. At first she was offered the very banalities she did not wish to hear. Then, when more details were offered that appeared to her mind contradictory in any way, they were challenged with further letters.

'I want to know exactly the time of death in action and ditto burial – extent and nature of wounds and manner of identification,' she wrote.

> I may say it was a great scandal that a mere boy should have been sent out so young and not two months after leaving Sandhurst, and those to blame will suffer a just retribution sooner or later . . . I am desolate but the matter is not finished yet . . . There is no

doubt in my own mind my slaughtered boy was pushed up into the line to save some one else.

In a brusque letter, Craigie-Halkett replied telling her little other than that a shell burst had killed her son. The Military Secretary at the War Office, through whom all correspondence was directed, regretted with Mrs Cottrell that no other particulars were forthcoming, other than his own 'deepest sympathy' in the loss of her gallant sons who, he felt obliged to say, 'died the death they would have preferred above all others'. This was hardly what she wanted to hear so she replied, this time in the third person.

She begs the Military Secretary to desire Colonel Craigie-Halkett, the most callous and cruel man she has ever heard of, to furnish her with the information she has so many times asked for. She does not wish any details withheld for fear of hurting her feelings. Having had both her brave noble sons sacrificed, nothing more can be done to hurt her.

If the last reply was noncommittal, the next was almost ludicrous, given the circumstances. It was written by the Reverend Horace Townsend who told Agnes that he was in the same trenches the day her son died.

Your son was a very gallant light-hearted fellow. I think ordinary common life was too slack for him; he longed to see and do noble deeds, and just at that time his regiment were holding a piece of front line in spite of all the Germans could do against them.

As I told you in a former letter of mine, he was knocked over by a shell earlier in the afternoon, and to a lad of his mettle this was just what made him feel he was really in the middle of great things . . .

While you his mother, must always feel his loss, you cannot but feel proud and deeply thankful to God that such a son was yours, and is yours still, though for a while removed from you – 'All live unto God.'

The Reverend Townsend had been able to discern much about Harold Cottrell in the handful of days the young subaltern had been in France. Mrs Cottrell did not believe what amounted in her eyes to more flannel. She also had no time for a chaplain who had made no effort to keep her son from going up the line; indeed, to her mind he had been complicit, having given her son the Holy Sacrament before he went forward.

There was an obvious lack of enthusiasm, though, interestingly, no refusal on the part of the War Office to pursue matters for Mrs Cottrell. The Commanding Officer in France might reasonably have felt that he had better and more important things to do than to answer correspondence from home. Nevertheless, the War Office still forwarded letters, albeit with a certain embarrassment. 'I am extremely sorry to waste your time by asking you questions about casualties . . .' the War Office official wrote, but Mrs Cottrell 'has been so persistent in her enquiries . . . it is evidently a case of a distraught mother who cannot control herself.'

Colonel Craigie-Halkett had by this time left to take up command elsewhere, though the next query from Mrs Cottrell was still sent out to the new CO. His reply to the Assistant Military Secretary, War Office, came in May, headed, 'In the field.' It was eight months since Harold had been killed.

Sir, with reference to your letter dated 19th April 1917 I regret that Mrs Cottrell feels that she has not been treated well, but I would like to point out that all her letters were answered, that not only did the Colonel Commanding the Battalion write to her, but the chaplain also, and not once, but several times. The chaplain is again writing to her regarding the points enumerated in your letter.

Whatever his letter said, it did not seem to mollify Agnes, for her letters continued well into July. There never could be any consolation for the loss she had sustained and her case showed where the limits were when it came to army sympathies and parental loss.

Both sides lacked the right words for any semblance of mutual comprehension. Her case simply underlined the divisions between soldiers and civilians so often referred to in diaries and memoirs of the time. Misunderstandings were destined only to continue.

When Sergeant William Andrews of the Black Watch wrote to the family of a comrade he could see dead on the German barbed wire, he thought his unsolicited letter would be welcomed. But his 'guarded account' of the man's death was far from appreciated; indeed the dead man's father wrote back full of suspicions not least because Andrews had failed to mention a funeral — 'surely his son received the tribute of a Christian burial'. Believing a funeral must have taken place and, as if checking the veracity of the story, he wanted to know which of his son's comrades had attended the burial. When Andrews replied that his son was in fact lying near the German trenches, the man angrily condemned him for not going out and collecting his son's remains. 'It seemed amazing,' wrote Andrews in his diary, 'that people at home should imagine we could risk the lives of three or four men to bring a body across No Man's Land.' A body lying on the German wire, and so close to the enemy, was not likely to be retrieved even if it belonged to the 1/5th South Lancashire Regiment, and its hapless Commanding Officer.

As well as commiserating with families, letters from the battalion served one other very useful purpose: they reassured those at home that no official mistake had been made. How commonly known it was that the War Office made errors it is impossible to establish, but, given that Britain was engaged in a vast and complex war, it was not unreasonable to suppose that mistakes did occur. Other than simple failures in administration, the War Office was only as good as the information supplied to it from the front. Anywhere down the line it was possible to confuse two similar names, even numbers, especially when such men were serving in the same battalion. One of those mistakenly reported to have died of wounds was the poet and author Robert Graves. His demise, officially notified to the press, was reported in *The Times* in July 1916; Graves later penned a disclaimer. This was also published in *The Times*, and informed friends that he was in fact recovering from wounds in a Highgate hospital. Such erroneous reports of death were inevitable, but some mistakes were more avoidable than others, especially when they originated from within the battalion itself.

The problem arose when assumptions were made that a soldier must have died of his injuries. Captain Maurice Turner, serving with the 1/4th Suffolk Regiment, was so convinced that a lance corporal serving in his company had succumbed to his wounds that he wrote to the man's father, Mr Hardy. 'It is with the greatest regret that I have to convey to you the sad news of the death of your son . . .' Like Private Cole's uninhibited letter to the Gardner family, Turner was explicit in the details, although this also helped leave little room for doubt. 'He was hit by a sniper just below the eye whilst doing his duty . . . I am sorry to say he was conscious when the SB (Stretcher Bearers) carried him away to the Dressing Station but I am quite convinced he did not realize the gravity of his wound.' Against all apparent odds, Hardy survived and was awarded the Military Medal in October 1916.

In September 1914, at the request of Lord Kitchener, a Red Cross Mobile Ambulance unit under the command of a former editor of the *Morning Post*, Fabian Ware, arrived in France charged with searching for missing British soldiers. Their search would take them along the line of retreat followed by the British Expeditionary Force after the Battle of Mons, and it was while they were conducting their work that they discovered a small group of British graves in a French cemetery near the town of Béthune. It was noticed that, although the graves were marked by wooden crosses, there was no evidence that their existence had been registered, and therefore it followed that no one was responsible for their upkeep.

Ware had been surprised at the lack of any official apparatus for such a job, and so he and his unit assumed the work themselves. Over the following months they noted the whereabouts of 3,400 graves before the idea of establishing an official body to undertake the necessary registration was sanctioned by the War Office. In April 1915, Ware was given the temporary rank of major and he and the men of his unit were transferred to the British Army to form the Graves Registration Commission (GRC), the forerunner of today's Commonwealth War Graves Commission. By October 1915, the Commission had registered 31,000 graves, and 50,000 by the following May.

In time, the GRC would employ almost two hundred men in several Grave Registration Units (GRUs) attached to the Army Service Corps, although its vehicles were supplied by a Joint War Committee formed soon after the outbreak of war by the Red Cross and Order of St John. The GRC would even begin to employ specialists, including for short periods an expert horticulturalist from Kew Gardens, who was sent to France to give advice on such matters as planting shrubs and sowing grass in cemeteries.

As the work of the Commission broadened and became publicly known, letters of enquiry were received and appeals made not only to send wreaths to place below the crosses of loved ones but to have pictures taken of their graves. By the spring of 1915, various requests, including those for photographs, were being channelled through the Joint War Committee to the GRC. The army had prohibited private cameras on the Western Front soon after images of British and German soldiers' cordial meetings in no man's land had reached the British press after Christmas 1914. However, in the case of the GRC this prohibition was waived for three professional photographers to travel under supervision around the Western Front taking pictures of graves.

It was soon realised that graves were spread so widely that it would be impossible to photograph each to order, so it was decided to take images of all registered graves in each cemetery so as to supply them to relatives as and when they cared to apply. The Joint War Committee would pay for this new photographic department of the GRC, so ensuring the images were free. By August 1915, 2,000 negatives showing 8,000 burial places had been safely filed, and 200 requests dispatched to families with a further 200 in the process of being fulfilled. Information as to where the grave could be found was also supplied with each image, with one eye already on post-war family visits.

The GRC had not publicised the work of the photographic department for fear it might be swamped with applications for images of graves that had not yet been photographed. Instead, the GRC relied on publicity by word of mouth until, in August 1915, Fabian Ware felt comfortable enough for a public announcement to be made through the Joint War Committee. From then on, the clamour for photographs steadily grew, and sixteen months later the GRC reported that 12,000 photographs had been dispatched to families, although delivery could take six months or even longer and the results were not always to the recipient's satisfaction.

A rider accompanied each photograph that underlined the difficulties faced by the photographers. 'Owing to the circumstances in which the photograph work is carried on, it is regretted that in some cases only rough photographs can be obtained.' Harry Wakeman, who lost his RAF officer son Malcolm in the closing weeks of the war, was one who was not impressed. In his view 'rough' should not mean undecipherable.

I am sorry to say that I cannot read the name or inscription on the cross and I should have liked a photo from which I could read the name and make sure that the photo was a genuine one of the actual grave. Under a magnifying glass the inscription does not look at all like Wakeman and seems to have 'St' at the end — sorry to trouble you but the photo ought to show clearly the name and whatever else is on the plate.

He received a reply assuring him the image was 'undoubtedly' that of the correct grave, although Harry Wakeman later paid a private photographer to take the image again.

Despite occasional reservations, the GRC received many letters of appreciation, as well as offers to pay. Sadly, in many cases, these treasured pictures would prove to be the only lasting record of a soldier's grave, for, as battles ebbed and flowed, a number of cemeteries established close to the front lines were damaged or destroyed in the fighting.

The work of the GRC was deemed extremely important for morale, as Douglas Haig, the Commander in Chief, made clear in March 1916.

It is fully recognized that the work of this organization is of a purely sentimental value, and that it does not directly contribute to the successful termination of the war. It has, however, an extraordinary moral value to the Troops in the Field as well as to the relatives and friends of the dead, at home. The mere fact that these officers visit day after day, the cemeteries close behind the trenches, fully exposed to shell and rifle fire, accurately to record not only the names of the dead but also the exact place of burial, has a symbolical value to the men that it would be difficult to exaggerate.

Haig also had an eye to a time when the war would be over.

It should be borne in mind that on the termination of hostilities the nation will demand an account from the Government as to the steps which have been taken to mark and classify the burial places of the dead, steps which can only be effectively taken at, or soon after, burial.

As there was little possibility of civilians physically seeing the graves of loved ones, the GRC received requests for wreaths to be laid at the graveside. Fabian Ware foresaw that this would cause any number of problems, not least ensuring that wreaths from Britain reached the Western Front in one piece. He did not want to say no, for both he and the Red Cross recognised the public disquiet about the exhumation of Lieutenant Gladstone. This had caused, as Ware wrote, 'an administrative difficulty': his grave could have a wreath because he had been brought back to Wales. If exhumations were forbidden, then perhaps it was only fair that wreaths might be sent to France and Belgium. In the end, Ware had the idea that local people, led perhaps by the *curé* or mayor, could be prevailed upon to make and place the wreaths. The solution, at least in the medium term, was to allow wreaths to be laid at graves although there is no evidence that this question was ever satisfactorily answered.

Even paying for a wreath would have been beyond the pockets of many poorer families and a not inconsiderable expense for those a little better off. By contrast, there were a small number of wealthy individuals who sought to pay tribute to their dead in a way that involved a financial commitment far in excess of anything that might be contemplated by the vast majority of grieving relatives. Their fervent wish was not only to buy the land where a son or husband had fallen but to erect a memorial there to his memory.

In some cases the purchase was made in order to keep the body where it lay and forestall any attempt to remove it to a war cemetery. For others it was simply to commemorate in stone, for posterity, the brief life of a soldier, irrespective of whether he was missing or occupied a known grave.

Stockbroker Edward Rae lost his son Lieutenant Keith Rae in July 1915 during fighting near the village of Hooge in the Ypres Salient. For a while the family harboured hopes that Keith might still be alive, perhaps as a prisoner, but any optimism quickly faded. Realistically, as Edward Rae knew, his son was almost certainly dead and so he proposed to purchase the land on which his son had fought and where he was last seen wounded, still firing his revolver over the parapet.

Buying the land would have to wait until peacetime, but in the meantime a temporary memorial could be raised until Edward Rae could visit Belgium. In a letter written after the summer offensive of 1917, he sent a letter to a person of obvious influence but whose identity is unknown:

As Hooge is now so definitely behind our line, do you think it would be possible to write to any officer who you know within Ypres neighbourhood asking for information as to the ownership of land in the village? Should an armistice be declared, with the withdrawal of the Germans, I might by grace and favour get permission to go to Ypres . . . I am eager, as you know, to get permission of, or rights over, the little piece of ground where Keith's trench was. His Colonel and other officers gave us plans and indications by which I could identify it. The cross has long been ready, but it might be difficult at the moment to get leave to ship it. I would be more than content in the meantime to set up a wooden cross.

In 1921, Rae was able to come to an arrangement with the owner of the land, a Baron de Vinck, and a Celtic stone cross set in a small garden was unveiled with words that paid tribute not only to Keith Rae but to all the men of his battalion, the 8th Rifle Brigade, killed on the same day. The memorial was moved many years later for reasons of care and of safety, and now stands next to the British cemetery at Sanctuary Wood, still only a short distance from where Keith had been killed.

There was one civilian who could visit his son's grave during wartime: Sir Harry Lauder. In 1917 he had been travelling around the Western Front giving concerts to soldiers but always with one eye on a visit to the cemetery on the Somme where his son was buried. His grave had been registered by the GRC and an

impressive wooden cross erected by the men of John Lauder's
battalion. Harry was also fortunate in that in the spring of 1917
the Germans had pulled back more than thirty miles from their
trenches on the Somme to a new defensive position known as the
Hindenburg Line. Not only was it safe to visit the grave in peace
but the cemetery was now out of range of enemy fire.

Sir Harry had noticed that one of the officers accompanying his
tour had been looking at him in a 'curiously intent fashion' before
approaching to ask, 'Where do you go next, Harry?'

His voice was keenly sympathetic, and his eyes and his manner
were very grave.

'To a place called Ovilliers,' I said.

'So I thought,' he said. He put out his hand, and I gripped it,
hard. 'I know, Harry. I know exactly where you are going, and I
will send a man with you to act as your guide, who knows the spot
you want to reach.' . . .

I certainly was not disposed to chat, and I suppose that sympathy for my feelings, and my glumness, stilled the tongues of my
companions. And, at any rate, we had not travelled far when the
car ahead of us stopped, and the soldier stepped into the road and
waited for me. I got out when our car stopped, and joined him.

'I will show you the place now, Mr Lauder,' he said, quietly. So
we left the cars standing in the road, and set out across a field that,
like all the fields in that vicinity, had been ripped and torn by
shell-fire. All about us, as we crossed that tragic field, there were
little brown mounds, each with a white wooden cross upon it.
June was out that day in full bloom. All over the valley, thickly
sown with those white crosses, were wild flowers in rare profusion,
and thickly matted, luxuriant grasses . . . It was a mournful journey, but, in some strange way, the peaceful beauty of the day
brought comfort to me. And my own grief was altered by the
vision of the grief that had come to so many others. Those crosses,
stretching away as far as my eye could reach, attested to the fact

that it was not I alone who had suffered and lost and laid a sacrifice upon the altar of my country . . . I knew that he was only one, and that I was only one father. And there were so many like him – and so many like me, God help us all!

So we came, when we were, perhaps, half a mile from the Bapaume road, to a slight eminence, a tiny hill that rose from the field. A little military cemetery crowned it. Here the graves were set in ordered rows, and there was a fence set around them, to keep them apart, and to mark that spot as holy ground, until the end of time. Five hundred British boys lie sleeping in that small acre of silence, and among them is my own laddie. There the fondest hopes of my life, the hopes that sustained and cheered me through many years, lie buried.

No one spoke. But the soldier pointed, silently and eloquently, to one brown mound in a row of brown mounds that looked alike, each like the other. Then he drew away. And so I went alone to my boy's grave, and flung myself down upon the warm, friendly earth. My memories of that moment are not very clear, but I think that for a few minutes I was utterly spent, that my collapse was complete.

No sooner was a soldier interred than the process to return his possessions to the family began. In principle, personal items would be passed on with a statement of what had been found and removed. These inventories for both officers and other ranks varied greatly in length, although for content Lieutenant Harry Armstrong's was not untypical. This subaltern died in a Casualty Clearing Station and his effects noted: a bundle of letters and photographs, one tinder lighter, wire-cutters, binoculars with strap, identity disc, compass, spirit flask, map case, safety pen, safety razor, comb, scissors, twenty-six francs and fifteen centimes, two wristwatches, an electric torch, two cap badges, silver ciga-rette case, pencil and case, pipes, clasp knife, two tobacco pouches, whistle, two cheque books, a metal mirror, a medicine case, leather pouch, piece of shell, one small box and six penny stamps.

During the war, the majority of officers conducted their financial affairs through a bank, Messrs Cox and Co., and it was through an arm of this company, Cox and Co.'s Shipping Agency, that the War Office instructed that all officers' personal items were to be packaged up and returned.

Packages might number one, two or even several, for, unlike other ranks, officers bought and paid for their own kit, and therefore it was considered rightfully the property of the next of kin. Unfortunately this was taken literally, and blood-soaked tunics frequently arrived along with the officer's other effects. This did not necessarily upset everyone's sensibilities. The mother of Lieutenant Charles Brooke, killed on 1 July 1916 with the Yorkshire Regiment, took his soiled and shredded tunic and set it in a frame to be hung in the hallway, so proud was she of her dead son. Her reaction can safely be regarded as unusual. A more likely response was shock and horror. Lieutenant Roland Leighton's blood-caked uniform was sent to his mother's home, as Vera Brittain recalled in her memoirs. She found Roland's mother and sister 'standing in helpless distress' among his kit lying on the floor, the 'tunic torn back and front by the bullet, a khaki vest dark and stiff with blood, and a pair of blood-stained breeches slit open at the top by someone obviously in a violent hurry'. Roland's 'gruesome rags' were burned in the back garden.

The number of packages received at home would reflect something of how, when and where the man had died. Perhaps the greatest loss of personal items can be attributed to souvenir hunters or battlefield scavengers, German or British. Yet they were only one piece of a fragmented picture where personal possessions were concerned. Items could be dropped or lent; in battle they might be forgotten or abandoned when a trench or dugout was hurriedly evacuated; if a man was cornered, his possessions might have been bartered, perhaps in exchange for his life.

The best chance a soldier would have of his personal items reaching home would be if men of the same platoon or company buried him. Then the comradeship in life was simply replaced by one in death: 'Ere's old Fred, poor devil, let's make sure his missus gets his belongings back.' Sadly, this bond did not extend much beyond the company or battalion, at best. Bodies that did not belong to the regiment conducting the search were more likely to be handled roughly, examinations to be more cursory and souvenir hunting altogether more likely.

Corporal Fred Hodges had definite views on what was right and wrong. His own self-imposed high standards, and the authority he held with two stripes, ensured that he was not going to abandon those standards with men under his command. He might turn a blind eye to some things, but not when it came to looting the property of the dead.

I was leading a party of men when we came across a lot of dead – our own men – nine of them hit by one shell. They were just all funny shapes, and as I glanced round I saw one of my party taking a badge off an arm. It was a Lewis Gun badge, L.G. in brass with a wreath around it, a pretty badge and he wanted it. I told him to leave it alone, and he sullenly put it down. 'I won't have any loot-ing.' I was strict and stern and I shouted at them. I realize now that we were all mere boys of eighteen and nineteen, and how understandable it was at that age to covet a nice brass badge. An NCO has to be a bit of an actor to get a point across, but looting was totally against my beliefs.

I also discovered that two London boys in the Regiment had been looting graves, getting rings off corpses. That shocked me. It didn't matter whether they were British or German, if they were dead and there was money, they'd take it.

Not all taking was looting. Helping oneself to a water bottle, or a pack of cigarettes, was a benign activity and did not normally rob a man of his identity; looting did and often denied a man, and therefore his family, a known grave. Engraved rings or inscribed fob watches would give a name to a man whose identification tags or pay book were missing. The simple fact was that the less that remained on the individual, the greater the chance his name would remain 'known unto God', friend or foe. Even the very act of rifling through a body's pockets ensured that identifying possessions of no value whatsoever were cast aside. 'It was curious,' wrote Scots Guardsman Stephen Graham,

> what a great number of letters, both British and German, lay on the battlefield. These had been taken out of the pockets and pocket-books of the dead and since they were no use had been thrown to the winds – literally to the winds, for when the wind rose they blew about like dead leaves. There were photographs, too, prints of wife or sweetheart, of mother, or perchance of baby born whilst father was at the war – the priceless, worthless possessions of those whose bodies lay on the altar.

After death, bodies were frequently blown apart or buried by spoil, so that recovery was difficult if not impossible. Even when a body was located, in what state was it found? Battlefield clearance was a horrific job. It was one thing to handle a corpse killed a day or two earlier by a single bullet to the heart, quite another to touch a body that had been mangled, perhaps dead for a week or more, stinking in the summer sun, and covered in flies. Only men who had grown accustomed to such sights and smells would bother to examine a body properly under such circumstances and many personal items were undoubtedly missed.

Twenty-eight-year-old Ernest Colquhoun was killed in the bitter fighting around Ypres in September 1917. His body was located, his possessions removed and then he was buried. Only in 1923, when his remains were exhumed from an outlying cemetery to be reburied in Poelcappelle British Cemetery, was his fob watch discovered. It had been given to him on the day of his marriage in 1913 by his brother Julian, and had been overlooked when he was found. The watch was returned to his family and years later passed down to his only son, Gordon.

For every overlooked fob watch, many more ended up in the pockets of the living and many pathetic letters survive, written by grieving next of kin, appealing for information about missing items while clearly ignorant of the brutal realities of the battle-field. Captain Sidney Rogerson recalled one incident concerning a man in his company named Robinson. Robinson liked nothing more than to crawl around in no man's land looking for trophies. He was allowed to go on condition that, if he came across any British dead, he would retrieve their identification and not take personal possessions. Rogerson also insisted he wrote to the relatives of those he found.

> Robinson did write to several wives and mothers only to get letters back asking, for example, if he could please forward 'our Jim's watch', or 'what became of the money my Albert had on him when he was killed?' . . . The requests showed clearly how little idea they had of the circumstances in which the identity of their loved ones was established – hurriedly, and under shell-fire, by a corporal grubbing about in the darkness for souvenirs.

Percy Boswell, an officer serving with the King's Own Yorkshire Light Infantry, was killed at the age of twenty-two on 1 July 1916. The casualties in his sector had been very heavy, with few men reaching the German wire in the attack. Although Boswell's name appears today on the Thiepval Memorial, his body was found (though subsequently lost) and personal items returned to his family in Streatham, south London.

Items returned included letters, a pocket book and photographs. Items missing included a wristwatch, gold scarf pin, a silver and leather flask, silver cigarette case and matchbox, fountain pen, field glasses and compass. There is no apparent connection made by the father between the nominal value of the items found and the high value of those that were lost. His appeal for any news, written on 18 November, the day the Battle of the Somme was officially closed down, is almost touching in its naivety:

> None of these [items] have been returned to me although I have made repeated application for same, I enclose a list of them as far as I can remember. I shall be obliged by your having the necessary enquiries made so that they can be returned to me . . .

The army's reply was a little vague.

> It appears that it was not possible to recover any of the deceased officer's effects, other than those which have already been forwarded to you . . . I am to add that although every endeavour is made to safeguard the collection and transmission of a deceased officer's effects, it is impossible under the conditions of Active Service to guard entirely against the losses which sometimes occur . . .

The sad truth about such 'losses' was transparent in the case of a Bedfordshire Regiment officer, Second Lieutenant George Smith-Masters, who was killed in mid-August 1915. Like Percy Boswell's, Smith-Masters' possessions were collected and sent back to the base for forwarding to Cox and Co.'s Shipping Agency in England. Nothing more was heard until three weeks later when John Smith-Masters, George's father, wrote to his son's battalion CO, Lieutenant Colonel Roundell Toke, to report that many of the items sent back from France had clearly been stolen in transit. Toke sent an immediate reply: it was both sympathetic and furious.

> Dear Mr Smith-Masters
>
> I am very sorry to learn that your son's things have been stolen on the way to the base.
>
> Everything was done in accordance with the regulations and I have a receipt for the things.

It is worse than scandal that officers up here in the trenches should have their kits rifled by individuals at the base, but it is only too common. I am going to report the matter officially in the hope that something may be done.

With many regrets, yours sincerely

RT Toke, Lt Col.

Soldiers were normally blamed for such thefts, but this case was not quite as it first appeared. On investigation, it was discovered that the subaltern's personal items were supposed to have been sent by registered post from the railhead, where the Regimental Post Corporal took them, to be sent to the base and then onwards to England. However, the weight of these possessions had exceeded the maximum allowed and so instead they had been placed inside an army sack along with other non-valuable items of kit and fastened with a metal seal. This bag had then been sent by stages to Cox and Co.'s warehouse in London. Here the seal was noted as being intact before it was sent to the receiving depot of the Great Western Railway prior to its last journey by passenger train to the Smith-Masters' home in Banbury.

John Smith-Masters received the sack but the wooden box in which the valuables had been stored within a brown paper bag had been smashed and, except for a letter and two cheque books, nothing remained. Personal items as listed in the accompanying document, such as his son's revolver, silver cigarette case, silver wristwatch and his whistle, were all missing. John Smith-Masters was livid and he wrote to the War Office that evening:

Unless I receive immediate satisfaction I shall write to *The Times* detailing the circumstances. The intrinsic value is considerable [later put at £23 10s. 6d.], but the value to us is far more. The articles were nearly all special presents made to my son.

All the evidence pointed to a theft that could only have taken place in England and not at the base in France. The Great Western

Railway was ordered to investigate not just this case but four others where items had been reported stolen, including possessions belonging to a Second Lieutenant Alexander Tippet, killed around the same time as Smith-Masters, and Lieutenant Cecil Parry, who was killed in July.

In October 1915, Albert Allen and Richard Quartley, employees of the Great Western Railway, were arrested. They appeared at Marylebone Police Court charged with the theft of field glasses, a compass, a silver watch, cigarette case and revolver. All were reported to have been possessions of a Second Lieutenant George Smith-Masters, although when his father was asked to go to Paddington Railway Station to identify them, he could see nothing that he could say for certain belonged to his son, although other property was later identified as belonging to Tippet and Parry.

What became abundantly clear was that these were not the only thefts, the men admitting to having opened about twenty bags of officers' kit: the *Daily Mail* later reported that the pair had opened forty bags. Whatever the final figure, subsequent enquiries led to a large quantity of property being removed from Allen's house, and a Bury St Edmunds publican named Fountain also being charged with handling stolen property. In all, police believed they had uncovered evidence that at least £200 worth of property had been stolen.

'I am so devoutly thankful that the suspicion, which so many people thought attached to some of our men in France, has been removed,' Smith-Masters wrote to the War Office. Sadly there is no evidence from surviving papers that he got back any of his son's missing possessions.

When arrested, Allen accused Quartley of being the ringleader. Quartley was wearing a silver wristwatch when apprehended and had a silver cigarette case in his pocket, both of which he claimed 'had dropped out of bags'; he also spuriously pointed out that officers' bags were not very securely fastened. Rather surprisingly, both men pleaded 'not guilty' to the crimes but were convicted nevertheless.

It is interesting to highlight but not to overstate the incidence of theft. Many thousands of items were handled by numerous individuals between the battlefields and Britain, and there are many stories of items obviously of great monetary, as well as sentimental, value making their way back home. George Musgrave, whose father was killed in 1917, remembers his mother mentioning how she received her husband's watch and chain.

> One letter she received after he died was a letter from the War Office sending the remainder of his possessions and they came in a little brown paper parcel and included his gold watch, the chain of which was hanging out of the brown paper. It had come through the post and nobody had stolen it. That was a vivid memory she had.

*   *   *

In France that summer of 1917, Sir Harry Lauder was at his son's graveside in a cemetery created in the land between what had been the former British and German front lines before the Somme offensive began. From there he could see across a vast expanse of land, heavily pockmarked from shelling, land every yard of which had been contested. However, at that moment his only thought was for his son, John.

> As I lay there on that brown mound, under the June sun that day, all that he had been, and all that he had meant to me and to his mother came rushing back afresh to my memory, opening anew my wounds of grief. I thought of him as a baby, and as a wee laddie beginning to run around and talk to us. I thought of him in every phase and bit of his life, and of the friends that we had been, he and I! Such chums we were, always!
>
> And as I lay there, as I look back upon it now, I can think of but the one desire that ruled and moved me. I wanted to reach my arms down into that dark grave, and clasp my boy tightly to my

breast, and kiss him. And I wanted to thank him for what he had done for his country, and his mother, and for me.

Again there came to me, as I lay there, the same gracious solace that God had given me after I heard of his glorious death. And I knew that this dark grave, so sad and lonely and forlorn, was but the temporary bivouac of my boy. I knew that it was no more than a trench of refuge against the storm of battle, in which he was resting until that hour shall sound when we shall all be reunited beyond the shadowy borderland of Death.

How long did I lie there? I do not know. And how I found the strength at last to drag myself to my feet and away from that spot, the dearest and the saddest spot on earth to me, God only knows. It was an hour of very great anguish for me; an hour of an anguish different, but only less keen, than that which I had known when they had told me first that I should never see my laddie in the flesh again. But as I took up the melancholy journey across that field, with its brown mounds and its white crosses stretching so far away, they seemed to bring me a sort of tragic consolation.

I thought of all the broken-hearted ones at home, in Britain. How many were waiting, as I had waited, until they, too, – they, too, – might come to France, and cast themselves down, as I had done, upon some brown mound, sacred in their thoughts? How many were praying for the day to come when they might gaze upon a white cross, as I had done, and from the brown mound out of which it rose gather a few crumbs of that brown earth, to be deposited in a sacred corner of a sacred place yonder in Britain?

He will stay there, in that small grave on that tiny hill, I shall not bring his body back to rest in Scotland, even if the time comes when I might do so. It is a soldier's grave, and an honourable place for him to be, and I feel it is there that he would wish to lie, with his men lying close about him, until the time comes for the great reunion.

6

The Missing

'He stands by my side and whispers
Dear mother, death cannot divide'

2204 Lance Corporal Clarence Quarrell
28th Battalion Australian Infantry Force
Died of wounds 17 November 1916, aged twenty-three
Buried Heilly Station Cemetery, Méricourt-L'Abbé

Second Lieutenant Hubert White of the 2nd Essex Regiment had been reported missing in action since the first morning of the 1916 Somme offensive. After the carnage, a number of men from his platoon had been asked to give accounts of the day and the whereabouts, if known, of their platoon officer. This was a normal procedure in the search for missing officers, and was frequently in response to enquiries made by their families at home. The following accounts were taken from survivors, men who served under the missing officer in A Company's 2nd Platoon.

'We left our trench which was known as "Toppin Trench" about 8.30 in the morning and we got past our barbed wire and the German barbed wire and had also just passed the 1st line of German trenches when the Lt. was shot through the head and killed instantaneously . . . I saw him fall,' testified Lance Corporal Farrer. 'I saw him fall' was unambiguous, but this sighting was contradicted by Private Catchpole who, in reporting conversations with other men in the platoon, stated that Lieutenant White was in fact wounded 'in our lines before we started advancing'.

Private Catchpole even recited the words given by their wounded platoon officer as he urged the men forward. 'The men told me that the last words they heard the officer say were: "Carry on; do your best; I'm finished."'

These were far from the only conflicting accounts. Private Robbins was next. 'This officer's servant came up to me at Colincamps near Beaumont Hamel,' he declared, 'and said "My chap's gone,"' and when I asked him for an explanation he said that 2nd Lt White had been shot in the head. At the time we were in the 2nd line German trenches . . .' Really? Not according to Private Friend, who had yet another version of events.

> He was my platoon officer, A Coy. He went over in the 2nd wave [and] got to about three quarters of the way between our 1st and the German 1st line. He had a stick in his hand pointing half left as if he was going to shout something, when he was struck by a bullet and fell.

In no man's land, 'near our trenches', is where Lance Corporal Bailey placed the officer, broadly agreeing with Private Friend. 'I saw Lt White go down . . . He fell as if killed outright.' Only Bailey added that White was not in A Company at all, but in C Company, Bailey's company. Finally, in another report that did not go into many details, Private Lucken remembered that the officer had 'only joined the battalion about a week before the advance on July 1st'. Even this small detail seems at variance with Private Friend's closing testimony that Lieutenant White was much loved: 'It broke the men's hearts when they heard he was killed.'

Did Second Lieutenant White fall in the British front line, three-quarters of the way across no man's land, or deep in the German trench system? Was he in the second or fourth wave of the attack, or even in A Company at all, and what were his last words? Given that his platoon was probably no more than forty-five strong, and that all the men would be likely to be in fairly close proximity to one another, the eyewitness accounts are seriously inconsistent. In Lieutenant White's records, an official note says that Private Friend's account was 'certainly hearsay', but because he had held the officer in high esteem he had made it his duty to find out what happened. This is a curious note, given the very specific nature of the recollections.

Here, in this one officer's records, lies the problem that beset the authorities when they tried to locate soldiers missing in action. White's may have been an unusual example for its number of blatant contradictions, but it is by no means a rare record of confusion and misinformation. Corporal John Lucy summed up that confusion well after he lost his brother Denis, killed in an attack in which both siblings were heavily engaged.

Following my own experience of hearing that my dead brother was alive and only slightly wounded, I found it hard to believe many of the stories bandied about. The troops, I am sure, did not lie deliberately, but their imagination, in the stress of battle, often played strange tricks on them.

Robert Graves, the soldier and poet, agreed. He wrote that men who had gone through the worst of trench warfare could not remember anything truthful if that memory did not also contain falsehoods. 'High explosive barrages will make a temporary liar or visionary of anyone; the old trench mind is at work in all over-estimation of casualties, "unnecessary" dwelling on horrors, mixing of dates and confusion between rumour and scenes actually witnessed.'

Men naturally sought to rationalise that confusion. Lucy recalled how, after battle, his depleted company was withdrawn from the front line and moved back the short distance to reserve, where he saw how men 'grouped in little parties to discuss their experiences'. Such discussions were as likely to confuse further as to clarify, for as men tried to make sense of their own hazy recollections they began to form a collective rationale for events that were almost entirely chaotic. Despite subsequent attempts to recover the battalion's dead, Denis's body was never recovered and he has no known grave.

The British Army suffered, on average, around 2,000 casualties a day, every day for 1,559 days. Those figures shrank or rocketed according to the time of year and whether an offensive operation was under way. The army's losses in February 1915, before the fighting awoke from its winter slumber, were but a tiny fraction of its losses in April 1917 when the Battle of Arras was in full swing and casualties could run not just into thousands but into tens of thousands in a day. It stands to reason that the pressure on the administration that dealt with those casualties was simply phenomenal.

After any action, the immediate job of the NCOs of each platoon was to undertake a roll call. In the British Army, a casualty was simply a man who failed to answer his name on the NCO's list. Lucy recalled the procedure after the attack in which his brother died.

The senior NCOs listed our casualties from information given by the survivors: '08, Corrigan?' 'Dead, Sergeant, I saw him too.' 'Right, killed in action. Any one seen 23, Murphy?' No answer. 'Right, missing.' 'What about MacRory? Any one see MacRory coming back after he was hit?' No answer. 'Right, wounded and missing,' and the Sergeant's stubby pencil scribbled on.

A casualty could mean the man was killed, wounded, taken prisoner or missing. 'Missing' might well mean nothing more than that the man was not wounded but lying in a shell-hole waiting for an opportune moment to come back in. Equally, he might have become disorientated and ended up in neighbouring trenches. Either way, after any attack, men slowly dribbled back to their units over the following hours.

After a day, or possibly two, when stragglers had returned, it was up to the officer commanding a battalion or unit to ascertain from the survivors if any information was forthcoming about those who had failed to reappear, upon which he filed a report that was dispatched up the chain of command.

These lists of missing were subsequently supplied to the War Office, which forwarded them to the Enquiry Department for Wounded and Missing run by the Joint War Committee of the Red Cross and Order of St John. From there, representatives were given access to hospitals and camps at home and overseas to collect information from wounded soldiers. Normally any new information would then be passed back to the War Office which would communicate the details to the families concerned. In all, the Enquiry Department received over 340,000 enquiries and obtained nearly 385,000 eyewitness reports, interviewing, as estimated by the Department's Director, Lord Lucan, a staggering four million servicemen throughout the war.

In 1917, Arthur Barraclough was in hospital in England recovering from wounds when a list of names was read out on his ward. All were names of men missing in action and those on the ward were asked if they had any information in addition to what little, if any, was already known. One of the names was very familiar to Arthur and he knew that the soldier was not missing but had been blown to bits.

'Would you like to go to Chesterfield?' they asked me. 'That lad you just named lived in Chesterfield and it would be a great pleasure to us if you could go and tell his mother, tell it to her nice, that he isn't a prisoner of war or anything like that, that he is dead and won't be coming home.'

After recovering from his injuries, Arthur went and found the house. 'It was a bit of a hard do for them. He was only a young man like myself, about twenty. They were heartbroken really, but they thanked me for going to tell them.'

Lists of missing men for whom there was no information were automatically printed and sent once a month to the Foreign Office for transmission through the neutral Dutch government to

Germany. Despite the ferocity of the fighting in France and Belgium, there was a regular diplomatic exchange of information between the two belligerents through the offices and embassies of neutral countries, usually Holland, Switzerland and, until it joined the war on the side of the Allies, the United States. Britain and Germany exchanged lists of prisoners and information on the dead as well as questions regarding the missing.

These lists of the missing would be circulated among prisoner of war camps in Germany and were accompanied by forms on which any prisoner could volunteer information, before they were collected and sent back via Holland to Britain. In the vast majority of cases, these forms only confirmed the suspicion that the missing men were in fact dead, for it was found that in the main any missing man who had survived would already have communicated with his home. In the case of Second Lieutenant Hubert White, the only uncontested fact was that this missing officer was very evidently dead, a fact that may actually have brought some relief to his family, reassured by the knowledge that any suffering he might have experienced was now over.

The ratio of officers to other ranks, as already noted, was broadly 1:40. Given the number of men who could disappear in an attack, finding information on a private or NCO was generally a more protracted undertaking for his worried family than if he was an officer. This fact was exacerbated by an administrative deference to the social importance of officers' lives over those of privates and lance corporals: it was inevitable that more effort would be expended in the search for missing officers. In many ways that deference was reciprocated by the wives of missing privates and NCOs who wrote to the War Office. Time and again one finds among records held at the National Archives letters written by wives, many semi-literate, letters that remain courteous and mindful of how many cases the War Office had to handle; letters from wives who did not wish to be a nuisance.

The sad case of Fanny Dorrington is just such an example. Her problems began soon after an official letter disclosed that her husband had been wounded on the eve of the Loos offensive in September 1915 while serving with the 1st King's Royal Rifle Corps. There was no reason to doubt the War Office report, based on specific details contained within her husband's medical records. According to these, he had been wounded in the head and admitted to the 6th Field Ambulance before being transferred to the 1st Casualty Clearing Station and then onwards by Ambulance Train to a Base Hospital. In time this report proved entirely false. Rifleman George Dorrington was missing in action and he may not even have left the front line trenches. For six months, as she looked after her infant son, Fanny remained bewildered as to why she could neither receive news directly from her husband nor from any hospital. Nevertheless, her tolerance when writing to the War Office is remarkable. 'Dear Sir', she wrote at the end of September 1915,

> Being as I have not heard from my husband and I see his name on the casualty list, I thought I would write to see if you could help in any way of hearing from him. It is nearly a month since I heard from him . . . If you could kindly try and let me no [sic] where he lies I should be very grateful to you indeed. Hoping this will not be giving you any trouble . . . Mrs Dorrington.

Fanny Dorrington had had previous experience of the slowly turning cogs of military administration. Earlier that year, in March, she had twice written in pursuit of the extra allowance payable after the birth of her son in February. There had been no response to her first letter, hence the second; it may not have been entirely a surprise that no answer was received from the War Office to her letter in September.

Fanny was clearly a patient woman, for her next letter, dated 19 November, remained polite, noting that while she had been informed that her husband had been wounded she still did not know where he was.

Of course I no [sic] there are other things for you to do but as I cannot get a letter from him I am rather anxious about him so if you would be kind enough to help me in any way I should be very grateful.

Once again she received no reply so she wrote again, this time in January. Understandable exasperation was setting in. Furthermore, ninepence had been stopped from her Separation Allowance of fourteen shillings, deducted without explanation. Only much later that month did she receive a reply, though only to address the question of her allowance. It was not until the beginning of February that any decision was taken to report Rifleman Dorrington as not only wounded but 'missing'. Fanny wrote once more in March 1916:

Dear Sir or Madam: I am writing again to see if you have yet received any information concerning Rfn G Dorrington. I have had a report from the War Office stating that there is no trace of him anywhere. Surely something can be done by now it is six month since he was wounded and he cannot be found. I have done all I can possibly do. Other wives can get to know there [sic] husbands and surely I can know where my husband is. I have been ill with constant worrying which of course no wife can help doing. Will you kindly see into this case for me as you receive all information before I do. Hoping you will be good enough to let me no [sic].

    Yours truly F E Dorrington

Finally, towards the end of that month, Fanny was informed that her husband was, for official purposes, to be accepted as having died of wounds in September. The search was over. Then, curiously, in May 1916, there is a final letter in which Fanny asked when she might receive her husband's effects. Given the army's utter confusion over Dorrington's whereabouts, it may have surprised Fanny that a purse, letters, photographs and a pipe were forthcoming, though no explanations were ever asked for or given. In that last letter, Fanny enquired, too, as to when she might expect the return of her marriage certificate supplied during the processing of her pension, and, as always, she remained entirely respectful and patient. 'Of course I know you have a good deal more to do.'

In cases such as Fanny's, the government's policy was to continue paying Separation Allowance for thirty weeks after a wife was first notified that her husband was missing. Only then, in certain cases, did she become eligible for a pension or gratuity. This new payment did not necessarily signify that the missing soldier was considered dead and no certificate of death would be issued until the authorities were satisfied that for official purposes he was no longer alive, at which point any articles of personal property that might have been recovered could be disposed of.

Finally, in October 1916, Fanny received official notification that she would receive £52 gratuity and five shillings' pension a week for her and her eighteen-month-old son. If Rifleman George Dorrington ever had a marked grave, it did not survive and his name is now on the Le Touret Memorial to the Missing.

In the example of Lieutenant White, the officer's death was certain despite the absence of a body, while, in the case of Fanny Dorrington, she appears to have accepted her husband's death and moved on: she married again before the end of the war. For many people there was no clear-cut answer and 'missing' remained 'missing', though the individual was officially believed to be dead. Reports of the last sightings of any soldier could range from one that was seemingly uncontestable and fully verifiable, to one that was simply a vague impression, though just occasionally an identification could be made by a specific and personal item that by its very nature could distinguish one man from all others. The body of one young officer, Laurence Forrest, of the 16th King's Royal Rifle Corps, was identified through a trench periscope by the characteristic black armband he had worn in remembrance of a sister-in-law who died on the RMS *Lusitania*, the passenger liner sunk by the Germans in 1915. His body hung on the enemy wire, and the witness, another officer, Walter Hill, did not need to inspect the body at close quarters. Forrest's body was never recovered.

Inevitably, most cases could not be confirmed in such a calm and rational way. Normally both judgement and memory were clouded in the turmoil and adrenalin rush of battle; unreliable sightings offered hope to families while at the same time unleashing years of unremitting mental torture. 'She doesn't understand why there isn't a body for burial' is one comment on a missing officer's file.

In the light of optimistic reports, a family would be condemned to search in vain for their loved one for the entire war and often beyond. Angus Macnaghten was a thirty-one-year-old officer in the Black Watch when he was reported wounded and missing during the First Battle of Ypres in October 1914. The fighting that month had been protracted and fierce, with the Germans straining every sinew to break the thinning British line. On the morning of the 29th a successful attack had been made on the Black Watch trenches and the Highland regiment pushed back with many casualties. The first news concerning Angus's whereabouts was extremely positive. In a note marked 'Urgent' and sent to Angus's wife Hazel, a battalion officer wrote: 'Angus was captured yesterday but is quite safe and from questioning a fellow who escaped they were very kind to him so no need to worry. He will appear as "missing" in papers.'

Days later another officer concluded, 'He [Angus] is captured I know, and I hope unwounded. But there is a possibility he was hit in the leg which would not be serious . . . He is safer now than he was before.' There was every reason to be happy and hopeful and, in writing to her aunt, Hazel could not help but show her relief; she was 'so *utterly* thankful'.

From this high point, the news slowly began to dim. Reports remained hopeful but became more circumspect. By December there was still no news and so Hazel placed an appeal in the personal column of several national newspapers while Angus's bankers, Coutts, were put on alert in case any money should be drawn on his account, a strong indicator that he was alive.

Hopes continued to be raised and dashed. New eyewitness statements seemed to confirm that Angus had been lightly wounded in the leg. Yet if that was the case, why had he not himself written? There were 'helpful' suggestions, with no evidence, that wounded prisoners kept in Belgium were not allowed to write; perhaps that was the reason, thought Hazel, but, as weeks turned into months, it seemed less and less likely. 'I fear that if your husband had survived he would have found some means to let you know it since Oct. 29th,' wrote the Anglican Bishop for North and Central Europe, whose contacts in Germany had drawn him into the search. 'It grieves me to write it, but that is what experience tells me in this sad, sad war.'

His opinion was read but not accepted. Early confident replies had set the framework for Hazel's mindset and therefore for her hunt; and not only Hazel's, but those of other family members, too. The idea that Angus would have written, if he were alive, could be spun from a negative into a positive. 'Everybody says – and I'm sure it's true – that if anything dreadful had happened we should have heard sooner,' wrote Angus's sister, Lettice. There was an inclination to disbelieve or downplay pessimistic news. One gunner with the Royal Field Artillery gave evidence that was immediately disregarded by Lettice. 'He actually said he had seen a grave at La Ferté with A's name upon it dated Nov. 5th. I *absolutely* refuse to believe it.'

There were so many eyewitnesses, but the most plausible account had placed Angus at one end of the trench with just two other men. There were other issues, too. Rumour and second-hand information were being recounted as if they were first-hand, and the sense that embellishments were occurring was strong: 'He went on firing long after everyone had finished,' reported Lance Corporal Mackay, who, as it turned out, was not a direct witness. Privates Small and Weir both testified that Angus had refused to surrender until shot through both legs and taken prisoner. Regardless of a soldier's natural inclination to get down when bullets and shell fragments were flying around, it increasingly appeared as if half the British Army had been watching Angus Macnaghten.

Hazel Macnaghten never gave up hope of finding her husband, although in early 1916 she reluctantly agreed that his death could be announced for official purposes. Even then, after eighteen months, tantalising news would still come to reawaken her hopes and fears, including a statement from an exchanged prisoner of war who had seen a name 'very like Macnaughton', in a hospital room containing three Black Watch officers. Nothing came of the sighting but not for want of investigation.

Asking for eyewitness accounts was important but they were problematic. The issue of confusion was very real but, just as importantly, there was the risk that hope sprang where none was warranted. If witnesses positively saw a man killed in front of their eyes, they were likely to say so, and offer no opportunity for hope. But anything less than a clear sighting could be couched in ways that left room for expectation. No one wanted to seal a man's fate when they were not entirely sure, and so a remote chance he was not dead was inverted into a possibility that he was still alive. Any new report could revive interest in a case that seemed forlorn and so it was imperative that people were responsible with information. It was a vain optimism, for, unfortunately, nowhere did that onus of responsibility lie more heavily than on the shoulders of newspaper proprietors and their journalists.

Newspapers were not just pre-eminent in the dissemination of information to the public, but had a virtual monopoly, for there was no other means by which the authorities could communicate on a daily basis with people at home. It was newspapers to which the War Office turned to print the lists of casualties that were scoured by civilians. It hardly needed saying that certain stories published by newspapers had to be handled with great care, especially those that dealt with such sensitive issues as the missing.

For news of the front-line war, the press was almost entirely reliant on information given to them by the War Office. Details as to how the conflict was being prosecuted and won were passed on and published with almost no contradiction. It mattered little whether the newspaper's editor was staunchly patriotic when there was no alternative source of information to the official line. Press barons like Lord Northcliffe and Lord Beaverbrook were invited into government and those journalists who were allowed access to the Western Front, and elsewhere, were shepherded around safely behind the lines and monitored for their compliance. The tabloid press in particular liked to trumpet the stories of Britain's heroes and to denigrate the enemy whenever possible, and lurid stories of German atrocities were widely publicised. The press reporting of the sinking of the *Lusitania* and later the execution of the nurse Edith Cavell induced noticeable spikes in army recruitment.

Lurid details were always good currency in Fleet Street, but blowing a story out of all proportion to its actual importance was a recognised ploy of the press. A story such as the 'miraculous' reappearance of a missing soldier would have been newsworthy and one bound to be of great interest, not just to those whose relatives were missing but to the wider public who were keen to read positive, heart-warming stories of survival against the odds. Accuracy was important for journalistic integrity, although in a sense that did not matter; either way, correctly or incorrectly reported stories would still cause a stir, igniting hopes that other missing men might still be found. In early May 1917 the *Pall Mall Gazette* (a London evening newspaper that eventually merged with the *Evening Standard*) published a short piece entitled 'A War Complication'. It was meant to be humorous, and might have been taken as such had it not been so ill-advised, ill-judged and, in its inaccuracy, inexcusable.

'I hear news has been received that the son of a well-known peer, who was reported killed at the beginning of the war, has been a prisoner all the time, but has only just been able to write home,' wrote a journalist in his column. 'Unfortunately, during the period that has elapsed, complications have arisen owing to the fact of his wife having got married again. There is naturally considerable commotion in the families concerned.'

It was in essence society tittle-tattle but the Army Council (which advised the War Office on military matters) was furious and demanded confirmation of the facts from the correspondent who had filed the report. 'Failing this, in view of the false hopes raised among relatives of missing officers by this paragraph, I am to request that you will publish a withdrawal in an early issue of your paper.' The article had drawn inevitable interest from families, including, once again, the Macnaghtens, and not only the family, but also the executor of Angus's estate who now questioned whether he was being premature in its division.

On advice from the Army Council, the War Office issued a stiff rebuke to the paper: 'No instance of a British Officer being a Prisoner of War in Germany for such a period as you mention, without being enabled to communicate with his friends, has come to the knowledge of the Army Council . . . Enquiries are being made as to the foundation for this statement in the *Pall Mall Gazette*, but it is believed to be baseless.' It was.

The authorities were angry in part because the *Pall Mall Gazette* had published misinformation of the wrong sort: misinformation that caused nothing but anxiety and upset. When another newspaper reported that commandants of POW camps saved themselves the bother of censoring British officers' letters home by burning them, this did not arouse any anger from the Army Council. This story was as potentially damaging as the *Gazette*'s. It encouraged people to believe that here was the explanation for their loved ones not being in contact. The *Daily Graphic* ran a story in December 1914 that made a comparable though more prosaic clarification. 'Thousands of anxious people in this country are puzzled to know why they do not receive news of their friends in the war who have been reported "missing". The fault lies with the Germans whose boasted efficiency is singularly lacking in the Prisoners of War Bureau.' In these cases the accusations were accepted without a murmur by the authorities as both stories were solidly anti-German in rhetoric.

In reality few prisoners were ever stopped from writing home for very long and silence had little to do with supposed German inefficiency or commandant vindictiveness. In the vast majority of cases loved ones were missing because they were dead. Irrespective of the miraculous reports of survival in the press, there was no other explanation for all but the smallest fraction of those who yearned to hear from a missing relative.

After all the government-inspired rumours and tales of German atrocities, all the posters that portrayed Germans as snarling, mad, gorilla-like creatures rampaging across the globe, it might have surprised a large segment of the British public to discover that diplomatic contact between Britain and Germany was constant, necessarily cooperative and even occasionally cordial. Communication might be through a third party, but it was essential if the respective governments were to keep track of a whole host of 'interests' trapped overseas. News about men taken prisoner, and as a consequence their welfare, was of great importance. Equally, there was the exchange of lists of the missing and the dead, as well as of the property of the deceased.

For those whose loved ones had simply vanished, there were few personal items that made their way home. It was as if these families had lost twice over, and so when the property of the missing did resurface, it was treasured no matter how banal it was or what condition it was in.

In an extraordinary but not unique case, enmity was put aside for a moment as property was exchanged between families on opposing sides of the line. This was a private not a government initiative, although the transaction had necessarily to pass through official channels.

The process of exchange began on 27 July 1915 with the death near Ypres of a German pilot named Roser. His plane had been seen to crash behind British lines at Sanctuary Wood though Roser was known to have fallen out of the aircraft and landed near trenches occupied by the 6th Sherwood Foresters. The battalion's Commanding

Officer, Colonel Godfrey Goodman, gave an order that personal items belonging to the dead flyer should be collected and brought to him. The German officer was buried with military honours.

On his own initiative, Goodman sought to return Roser's private belongings to his widow through the offices of the United States' Berlin embassy, forwarding detailed information as to the position of the pilot's grave. What followed next was an extraordinary act of reciprocation. Lieutenant Reinhardt, the brother of Roser's widow, heard about Goodman's actions and forwarded information about a British officer killed in October 1914. In a letter, Reinhardt paid tribute to Goodman's 'chivalrous service' before turning to the issue of the British officer he had found. The man, forty-two-year-old Captain Henry Maffett of the 2nd Leinster Regiment, was missing, believed killed. Through American diplomatic channels, Reinhardt could 'convey news of the fallen English comrade in arms to his widow who has probably remained in complete ignorance of his fate since 1914'. He went on to explain that Maffett was killed by a shell splinter as he advanced at the head of his company. His death 'must have been quick and painless, as he still held a pencil and half written dispatch in his hand'. Reinhardt's men buried Maffett and he gave the location of his grave. Reinhardt confirmed, too, that he had Maffett's wrist compass and two hand-written dispatches which he promised to return.

The message was communicated to Captain Maffett's sister, Mrs Emily Harmsworth, who requested 'that a message of appreciation be conveyed to Lieutenant Reinhardt for his great courtesy in this matter'. The belongings were, it is assumed, duly returned to the family.

The offer to return Maffett's possessions was as extraordinary as another case was entirely strange. After the news of the death of her brother Peter in September 1916, Emily Miller and the rest of her family heard nothing further, at least officially. Then, in early October, they received a private letter of great emotional importance.

More than two weeks after Peter's death close to High Wood,

his best friend, Raymond Singleton, returned to the trenches. It was a position, he wrote, that was 'considerably in advance [a thousand yards] of that we occupied on our previous action'.

> One morning, am not sure which, while off telephone duty, and resting, I noticed a rifle bolt cover lying near my feet. Being in need of one I picked it up; when imagine my surprise at seeing it marked 'P[eter].M[iller]. 14624.'! A strange coincidence indeed. It had not lain there for long, or it would have been noticed by somebody else, and picked up. I could not find the rifle. Probably the rifle, with cover, was salvaged, and by some means the new owner had dropped the latter so opportunely. I have another myself now, and am preserving that one as the only possession of his recoverable. Being Government property, I may not send it to you. But as I expect you will value even so slight a remembrance, I will endeavour to keep it safe until after the war.

A further attack on 15 September had pushed the Germans back over a mile, leaving Peter's body well within British lines, when his rifle was probably picked up. It is a remarkable coincidence that another soldier should have dropped the cover next to Peter's great friend.

Raymond survived the war and forwarded the cover to the Miller family. The story emerged only after the death of Emily, aged 108, in 2003. It is likely that only then was the item disposed of before anyone had time to realise its astonishing significance.

The strong pre-war social and economic ties that had existed between Britain and Germany enabled a certain amount of cross-border cooperation to continue long after the guns began firing. This was more concentrated the higher one ascended the social scale. There had always been an extraordinary level of inter-marriage between the families of senior politicians, as well as among those of the military establishment, indeed of the social elite in general. This meant that once the sons of these men went missing, there was an equally high level of inter-communication between families, each reporting to the other their search experiences, passing on details of influential friends who might be contacted for help. By their very nature, these connections were not available by and large to the ordinary ranks, or to the officer sons of lower-middle-class families.

The daughter of an Indian Army colonel, Hazel Macnaghten was well connected: her son, for example, was the godson of Sir Iain Colquhoun, a Scottish baronet and Commanding Officer of the 1st Scots Guards, and she spared no effort in networking, joining, in effect, the 'bush telegraph' of the upper class. In one letter, she wrote to the wife of a Colonel William Dooner asking whether he might be able to help. He replied in May 1915, offering some interesting advice.

My wife has asked me to reply to your letter explaining all the steps we took to get information about our dear boy. A German Governess who used to live with us, and who is now in Switzerland, through a sister who is in Berlin, managed to get an advertisement inserted in the best papers there asking for any information about our son (AECT Dooner) . . .

Such pre-war German connections worked well, although in Colonel Dooner's case the news was distressing: his son was dead. After passing on further information, he wished Hazel the luck in her search that had eluded him.

Private enquiries would be made throughout the war, revealing, if nothing else, that when it came to the missing, enmity could be put to one side. The charitable actions of men such as Colonel Goodman and Lieutenant Reinhardt showed that even in the depths of a bitter war, soldiers on each side of the line could act in a way that transcended the day-to-day job of orchestrating the brutal downfall of the other. But if war was able to bring out the best in individuals, it was just as likely to bring out the worst and not only on the battlefield.

Families of the missing were particularly vulnerable to exploitation by individuals who set themselves up in the chaos of war to act as kind Samaritans, though their motives were anything but charitable. Families like the Macnaghtens, who had been so tenacious in following every lead, were targets for those who claimed to have 'special access' or 'contacts' that others, including the government and the Red Cross, did not. When a newspaper article suggested that Edward Page Gaston, an American living in London, might be able to help find missing soldiers, people beat a path to his door, among them Hazel Macnaghten.

As a citizen from a neutral country, Gaston laid claim to having made four humanitarian trips to Germany in 1914, distributing parcels and money to prisoners of war. According to the press he was intending to expand the operation to open a 'relief base' close to the Rhine, to which shipments of parcels would weekly be made from his offices in Salisbury Square in London. This ambitious relief project was not all he was proposing for, as advertised, he was planning another visit to Germany to locate missing soldiers who might have been captured.

Gaston was not the only neutral proposing such help. Advertising in the *Daily Mail*, a Mr C. A. Hamm, living in Copenhagen, offered to find information about the missing through the Red Cross in Berlin. It is not known about any payment he might have required. Similarly a Dutchman, Mr van Wyck, could apparently gain access to small hospitals behind the lines for those willing to subscribe £5 towards 'his expenses'. He expected to leave for Germany once he had the requisite permissions from the authorities and enough subscriptions to finance the trip.

Of all the charlatans, Gaston had by far the greatest prominence. In slick self-promotional literature, he was pictured standing next to the grave of a fallen British soldier; in another, he was sitting at a desk surrounded by the personal property of fallen or missing soldiers, property he hoped to return to rightful owners. He maintained that he had the backing of the American Embassy in Berlin, and with a certain amount of bluff and charm he managed to ingratiate himself with senior British politicians such as Sir Edward Grey, who began recommending his offices. 'My dear Kitchener,' Grey wrote in early October 1914, ' . . . will you send me a line to say who at the War Office will see him?' Gaston met Lord Kitchener himself, and reassured the Secretary of State for War that he could reach parts of Germany that the British authorities could not. By then he was able to demonstrate considerable success in retrieving American property stuck in Germany since the outbreak of war. Through his work, he had secured the return of a great deal of baggage across the Atlantic, levying an additional, and unadvertised, hefty fee for himself.

Gaston's excessive fees had not come to light when he offered to supply parcels and money to British prisoners in Germany. He claimed to know that a number of British soldiers were wounded, lying unrecorded in Germany and unknown to the Red Cross. He could find the missing, and boasted in his literature how he had 'several of the most famous names in Great Britain on my list to be sought for . . .'

I have already organized in Germany a comprehensive searching service . . . No doubt there are hundreds, perhaps thousands of officers and men who have been wounded and placed temporarily in peasants' cottages, farmhouses, small hospitals, and other places where they are for the time being lost to those at home. For instance, a man with a bad shrapnel wound in the head might suffer temporary loss of memory and lie for a month or more unknown and unknowing. Such cases have come to my notice, and I have searches looking for others in the Belgian and French territory held by Germans. A number of private funds have been placed in my hands, not only to repay the expense of special searches, but also to provide clothing and ready money for those who may be found.

'I have been instrumental in the past,' he bragged, 'in bringing news of a considerable number,' adding, 'I should like to say, for the reassurance of those whose friends are missing, that I believe many of them will reappear before long, well and relatively sound.'

There was no evidence to back up this wild statement but in February 1915 it was enough for Hazel to send Gaston £50 (around £2,150 today). This money was to make a special search for her husband, and she forwarded an image of him that would be duplicated and distributed all over Germany. 'One or two other people have done this too,' wrote Hazel, with Gaston promising to give Angus money 'when he finds him'.

Her payment was made around the time of the first serious disquiet about the work of Gaston and others. 'Do you know some people are starting an idea that Page Gaston is a fraud,' wrote Hazel in March, 'but I don't think they have any grounds for their alarm.' There was every reason to be alarmed, as the British government well knew. As far back as mid-January 1915, the War Office had released a notice to the newspapers with a warning:

> It appears that the anxiety of relatives is being taken advantage of to get money from people who cannot afford it, with the pretended object of searching for the missing. A hint from the press might save money and disappointment in the case of those who otherwise may be misled by designing persons claiming official recognition which they do not possess.

The War Office had Gaston in mind but chose not to name him. The Foreign Office had already received a number of letters from disgruntled prisoners and their families claiming Gaston's parcels had arrived weeks late; parcels had never materialised; monies from relatives were missing or greatly diminished.

One letter from the mother of Stanley Warren, who was languishing in Doberitz prisoner of war camp, was typical. Her son had written to say that none of the parcels or money his mother had sent between 27 October and 19 December 1914 had reached him until January 1915. Even then only four of the seven parcels had arrived and just 10 shillings of the £3 10s. she had sent. Mrs Warren had also paid a further 7 shillings in fees to Gaston towards the transportation of the parcels.

> My poor boy must have suffered terribly in waiting between October and January for a change of clothes, and I am, as his mother, deeply distressed . . . I was assured by Mr Gaston that it was no good sending by S.P.O. [the Army postal service] but that Mr Gaston could deliver personally to any prisoner of war at Doberitz – both money and parcels in six days to a fortnight, and that if I left anything for my son weekly, I could be sure of his getting it, and very quickly too.

Despite the growing evidence, the government preferred to tip off the press for fear of embarrassment should their honest yet gullible cooperation with Gaston be made public. Only in June did the national newspapers follow up the War Office's warning when they chose to print an open letter from James Gerard, the American Ambassador to Berlin:

> I desire to warn friends of British prisoners in Germany against confiding anything to this man [Gaston] – he has no connection with this Embassy, and I will not even permit him to enter it. He has been required to leave Germany and Belgium by the German authorities. I most earnestly beg the British public and the friends of prisoners to have nothing to do with him.

With influential help, Hazel was fortunate enough to recover £35 of the £50 she had sent. Meanwhile, Gaston threatened to sue the newspapers for libel over Gerard's published warning, although, after much wrangling, the threatened court case came to nothing. Gaston was finished and eventually returned to America maintaining his innocence and cradling his wounded pride.

As a footnote to the story, several hundred prisoners of war exchanged with German prisoners were interviewed on their return by a committee set up to examine the treatment of British soldiers in Germany. Several mentioned the presence of Page Gaston in one camp in particular, Torgau, and no one interviewed had anything positive to say about the man. Captain Thomas Butt, captured in August 1914 while serving with the 2nd Kings Own Yorkshire Light Infantry, recalled that 'nearly all parcels entrusted to Mr Page Gaston failed to arrive . . .', while Captain Philip Godsal of the 2nd Oxfordshire and Buckinghamshire Light Infantry, captured the same month, was scathing about the stranger in their midst who had speciously claimed to be represented by the American Embassy:

His name was Page Gaston, and the Germans must have believed that he represented the Embassy, but the prisoners believed that he was an imposter, and it was reported later that the American Embassy were looking for him. He seems to have advertised in England that he had special facilities for transmitting parcels to prisoners, but we never knew to what address he invited parcels to be sent to him. As a matter of fact, many parcels sent through him were delayed for months, some even for over a year and some never arrived at all.

In the end Hazel contacted not only Gaston, but also van Wyck and Hamm. She had almost decided to send van Wyck's 'subscription' of £5 when she was warned against such action by her solicitor.

I most strongly advise you to give no subscription as I feel confident that it would be simply throwing away money. You may take it, that as people know your husband is 'missing', you will have continual applications from all sorts of persons who wish to help to find him for a pecuniary consideration.

In the case of Mr C. A. Hamm in Copenhagen, Hazel did seek his help though there is no surviving record of any payment, or of a request for payment. There is, however, a letter from Hamm written at the end of May 1915 in which he says his search has so far been 'fruitless'. As with all these individuals, their attraction, or lure, was their claimed insider knowledge and influential contacts. Hamm's letter is interesting, for if any letter was an enticement to a client to keep searching, and probably paying, this was it.

As you know, the Germans say that he [Angus] is not in any of the prisoners' camps or hospitals in Germany which I quite believe to be true, but there are camps and hospitals (German) in Belgium and Northern France, only the Germans strongly discourage enquiries in that direction.

I have received certain reliable but entirely confidential information to the effect that a very large number of British officers are now in Belgium (I know where) whose names the Berlin War Office will not disclose. I have also heard, confidentially, that there are a good many British officers at a certain place near Lille, including some captured about the end of October, which is of such special interest to Lieutenant Macnaghten's relations . . . I have tried advertising but the German press declines to accept advertisements about missing British soldiers.

That last statement was not strictly true as the Dooners had proved. Unfortunately, the charlatans never quite disappeared. In October 1915 Harry Whiting, a forty-two-year-old former soldier and, from 1909, an employee at the War Office, was convicted and sent to prison for receiving fees of £114 from 'distressed and anxious relatives' of missing soldiers and officers. In each case he had taken photographs of the missing and promised to make enquiries, none of which was undertaken. Even as late as March 1918, the War Office was advising relatives to 'be on their guard' when advertising for information. 'Fictitious particulars have been supplied by fraudsters with a view to obtaining money.'

If it was money that one Private Broomhall was after, the evidence is not conclusive. He was certainly peddling in 'fictitious particulars' when he arrived on the doorstep of a Weybridge family in March 1916, and, whatever his ulterior motives, his actions were dubious at best.

The story concerned the family of Lance Corporal Edward William Plant, known to all as Bill, an under-age volunteer in 1914, who was still only seventeen when he was badly wounded in the head, chest and right shoulder on 17 March 1916. Plant, who had been serving in the 7th East Surrey Regiment, had been evacuated to the 33rd Casualty Clearing Station near Béthune. A day or two later Private Broomhall, claiming to serve in the same regiment and home on leave, arrived unannounced at the home of Plant's parents. He brought the terrible news that their son was dead. He had seen the private's name posted on a list outside the CCS as having succumbed to his wounds. Furthermore, he had stood in front of Plant's actual grave, close to that of another Weybridge man he named as Private Leslie Caulder. The parents received this appalling news but there was a frisson of curiosity, too, for neither had had any information that Bill was dead, although hours later letters arrived reporting his injury.

As if matters were not confusing enough, Plant's parents received a note purporting to be from their son; he had got through an operation, he said, and was 'getting on satisfactorily'. The words would have been consoling but they were not in their son's handwriting. The note had almost certainly been dictated to a nurse, though she could have avoided much upset had she made that clear. The story was published in the local press as a 'Mystery', the journalist reporting that, quite understandably, Mr and Mrs Plant were 'suffering great anxiety'.

Why did Broomhall make such a catastrophic error? He was clearly a man with local knowledge. A Broomhall family did live in the town in the 1880s although there is no reference to them in the 1901 or 1911 Census. Presumably Broomhall was on his way home to Surrey on leave on or around the time of Plant's injury, but why had he been at a CCS in Béthune, and what possible reason could there be for his assertion that the CCS posted up lists of the dead? There was *no* reason for doing so.

Broomhall had accurately given the date of Plant's injury and he seems to have been in Béthune Town Cemetery where Caulder lay buried, killed in December 1914 [plot III, row B, grave 16], yet there was no other man buried there with the name of Plant that might explain Broomhall's error, and at the time the only man with a name in any way similar to Plant's was a Norman Planche. The incident remains a mystery, although one further detail seems to suggest that Broomhall was up to no good. There is no record anywhere that a Private Broomhall ever served in the East Surrey Regiment during the Great War.

There was one way of passing 'fictitious particulars' that was less liable to prosecution as the intention to deceive was harder to verify. People who professed to have extrasensory perception that was not proven could offer a range of services that once again offered another avenue of hope to those desperate for news. After falling victim to one man of doubtful character (Page Gaston), Hazel Macnaghten turned to someone who claimed to practise psychometry, the psychic ability to sense an object's past, present and future.

After contacting him, Hazel forwarded one of Angus's letters: his reply was positive and cruelly detailed. Angus was alive in a hospital and not able to walk. He was also unaware that Hazel did not know of his whereabouts. In the psychometrist's mind, he could track Angus's movements from Wittenberg to Friedrichsfeld, then onwards to Münster and Osnabrück. Inevitably, Hazel followed up all these leads through a contact in Basle. All the camps in these towns were checked, with the only useful information that all of them allowed prisoners to write four postcards and two letters home a month.

A well-meaning desire to help, and not for any reward, drew Mrs Kerry, a nurse, to her neighbour, Lily Jones's mother, Sophia. Her husband was missing after the fighting at Bourlon Wood, near Cambrai, and there had been no news for months.

This lady used to say to Mummy, 'Why don't you come along and see if you can get hold of John?' They had to go to a house in Tredegor, and they'd tap the table and call on certain names to see if they'd present themselves because this nurse had lost her son in the war and she was sure that he had come to talk to her. I think Mum went once or twice and I believe Nurse Kerry said Mum had made contact, but Mum told me she couldn't take it in and felt it was beyond her. I think she was a bit afraid to be honest and as she was Baptist she shouldn't believe in that sort of thing.

Sophia had been given to believe that her husband was alive. 'Mum was told that she was going to hear about Jack, and that he was still all right.' Whatever was going on in Tredegor, it was odd, for if John was alive then quite how contact was being made with him is not clear. 'It wasn't long before she did hear from the War Office and the news was that he was dead. I don't think she blamed Mrs Kerry.'

There are great monuments to the missing in France and Belgium: at Vimy Ridge, at Thiepval on the Somme, the Menin Gate at Ypres, and smaller but nevertheless impressive memorials such as Louverval and the dead of the Cambrai offensive of 1917, including the name of Lily's father, J. W. Jones. And then there are the panels: long friezes containing thousands of names at the rear of Commonwealth War Graves cemeteries such as at Tyne Cot, Vis-en-Artois, Pozières, Dud Corner and Le Touret: the list is long. They stand testament to the number of men whose bodies were never found, or whose graves were subsequently lost, in all around 50 per cent of those killed. And for almost every name there was a family not just torn by grief but numbed by the knowledge that there was no place to visit, no known resting place for their loved ones amongst their comrades.

7

Flagging Spirits

'My only beloved child
You have done your duty
I am waiting to meet you
Mother'

75524 Gunner Walter Seymour
88 Battery, Royal Garrison Artillery
Died of wounds 17 July 1916, aged twenty-three
Buried Acheux British Cemetery

Men facing battle were particularly keen to reassure their loved ones that, whatever happened, they would all meet up again in a 'better world'. Whether they actually believed what they wrote or not did not really matter. It was the confident reaffirmation of faith to worried-sick families of the Christian promise of life after death: the promise that Jesus Christ made to all who believe in Him, and proven through His own Resurrection.

Soldiers also appreciated letters in which their family and friends made clear their belief by praying for their loved one's safe return. Private Walter Shaw, a week before he was killed in 1916, wrote: 'It is a welcome thought when one knows his loved ones are commending him to the care of the Almighty.'

Facing the prospect of death or serious injury, many soldiers made it plain in their letters that they had attended church services and had taken Communion, placing their souls and bodies into God's keeping. Machine Gun Corps officer

Lieutenant Ernest Steele, writing to his parents on the eve of battle in September 1918, mentioned his talk with the padre about his proposed confirmation. 'He told me that it would be difficult to have it done out here, but he thought I could consider myself a communicant until it could be done. So I feel easy in my mind about that.' Those who failed specifically to mention any faith still wrote letters that were often spiritual in tone, even if it meant resorting to schoolboy Shakespeare: 'I have immortal longings in me,' wrote one young officer to his family, quoting from *Antony and Cleopatra* prior to going over the top.

At the outbreak of war, well over eight million people in Britain, nearly a fifth of the population, were active members of one or other of the main Christian denominations. Even among non-churchgoers, belief in God was still almost universal while atheism had only a small number of adherents. The truth of life after death was broadly uncontested across the country and gave courage to those families left to mourn.

Comrades' letters of sympathy would tend to confirm to the family that faith was present right at the end. The mother of Andrew Buxton, were she in any doubt, received a letter from the battalion quartermaster, Leonard Eastmead, in which he avowed that her son was 'one of the truest Christian soldiers I have met', adding: 'I wonder if it would comfort you to know that Andrew attended a Communion Service just before we moved into our battle stations?'

It stands to reason that grieving families were not only psychologically predisposed to believe that their son or husband was alive in the afterlife, they actively *wanted* to believe. To deny his continued existence was not only a denial of one of the tenets of Christianity but a rejection of their loved one's own confirmed faith and promise. In the foreword to a book dedicated to the memory of her son, Agnes Sanders spoke to other parents about loss and her belief in the life everlasting.

Being human we know the anguish of empty arms and eyes that ache with desire to see; but, in spite of that, we know a far higher thing. We know that there is no death. Leslie lives – a vivid, radiant life – free from all the fetters of time and sense, he lives and works and loves, as he could not do in their Time life; and we are content, and glad and proud.

People did not need to look far for good anecdotal evidence of a spiritual dimension to life that went beyond the everyday human understanding of existence governed by the known laws of science. After hearing the news of his son's death, Harry Lauder had a revelation.

He had been dead four days before I knew it! And yet – I had known. Let no one ever tell me again that there is nothing in presentiment. Why else had I been so sad and uneasy in my mind? Why else, all through Sunday, had it been so impossible for me to take comfort in what was said to cheer me? Some warning had come to me, some sense that all was not well.

That same feeling of deep despondency overcame Sir Oliver Lodge when his son Raymond was killed in France. Sir Oliver recalled that he was in 'an exceptional state of depression' that day. He was due to play a round of golf with an old friend at Gullane in East Lothian, Scotland, but: 'I could not play a bit. Not ordinary bad play, but total incompetence; so much so that after seven holes we gave up.'

Sir Oliver Lodge and his wife had always had the feeling that their son would return and only once had Sir Oliver ever dreamed of his son, although the dream had been vivid enough for him to record the details that morning (7 May 1915) in a letter to a friend. He had dreamed that his son was heavily engaged in action, but that he was being kept safe, by what, his father did not know. He told his wife who subsequently wrote to their son describing the dream.

Raymond replied four days later.

I was awfully interested in father's dream. Your letter is dated the 8th [May], and you say that the other night he dreamt that I was in the thick of the fighting, but that they were taking care of me from the other side.

Well, I don't know about 'the thick of the fighting,' but I have been through what I can only describe as a hell of a shelling from shrapnel. My diary tells me it was on the 7th, at about 10.15am.

The date of the dream and the date of the shelling coincided precisely.

Dreams, visions, or presentiment: irrespective of whether they occurred to the recipient in a conscious or unconscious state, they all seemed to endorse the belief that a sixth sense existed, not least among the soldiers themselves, including those who, after long periods of trench service, became convinced that they were shortly to die. In Lieutenant Basil Rathbone's case, it was a foreboding one step removed.

Rathbone, later the Hollywood actor best remembered for his role as Sherlock Holmes, served in the Great War as an officer in the King's Liverpool Regiment. His younger brother, John, also served, albeit in another regiment, although on one occasion when both brothers were in neighbouring French billets they were given permission to meet. They were able to enjoy the day together before turning in and sleeping in the same room. It was very late when Basil awoke from a nightmare in which he saw his brother killed. He lit a candle and looked at his brother who was sound asleep, but further sleep for Basil was impossible. 'A tremendous premonition haunted me – a premonition which even the dawn failed to dispel,' he wrote in his autobiography. Shortly afterwards while sitting in a dugout he felt an inexplicable desire to cry, and did. He wrote a letter to his brother but discovered that John had been killed.

The problem with all forms of visions or dreams was that they were taking place in times of war when families and soldiers were living under extraordinary pressures. Undoubtedly many visions were caused by fear, extreme fatigue or battle stress. They may have appeared very real and perhaps portentous to the witness, but that did not necessarily mean anything sinister was about to occur. Private Thomas Keogh, an under-age soldier serving with the King's Liverpool Regiment, had a vision while on guard duty in the front line.

As I was staring over the top a rocket went up from the Germans, and sent a broad path of light from their trench almost to ours. Right in the centre of that lighted way I saw somebody coming toward me. It was a woman with her arms stretched out, as if she were pleading. The light was shining full on her face, and I saw it was my mother.

I thought I heard her calling, 'Tommy, lad! Tommy, lad!'

But the artillery was going just then, and I knew I couldn't have heard her voice at that distance. Then the light went out, and she disappeared in the dark.

I believed that night that I really had seen her, and I wondered whether she was groping about for me out there in the dark.

Keogh felt afraid and conjectured whether his mother had died and her ghost had come to find him. The vision perturbed him greatly but had no obvious consequences. 'A week later I got a letter from her that told me she was as well as ever.'

Thomas Keogh and his mother survived the war, unlike Second Lieutenant John Rathbone, who was buried in a marked grave. In cases where no body was recovered, it was very difficult for civilians to accept that their loved one had just vanished. This absence of a body led many people to turn towards an alternative form of solace, spiritualism.

Spiritualism attracted some eminent supporters, including

close friends Sir Arthur Conan Doyle (creator of Sherlock Holmes) and Sir Oliver Lodge, the former Professor of Physics at Birmingham University, who had been a leading light in the development of wireless telegraphy. Both men lost sons in the war, although Conan Doyle was an exponent of spiritualism long before his son died in 1918. A committed Christian, he espoused the view that there was nothing contradictory in being both a Christian and a spiritualist; indeed, they were complementary. As early as 1916 he claimed to have definite knowledge of life after death, later touring the country to lecture on the subject. Sir Oliver had come to spiritualism after the death of his son Raymond in 1915. Through a well-known medium, Gladys Leonard, he had been put in contact with his son, convincing him of the probity of the subject and its value to the bereaved. In November 1916, his account of this contact was published in *Raymond, or Life and Death* and drew such interest that it was reprinted four times before the end of the year; in all, there would be twelve reprints.

Despite Conan Doyle's Christian beliefs, the established Church saw considerable dangers in linking itself with spiritualism. The Church was steadfastly against any attempt to communicate with the dead, deeming it a sin to seek to know the unknowable; overtones of the occult were obvious. Conan Doyle in reply argued that neither he nor Sir Oliver 'raised' spirits, which implied they had some control over the dead. Rather 'the most we can do is to make the physical conditions such that if they should of their own desire wish to manifest themselves to our senses, they may be able to do so'. This, he believed, was perfectly compatible with Christian teaching.

This was a problem for the Church. Those who grieved for lost sons or husbands had been told through Christian teaching of the certainty of life after death, and so they could not logically understand why they should be denied the chance to prove its existence through the offices of spiritualism. 'I can solemnly declare that, using an unpaid medium, I have beyond all question or doubt spoken face to face with my son, my brother, my nephew by marriage, and several other friends since their death,' wrote Conan Doyle. He also claimed that in seventy-two cases of bereaved parents of war dead whom he had sent to the same medium, six had had no result, six 'half and half', leaving sixty a 'complete success'. It must have been exceedingly tempting for anyone reading such a declaration to follow suit and reach out to a loved one.

If that was not enough for the established Church to contend with, it also had another intractable issue that appeared only to play into the hands of the spiritualists. While the Catholic Church had always prayed for the souls of the departed, the Anglican Church had, since its foundation during the Reformation, frowned upon such Roman practices. The dead could be remembered, tributes could be paid to them, but as they were already in God's care there was no point in praying for them. The dual ban on seeking to communicate with the dead and on praying for their souls did not sit well with all the bereaved parishioners who could read in books such as Sir Oliver's, or hear in lectures given by Conan Doyle, about the wonderful possibilities of communicating with the departed. When the bodies of those who had died remained abroad, and many would have no graves at all, spiritualism seemed to offer the only option to families who were desperate to have some link with the dead.

It was a dilemma that the Church would have preferred to ignore in the hope that it might go away. However, the Anglican Dean of Manchester Cathedral, William Swayne, was one of those willing to address the issue openly at the first Church Congress held after the war in Leicester. His view that prayers for the dead should be reintroduced was reported the following day in *The Times*.

The practice of silence with regard to the departed was not the practice of the primitive church [that is, in the early centuries of Christianity]. Why should they [Anglicans] commend their loved ones to God up to the moment they drew their last breath, and

then believe themselves to be prohibited from commending them
in prayer to the Father of Spirits?

It was not enough, he said, for the Church simply to condemn
spiritualism but instead it should ask itself whether it had inad-
vertently contributed to its popularity by 'maintaining silence in
their prayers on the subject of the departed'. It was probable, he
believed, 'that Spiritualism had come in to fill a void in the current
teaching and practice of the Church.'

With such highbrow exponents of spiritualism as Sir Oliver
Lodge and Sir Arthur Conan Doyle, the Church seemed to be
losing the argument. Despite its warnings, the public's willingness to believe in spiritualism seemed both insatiable and
understandable.

So certain was Sir Oliver of this newly popular discipline that he
was scathing not only of the Church's stance but also of fellow scien-
tists who doubted its truth. 'They [sceptical scientists] are governed
by prejudice; their minds made up . . . They pride themselves on
their hard-headed scepticism and robust common sense.' The truth,
according to Lodge, was that they were incapable of looking beyond
normal human experience. The evidence was there.

Communication is not easy, but it occurs; and humanity has reason
to be grateful to those few individuals who, finding themselves
possessed of the faculty of mediumship, and therefore able to act
as intermediaries, allow themselves to be used for this purpose.

The numbers discovering that 'faculty' grew and grew during
and particularly after the war. In 1914, the Spiritualists' National
Union could boast 145 affiliated branches. By 1919 this had more
than doubled, and, as if testimony to the influence of the Great
War on a generation, it had almost doubled in number again
before the Second World War. Books concerning dead soldiers
proliferated during and after 1914–18 and included titles such as

A Plain Record of the After Life Experiences of a Soldier Killed in Battle (1917) and *A Subaltern in Spirit Land* (1920). Then, in 1928, a small booklet appeared entitled *Listening In, A Record Of A Singular Experience*, the contents of which were published by a spiritualist magazine called *The Quest*. It was written by Olive Pixley and, like Sir Oliver Lodge, she told her story neither for self-publicity nor financial reward. Olive earnestly believed in her powers, and to doubt her integrity would have seemed misplaced. As a child, she explained, both she and her brother John were inseparable companions, and, as she discovered, the pair were possessed of 'a certain amount of psychic ability', but thought little of it.

In 1917 Olive's brother, a commissioned officer serving with the Grenadier Guards, was sent to the Western Front. 'He never thought he would be killed – nor did I,' she wrote, though they often discussed how and where he might be wounded. On the night before he embarked for the Western Front, John seemed to have doubts, asking his sister to ensure he had no memorial service should he die. 'They are so dreary and I'd hate Mother to go to it.'

In a week John Pixley was dead – 'killed in action' – the news arriving at the family home a few days later.

That was a Monday. On the following Thursday I was having breakfast in bed, with a bad cold. I was crying hopelessly and saying out loud, 'Jack, Jack.' Suddenly, in my head, I heard him say, 'Yes, I'm here.' I stopped crying, sat erect suddenly, upsetting my tray, and said, 'Jack, is that you?' Again he said, 'Yes, I'm here, sitting on the end of your bed.' It was unbelievably true – I couldn't see him but he repeated again and again that it was him and that he was just going to the dining-room to see the others who were having breakfast. There was a pause while I sat dazed and credulous, and then in a few minutes he returned and told me exactly where they were all sitting and what they were talking about and other details, all of which I verified later.

And so began an extraordinary ongoing dialogue in which John described his experience of the afterlife, and advised his sister on everything, from whether she should learn the piano, to how she should behave with others; in turn she asked whether he was still in uniform and if he had met Jesus.

By any stretch of the imagination her story seems bizarre, though to other spiritualists she was credible. In the preface to her story, Olive made explicit her initial reluctance to set pen to paper to reveal something 'so private and intimate', adding that she wrote 'not for the scientist, to whom I can prove nothing, nor for the intelligent sceptic for whom other people's experiences are valueless, but for all those who, like myself, have lost the dearest of companions'.

And there were plenty of sceptics, and not just in the Church. One of the better known, Walter Cook, put his thoughts in writing in a book, *Reflections on Raymond* (1917), that directly challenged Sir Oliver Lodge's beliefs and berated what he saw as the revival of a 'dangerous and deceptive anachronism'. His book attempted 'to dissuade the bereaved in this war from looking for hope where, as the Author believes, no real or healthy consolation can be found'. He continued:

The argument that 'evidences', accepted and endorsed by a leading scientist, are beyond refutation by an unknown layman, is indeed a strong one. The converse is, however, equally potent – namely, that if, as this book attempts to show, even a trained scientist can be deluded and mistaken in these matters, then Spiritualism is a danger which no one, however sane, can dabble in with impunity . . . Nothing can be conceived more disastrous to the mental well-being of the nation, or more derogatory to the dignity of our heroes' memories, than that whole households of mourners in England should be enticed from their proper sorrow by what is, after all, but that ancient Will-o'-the-Wisp 'Spiritualism'; or that we should conceive of the 'after-state' of our heroes as liable to intrusion by the summons of paid and professional mediums.

Evidence in support of Sir Oliver's contention that his son communicated with him appeared a classic case of the wish being father to the thought, Cook believed. Certainly wishful thinking appeared to underpin much of Sir Oliver's and Olive Pixley's belief that the missing, those men who had been torn and battered and ultimately lost in war, were entirely reconstructed in the afterlife. Sir Oliver's son reported to his father that not only did one man who had lost an arm and a leg in the war now have both once more, but that a missing tooth had been replaced, too.

This was no surprise to some. In his address to the Leicester Church Congress, the Dean of Manchester had indeed noticed that 'the communications professing to come from the departed were usually quite in harmony with the ideas prevailing in the circles from which they came'.

The dead, for example, inhabited environments that appeared rather like those on earth and being able to visualise loved ones living and socialising in everyday surroundings was comforting to grieving relatives, though it could also sound very peculiar. John Pixley was described as living somewhere that looked 'rather like Switzerland'; Oliver Lodge's son drank whisky and soda and smoked cigars.

Neither Sir Oliver nor Olive Pixley had wanted to talk publicly about their experiences but felt compelled to do so, as the former explained.

It is not without hesitation that I have ventured thus to obtrude in family affairs. I should not have done so were it not that the amount of premature and unnatural bereavement at the present time is so appalling that the pain caused by exposing one's own sorrow and its alleviation to possible scoffers becomes almost negligible, in view of the service which it is legitimate to hope thus be rendered to mourners if they can derive comfort by learning that communication across the gulf is possible.

Olive Pixley was just as forthright.

I have never cared, and do not care now, whether the following facts are believed or not. If the narrative be true, then those who read it will be glad one day of their knowledge. If it be phantasy, no one suffers.

Such an assertion would have appeared naive not only to the established Church, which battled hard against the growth of spiritualism post war (in June 1919, Conan Doyle claimed there were 352 'Spiritualised' churches in Britain), but also to others in the fields of science and medicine. In February 1920 Professor Robertson, physician superintendent of the Royal Edinburgh Mental Hospital, warned that spiritualism was dangerous, especially to those who were of a neurotic disposition. 'The tricks the brain could play without calling in spiritualistic aid were simply astounding,' and he believed that neither Sir Oliver nor Conan Doyle were competent judges of such phenomenona.

The eminent scientist Sir Edward Poulton, whose son Ronald had been killed in April 1915, stoutly resisted the ideas of spiritualism for a number of reasons. He spoke movingly of the great trial of bereavement; of feeling 'numb with despair' and of 'the awful silence that grows deeper and deeper'. This deepening silence may indeed have contributed to the growing post-war surge in interest in the new science. But that 'silence', he argued, was a genuine one, made more terrible by the youth and promise of those who had died, but a silence nevertheless. He found no comfort in the 'supposed instances' of communication with the dead and he did not believe that those who claimed to be able to reach out to the dead were plausible.

Even if, as Sir Edward Poulton said, the 'silence' could be broken by direct contact with the departed, 'What then?' he asked.

Should we be helped or hindered in doing our duty in the world? I cannot doubt that we should be hindered. If there were real contact with our loved ones gone, above all with the young, how could we give to our life here that continuous concentrated attention which is essential if the best is to be made of it?

Comfort was in the happy memories of the past, too poignant though they might sometimes be. To do justice to the dead, he argued, the living had to continue with life and not be drawn into a slough of despond but live as those departed would wish them to live. Sir Edward quoted from a letter he received after the death of Ronald from Lord Alfred Milner, a friend and member of Lloyd George's War Cabinet.

We owe it to the dead, above all to the heroic dead, not to let ourselves be crushed; saddened we must be . . . but not broken, not weaker, or less resolute to fight out to the end what is truly the Battle of Life. We cannot fail to find help when we realize that the comfort we receive is, on its other side, loyalty to our loved and lost.

The 'Battle of Life,' would have appealed to Sir Edward Poulton, a man who had spent the greater part of his own life in the study of evolution and natural selection, work for which he was knighted in 1935. The attitude of which Sir Edward spoke was exactly that exemplified by his family friend from Reading, Leonard Sutton, who worked tirelessly after the death of four of his five sons in the war, and Edward himself threw his energies into his discipline of science for the rest of his life, becoming President of the British Association for the Advancement of Science at the age of eighty-one.

Despite such views, it was difficult to argue against the fact that some people did gain great comfort from spiritualism. Florence Billington lost her boyfriend in 1915, but it was only years later that she met a spiritualist in Leeds who spoke to her about her lost love.

I met this man and he came to lunch with his wife, and while we were having a cup of tea this man told me he could see a very young boy in khaki standing behind me.

Florence was asked if she knew who he was. 'Yes, I know who it is,' she replied.

'Well, this young man is showing an awful lot of love towards you. He's here for you and he wants me to tell you that he loved you with all his heart and soul and had hoped to make his life with you, if he could have done.'

On occasions since, I have felt his spirit visit me, that he was thinking of me and was somewhere near. I liked it, it lifted my spirits no end, it was a lovely feeling to think that people can stay with you even after they've gone, that they're still there.

Florence found the incident in Leeds consoling and the circumstances, in her case, appeared benign.

By mid-1917 the British people were beginning to suffer from war exhaustion. The sense that the conflict would continue without end was taking hold, and the government feared a steady erosion of public morale. It was not just the emotional cost that seemed so high; the economy was also in difficulties, and the government introduced rationing for many basic foodstuffs.

Since the introduction of conscription in January 1916, the British Army had compelled men to serve who were often reluctant to fight. Long gone were the heady days of mass volunteering when men went gladly to war, supported by families ignorant of the consequences. Everyone knew what service at the front meant in terms of the risk to life and limb; to win the war would require sacrifice on an unprecedented level but also a dour determination to see the job through.

The government had been complacent about the realities of an international war until the shell crisis in May 1915, when *The Times* highlighted the desperate shortage of ammunition at the front. Since then, the authorities had become far more attuned to the need to mobilise both manpower and minds for the war effort. With the campaigns of 1917 at Arras and later at Ypres in the bloodiest of grips, the authorities understood the need to bolster public faith in the struggle. They had to convince people that their private loss, while deeply traumatic, was for the purposes of both national survival and worldwide freedom from the threat of German domination and tyranny.

Throughout the war, the government produced a number of armlets and badges to distinguish one type of person from another. Insignia were, by and large, issued as protection from misguided accusations that any individual was not an active participant in the war effort. Of course, such distinctions worked both ways: their absence, as the authorities well knew, would help point out a shirker or backslider, not doing his 'bit' for the country.

There had been no corresponding need to consider or publicly acknowledge the sacrifice of civilians not linked to the war effort in the traditional sense of a physical, work-related contribution. Yet the maintenance of morale at home was as vitally important as morale abroad and they were, of course, inextricably linked. If press reports were anything to go by, the government was increasingly concerned by ideas of subversive 'pacifist' agitation, which in actuality meant the work of any individuals or organisations united only by their reluctance to accept unquestioningly the government's prosecution of the war. Still, if ordinary citizens were to remain welded to the national cause, government thinking would need to be flexible and, crucially, appear more sympathetic. The formation of the Graves Registration Commission in 1915, and the willingness to photograph graves for families back home, demonstrated that the authorities were not insensitive to ideas and suggestions, but by 1917 they needed to be much more proactive than had hitherto been the case.

In mid-August 1917, during the British offensive near Ypres, the War Office announced a national competition to design a memorial plaque to be made in bronze. This would be given to the next of kin of all those who fell in the war. A total prize pot of £500 was on offer, with entries to be submitted by the start of November, the winner receiving £250. This date was then extended to the end of the year to allow, curiously enough, even those on active duty to compete: curious because designs had to be 'actual models in relief in wax or plaster' and finished with precision. The predetermined words 'He Died For Freedom And Honour' were to be included as part of the design. To eliminate any possible bias when choosing the winner, every competitor was to submit the work using a motto or pseudonym.

In the end more than eight hundred ideas were presented and the following March the successful entry was announced. Unsurprisingly, the winning submission came not from a soldier in the trenches but from a well-known professional sculptor from Liverpool: pseudonym 'Pyramus', real name Edward Carter-Preston. His circular design bore the image of Britannia holding forth a laurel wreath, while beside her stood a lion. Accompanying the plaque would be a memorial scroll that would carry the inscription:

He whom this scroll commemorates was numbered among those who, at the call of King and country, left all that was dear to them, endured hardship, faced danger, and finally passed out of the sight of men by the path of duty and self-sacrifice, giving up their own lives that others might live in freedom. Let those who come after see to it that his name be not forgotten.

It had been hoped that production would begin immediately, reported *The Times*, then added the corollary: 'In view of the probable scarcity both of paper and metal [the manufacture of the plaques eventually consumed 450 tons of bronze], it is at present uncertain when they will be available for distribution.' It was not until June 1919 that distribution began and was given to one family member in a descending list of importance, that is, the widow should come first, followed by the eldest surviving son, then daughter, father, mother, brother, sister, half-brother and, lastly, half-sister. In all, 1.365 million plaques were issued.

The final design was not to everyone's taste. 'The figure of Britannia may be very fine and dignified – which it ought to be; but what about the British lion – so called! What animal was the model? The lion ought to have been a magnificent production instead of the meagre-big-dog-size presentiment!' This letter was written and signed by both the Chairman and the Head Keeper of Clifton Zoo, Bristol.

'Let us roughly scale it,' the letter continued. 'It is only one-third the height of Britannia, and if we assume Britannia to measure 6ft, then the lion is only 2ft in height.' Other failings were observed: the neck was wrong, the mane was 'paltry', as was the head. 'Surely a better-constructed plaque than this should be handed to the next-of-kin to perpetuate the memory of our departed heroes, and not one embellished with a lion which almost a hare might insult.'

The comments were well observed, from men who knew the average height of a lion, but no changes to the design were made. Such dissension was only a precursor to the time when thousands of publicly funded memorials would be constructed and unveiled, a time when emotions were still raw and disagreements often heated.

Three months after the idea for the Memorial Plaque, Lord Derby, the Secretary of State for War, came up with another proposal. The Ypres offensive had ended just two weeks earlier, with an additional 250,000 Allied casualties dead, wounded and missing. His inspiration came after a member of the public, Mr

Arthur Ripley, read a speech made by Lord Derby in the House of Commons. Derby had berated the work of 'pacifists', characterised as seditious individuals, who did not 'hesitate to enter the houses of many humble people trying to influence them against the carrying on of the War', and encouraging the belief that 'the whole of the sacrifice' they had made was in vain.

Ripley suggested that, in light of the speech, the government send with every notification of death a letter in the name of the Prime Minister expressing appreciation for 'the loyalty and self sacrifice of the deceased and of its sympathy with his family'. Ripley felt sure that if his idea was adopted it would go a long way towards 'comforting and uplifting the bereaved – inspiring the people with renewed courage and determination, strengthening the Government and counteracting the poisonous and pernicious operations of the Pacifist'.

No one could accuse the government of not listening. A week later, Derby wrote to the one man Britain had repeatedly turned to for appropriate words at appropriate moments – Rudyard Kipling. In a confidential note, Lord Derby set out his stall:

Now I want you to help me in another matter and which I would ask you to treat in strict confidence. At the present time when a letter goes to the next of kin of anybody who has been killed, the wording is very bald:

'The King commands me to assure you of the true sympathy of His Majesty and The Queen in your sorrow.' This letter is signed by me [as Secretary of State for War]. It is suggested that we ought to put something more in to counteract the Pro-German pacifist poison which is being freely scattered in stricken homes. I cannot myself think of the right words, but I am sure in this respect you could very much help me. One wants to put in something to the effect that the person to whom he is writing should be told that 'he whose love you mourn died in the noblest of causes and that the Country will be ever grateful to him for the sacrifice he has made'.

In other words, Derby did not want the grieving family to believe it was only royalty that appreciated the sacrifice, but the entire nation. Rudyard Kipling set to work and produced a piece very like that proposed by Derby but with slight literary adjustments:

> The King commands me to assure you of the true sympathy of His Majesty and The Queen in your sorrow.
>
> He whose loss you mourn died in the noblest of causes. His Country will be ever grateful to him for the sacrifice he has made for Freedom and Justice.

Kipling offered to work further on the text if Derby so desired, adding,

> Don't you think it would be good if the King – unmistakably the King and not the Government – were to issue a personal medal to relations of the dead – a medal for the males and a brooch for the women. Plaques etc are left about on mantelpieces and get lost, nor are they available in public places such as churches: but a medal and especially a brooch is a sign of distinction and (which is important) entitles the wearer to look and talk with contempt at people who have not sent their sons.

Kipling suggested medals and brooches were to be given to the nearest male and female relatives and the mother and father if they were still alive. 'People would soon learn to wear their medals. They would begin in the villages etc where there are regular Sunday services preached on the dead,' Kipling indicated, adding rather ominously, 'and by the time we got to making village and town memorials to the dead pretty nearly every one would be badged members of the order.'

It would be easy for critics to be entirely cynical about the motivation of Lord Derby and the government in which he served.

The decisions may have appeared hard-nosed and practical but a war had to be won and any new idea that helped facilitate ultimate victory was worth considering. It was about using all the weapons at the state's disposal so that the war might best be prosecuted.

Machiavellian though the government might seem, it also made a seemingly magnanimous gesture that was not dedicated solely to winning; in fact, some would argue, as they did, that the gesture in question potentially inhibited ultimate victory.

At the end of November 1917, the War Cabinet discussed the way in which families were informed about the death of an individual executed for cowardice, desertion or some other serious misdemeanour. The policy had always been for the Army Record Office to tell the family without any attempt to mask the fact. In March 1917, for example, Alice Jones learned with the authorities' 'very great regret' that her husband, Private Richard Jones, 'was sentenced after trial by Court Martial to be shot for Desertion . . . and the sentence was duly executed on 20 Feb. 1917'.

Questions had been asked before regarding the information conveyed to relatives, but the issue had apparently gone away until raised repeatedly by a small number of backbench MPs in October and November 1917. This time the questions led to a swift change of policy. At a Cabinet meeting it was agreed, though not unanimously, that those soldiers shot after court martial would now be reported only as having died on active service.

In January 1918 Lord Derby informed the War Cabinet that he had implemented its decision. He had disagreed with the change, believing it a matter of mistaken kindness when, 'by some means or another, at a later date the relatives become acquainted with the reasons which led to the death of the man in question'. The problem was that details of any execution were carried in General Routine Orders and read out to the men at the front for their deterrent effect. The promulgation of an execution was therefore the primary reason for capital punishment. Forbid this, and discipline in the British Army would be seriously undermined: allow the circumstances of a man's death to be widely circulated, and the chances of a family member discovering a loved one's execution, perhaps through a soldier on leave, would be considerable.

Like Lord Derby, the army was against the change. As well as agreeing with him, the army also reasoned that a man shot for cowardice would now be treated in just the same way as a man who died fighting to the last 'both as regards the notification of his death and benefits for his dependants'. Campaign medals would also have to be issued, undermining army cohesion and discipline.

The Cabinet's view, ill-advised or otherwise, was that if a man's life was taken for disciplinary reasons, the relatives should not be made to suffer, and their decision stood for the rest of the war.

News that compassionate allowances were to be made also to the widows of executed men must have come as a huge relief to those affected, especially those with children. Gertrude Farr had been in desperate straits after news of her husband's execution in 1916 had been handed to her in a letter at the post office. Her shame was total and she had stuffed the envelope down her blouse before making her way home.

'Six months after my father was killed my mother's pension and my allowance was suddenly stopped,' remembers her daughter, also named Gertrude.

Mum went back to the post office and asked the postmistress who obviously knew my mother, and said 'I am ever so sorry, Mrs Farr, but there is nothing for you.' She must have inquired, of course, and told Mother 'that owing to the way your husband died, you were only allowed a pension for six months and nothing for me.' So there she was aged twenty-one with a three-year-old child.

We lived in quite a poor part of North Kensington, a working man's area, and most people lived in tenement blocks with only one room. Well, Mother had a room for which she paid 2/6d. a week but because her pension was stopped it was soon obvious she did not have any money, we had nothing. The landlady knew the circumstances, she knew, but all the same she said it was her living and she asked my mother to go.

We were homeless and Mother, in looking for work, had to explain why she needed to go into service with a young daughter. I know we lived for a short while in a house in Ewell in Surrey, with a very elderly Scottish couple. All their staff had been called up so she was taken on as a general dogs-body there. Then eventually my mother got a job at the home of Lord and Lady Arkwright in Hampstead and they were willing to take me, which in that era was a wonderful thing as it was unheard of for a child to go into service, none of the other staff had children.

One evening when mother was waiting table there, Lord Arkwright told the story of Mum's predicament to the 7th Earl of Clarendon. He was most interested as to why we had no money, no pension or allowance, and he said: 'Give me any evidence you have,' and that meant including postcards a nurse had written on behalf of my father when he was in hospital shell-shocked. These with any other evidence of my father's condition were sent off to the Ministry of Pensions.

The Earl of Clarendon fought mother's case. He couldn't get her pension back but he did get my allowance [5s. a week for the first child] so she had that until I was 16, although the postcards were never returned.

The War Office dealt with the award of widows' pensions, and the Board of Commissioners of the Royal Hospital Chelsea was responsible for the award of disability pensions. Then, in February 1917, the newly formed Ministry of Pensions took over this work but the somewhat archaic system of granting all pensions under

Royal Warrant continued, ensuring that pensions were not a stat-
utory right. Ministers believed that if pensions were resolved by
parliamentary statute then political parties might seek to influence future voting patterns by promising ex-servicemen and
widows pension increases. As pensions were not a right, they
could also be withdrawn, just like Separation Allowances, if an
individual were deemed to be no longer worthy of the money.

Widows' pensions were not paid automatically when a man
died. Separation Allowances continued for a further twenty-six
weeks after notification of death (and, as we have seen, thirty
weeks after notification that a man was missing), during which
time the widow's pension was calculated: the final payment
depended on a number of variables, such as the rank of the
deceased, the age of the widow and the number of dependent
children.

Pensions were always miserly. Soon after the war broke out,
they were set at a new base level – that of a widow of a private – at
7/6d. for the widow and 5s. for the first child, and incrementally
smaller amounts for each additional child. This sum rose periodically during the war to a minimum of 10s. for a widow in March
1915, so that in that year a widow of a private with one child
could expect to receive 15s. a week; there were further sums for
other children. By March 1916, just over 23,000 women were
receiving a widow's pension, while nearly 18,500 were still on
Separation Allowances awaiting a final settlement; eight hundred
pensions had been refused, in most cases because the marriage had
failed and the husband had no longer been supporting the wife
when he died. Furthermore, if a widow remarried she automatically lost her pension.

Widows' pensions were periodically revisited. By mid-1917,
the basic pension was 13/9d. for the widow, 5s. for the first child,
and in May 1918, although the widow's allowance remained the
same, the amount paid for each child increased, starting at 6/8d.
for the first child, still a pitifully small amount. Ironically, the

government thought it was being broadly generous, calculating that pensions should provide roughly two-thirds of pre-war income when, of course, there had been a husband to feed. In some cases where the husband was on very poor wages, such as those paid to agricultural labourers, the widow would be better off. To give some idea of prices in 1914, milk cost 2d. per pint as did a mackerel fish. Eggs cost 1/- per dozen and soap 3d. a bar; an average-sized frying pan was 1/2d.

Whatever increases the government sanctioned, they were not driven by generosity but almost entirely in recognition of rapidly rising prices. During the course of the war, widows in dire need could seek to have supplementary payments from the Royal Patriotic Fund Corporation, set up by Royal Warrant during the Crimean War and aided by a £6 million pound grant given by the government in 1916. However, no one got wealthy on a war widow's pension, and, with the man of the house gone, the mother had few options other than to go back to work. This might involve reviving former skills or domestic trades, enabling the mother to stay at home, but more often than not she was forced to go back to employment in a retail business or factory.

Letitia Sherington's husband eventually died of his crippling illness in August 1917. The family's income was small and their finances ever more squeezed, and anything that could be procured for free gratefully received, as eight-year-old Joyce knew.

We were all very much aware of the food shortages, particularly of meat and potatoes, although the shortages worsened through 1917. We were lucky as we were much helped by my brother Harry's boss at Park Farm who offered us a half hundredweight (56 lbs) of swedes to help with the potato shortage if he could get them from Cuffley to Hornsey. There was no transport so Harry carried the sack on his back to Cuffley Station and from Hornsey Station to our house. We none of us ever confessed that we did not like swedes in any form.

Despite the generosity of the farmer, Letitia was forced to return to work, taking a job in a local coal office. The job proved to be a lifesaver in more ways than one. Apart from providing badly needed money, the job also gave Letitia a focus that she had not had before.

> I am certain that going there saved my reason. The subject was sufficiently exacting for me to have to give it my whole attention. I had to stop pacing about. I had to meet dozens of strangers and try to help with their difficulties. For months I had lived with a weight on top of my head and a tight band round my forehead. I used to feel sometimes that it would be a relief when the knot snapped and I could give up. Gradually the routine of unhurried work exercised its curative influence and I grew to love my 'little 'ole'.

A death at the front could bring about a precipitous loss of income and with that a loss of status, too. Before her husband was killed, Dennis Gilfeather's mother had lived quite well.

Dennis's father, John, had begun life as a coal miner but had gradually managed to build a coal business. Four months after John Gilfeather had gone to France, he was shot at the Battle of Loos in September 1915. Suddenly Dennis's mother was left with four young children and a business she had no way of maintaining.

> Dad had left a good business but there was no way we could have taken over for we children were far too young, so his brother took control and two of my aunts. That's how the business disappeared out of our hands altogether. We moved house then and Mum received the magnificent sum of £1 2s. 6d., that was her pension every week for herself and us four kids. Life was very hard when suddenly Mum went down with erysipelas, an acute infection, and came close to dying.

I felt my whole world was changing. The sunshine was leaving my life. Your mother's in bed in hospital and they're prophesying her death. I remember saying to her, 'Now you canna go, Mum. I love you so much.' That's when she said, 'If anything happens to me, you'll look after the bairn and Annie' – that was the two youngest. I said, 'Yes, I'll do that.' And that's what I tried to do.

My father's relations had taken the business and now they were saying they were going to have me, and then my sister would go to my gran with the two young ones, but then a close friend of my mother's stepped in and said 'There's nobody taking anybody. If Mrs Gilfeather does not come back I'll stay here and bring them up.' Mum was terrified of the family splitting up. Then after about six weeks, she started to recover. She was a fighter and, although weak, she managed to come home again.

My eldest brother John was four years older than me, but he was a nervous lad, very quiet and so my mother began to lean on my shoulder, she got dependent on me after Dad died.

Those boys who took the role of man of the house were determined to help in any way they could. Donald Overall was aware of his duty not just to his mother, but to his younger brother Cecil, as his mother reminded him.

My mother was a seamstress. She used to buy army blankets and dye them blue or black. Then she would buy patterns and place them on the kitchen floor with the blankets and cut them out and stitch them with the sewing machine to clothe us kids and herself. Then she took it on as a part-time job as she was good at it. And she would make these clothes for other people and I used to deliver them to the house and collect the money.

We had a sitting room, a kitchen and a bedroom. We had a sink and a cold-water tap, no hot, and a gas cooker and Mother's sewing machine along one wall by the window so that she could see what she was doing. Even as a five-year-old I used to peel the spuds, cut up the onions, stick a fork in the sausages and when time permitted my mother and I would make blackberry and apple jam. Then there were the more tiring jobs. I had to clean the stair rods because our flat was the first flight up and to buff up the brass fender with metal polish. I had to brush up all the dust from the floor, on my hands and knees getting into the corners, and then I got the duster and went round. Every Sunday I would get milky water and go and wash all the leaves on the aspidistra; that became a ritual.

Lastly I had to go and do the shopping. I had a wicker basket with a big handle which I put over my arms, and Mum used to write the list of goods to be bought and the precise money to pay for each of them and I'd go round to the Old Kent Road aged no more than six, that's across two sets of tram lines to the row of shops; the shopkeepers used to treat us kids quite well, I wasn't the only one who had lost a father.

Then one day a policeman came round on a push-bike with a blue helmet blowing a whistle shouting air raid, take cover. I was standing there and I looked up and I saw all the Gotha bombers with their swept-back wings coming along the Old Kent Road towards London, quite a number of them. I was frightened and didn't know what to do, but a man came along and said, 'Where are you going, son?' so I told him and he put a dustbin lid over my head and steered me across the road and I walked home with my shopping basket with goods in my hands and a dustbin lid held over my head.

Ten-year-old Clara Whitefield's father died of wounds in hospital in Nottingham from a blood clot that had eventually gone to his heart. At the time everyone went haywire, according to Clara. 'Mother went out the house and was walking up and down the passageway at the side of the house like a mad woman,' until she finally calmed down. As the eldest child in a family of seven, Clara's life was about to alter dramatically.

Mother did what she could do, but she had to work all day, six days a week in those days and I used to do everything, cleaning, washing, shopping, standing in queues for things. My sister grew up thinking that I was her mother, because Mum was out all day and I'd got her from when she was first born.

My mother knew that the money coming in wouldn't keep us so she went to the school and she got permission for the eldest daughter to stay at home until the youngest daughter, Florence, went to school. So I stayed at home and I looked after her and I looked after the others. No school board inspector ever came to see me because Mum had gone through the process. I used to do everything at home because my mother was working so hard; there was no one else to do it so I did it and I enjoyed it. I didn't miss school because I knew what I was doing was right.

'The process', as Clara called it, meant official exemption from school attendance. Although the official school-leaving age was fourteen, those with excellent attendance records could leave at the age of thirteen. Furthermore, children could be employed as young as twelve, 'half-time' (up to thirty-three hours a week), as long as they continued to attend school part-time.

There was considerable local discretion allowing flexibility in child employment in industry but Clara was at least a year below even that minimum age. Interestingly, it was discovered in Birmingham that while the number of prosecutions of businesses employing school-age children actually fell during the war from 325 in 1914 to 93 in 1917, the prosecution of parents for withholding their children from school rose 60 per cent from 2,818 in 1915 to 4,706 in 1917. It would be astonishing if the rise were not due in part to the pressure placed on mothers, widowed or otherwise, to earn extra money, leaving children like Clara to stay at home to look after siblings and take on many domestic duties.

How far parents were really pursued by the school inspectors is not known. The government noted that, along with flexibility in child labour laws, there also came a considerable disparity between regions. In May 1916 it was observed that nationally 16,750 exemptions from school had been granted, including 546 to children under the age of twelve, yet in a number of regions it was also apparent that all requests for exemptions had been refused.

One area where a blind eye had been turned was the countryside, where child labour was deemed vitally important to the economy. In August 1914, just as the harvest began, farmers had been hit not only by the loss of agricultural workers to the army, particularly Kitchener's New Army, but also by the military's requisition of horses, robbing the land of natural power at a seasonally critical time.

In February 1915, the government's Board of Education conceded that statements made by both the Prime Minister and the Board on the outbreak of war

> had given encouragement to farmers to believe that the Government would look rather easily on any exemption of children from school attendance. The Government was naturally anxious that the harvesting should be carried on satisfactorily. The words they used applied to a particular emergency, which had been misconstrued as applicable to the whole farming year.

Asquith told the House of Commons (4 March 1915) that, when it came to farms, the government would 'not be bound by any pedantic regard for rules, conventions or usages which have prevailed when the circumstances were normal'. Local authorities were obliged to ensure that child labour was reasonably paid, used only when no other labour was available, and that work was light and suitable, and of limited duration. If these rules were followed, the government would not 'interfere with the discretion of the local authorities'. Numbers of children officially granted exemption from school to work in agriculture owing to 'circumstances created by the war' grew from 1,152 boys and 42 girls at the end of 1914 to 3,800 boys and girls by the end of May 1915 and 8,000 by the start of 1916, although these were official figures; how many were allowed unofficially to work in agriculture was never quantified.

Len Whitehead's father was a farmer. After his brother was killed, Len was needed to help out periodically, for not only had Len's brother left the farm but another lad had gone, too.

Two very strong able-bodied men going off to war and leaving the farm, well they hadn't got their labour you see, so we boys had to do our work, feeding the cattle, hoeing, getting in the mangels which we used as cattle feed. It wasn't a lot of help because we were only children really but if we did one row it was something. We used to work until dusk most of the time. We got tired; we never had to be told to go to bed, you were glad to crawl under the covers and sleep.

We were told at school that we were helping the war effort. There was a teacher, my father called her the governess, and he'd say, 'Ask yer governess if it's all right not to go to school tomorrow, I want you to drive the drill horse,' and I'd ask her and she'd say it was all right so I wouldn't go in. Education suffered of course, sometimes I'd be off two or three days, but there you are.

With income short, children were frequently expected to add extra hours to the working day. In 1918, the government became disturbed by signs that children were working long before and long after school hours. Although school attendance was in theory uninterrupted, teachers reported that many children arrived exhausted and incapable of learning properly, and there were fears, too, of a moral deterioration among children from associating with undesirable companions in the course of their work.

In March 1918 the MP for Flintshire and Parliamentary Secretary for the Board of Education, Sir Herbert Lewis, told Parliament that an education inspector had reported that a boy aged eight delivered milk from 4.45 to 8.00 each morning and was also engaged in delivering milk at weekends; another boy sold newspapers for thirty hours a week, and others were working up to sixty hours a week outside school hours. Len Whitehead was another of those who took on extra work before school.

One day the vicar and his wife arrived at the farm and I was called in and told that I'd been found a job at the vicarage. Get there at six in the morning and work till half past eight. I had to clean out the grate in the kitchen, light the fire, clean the boots and shoes, and then go to school. Then in the afternoon, go back to the vicarage at four o'clock and work till six as a kitchen boy, which meant emptying the ashes from the range and chopping wood ready for the morning. As well as that, I was supposed to work in the garden. Their gardener had been directed to work on a farm and the garden had gone to pot as the vicar had had to do it himself. He was incapable of doing anything, so they had me.

It was a beautiful walled-in garden with peaches and cherries and nectarine all trained on the walls, and of course they expected me to look after it, cut the lawns and all the rest of it. My wage was one shilling and sixpence a week and my breakfast and tea in the afternoon. I gave a shilling to Mum and kept sixpence myself. My mother was feeling the loss of the boys, you see, and their wages and we were very poor really.

Clara Whitefield had given up school altogether in order to bring in extra income to her cash-strapped family.

I was a slave. I went to work for this lady, cleaning. I was only a kid and I'd got to scrub this big floor and some back stairs and I got two shilling for that; they gave me it like it was £100. People used to come and have me cleaning for them and my mother had got to let me go because we wanted the money. She did not advertise me, of course, but people just got to know that I was around.

Old hands I'd got, ten years old, and old hands. They used to get cut or rather they'd crack down my fingers and nails because I was using soda in the water, it was cruel, and that was terrible for the hands and they'd be that painful. I used to get some Vaseline and rub it in but people reckoned it was your own urine that was best for your hands, made your hands tingle but it was good. Your own urine in a bucket and dip your hands in, that's what I was told.

At the end of the day I was exhausted, my bones ached, and the pain in my shoulder blades was terrible from using my hands such a lot, but when I went to bed I didn't sleep straightaway because my mind wouldn't let me, I would be thinking about what I had to do. Life! I could tell you something but I won't bore you with my tears.

The urban requirement for child labour, particularly in heavy industry, had been easier to monitor, owing to its concentration, than that in agriculture, and for this reason it was not judged by the government to be a significant problem. Although the labour shortage led to increased pressure to relax restrictions in the employment of children in industry, business interests often failed to get their way. In Durham, for example, a demand for boy labour for surface work at the mines was refused by the local education authority.

According to President of the Board of Trade William Hayes Fisher (*Hansard*, 17 August 1917), 600,000 children 'had been drawn prematurely from school and had become immersed in industry'. Although he did not specify the precise age of these children, it was almost certainly those under the 'official' school-leaving age of fourteen rather than under twelve. In Bradford, for example, employers agreed to give up the half-time employment of children as young as twelve in exchange for a system allowing child employment from the age of thirteen and not fourteen (*The Times*, 19 July 1916).

Hayes Fisher's figures cited the number of children legally withdrawn from school to go to work, but they did not include all those taken on in flagrant violation of employment laws. How many tens of thousands of children were employed in this way was anyone's guess. Dennis Gilfeather was one of them, and desperate times meant desperate measures.

My mother depended on me, telling me her troubles, then she said, 'You could get a job in the mill.' I was just a wee boy, I was only nine when I started in Cox's mill that employed six thousand people processing raw jute into things like sandbags for the soldiers. They badly needed the labour because all the men were gone.

My pay was one pound and one penny a week; boys' pay was one pound so that extra penny meant that they could hide the fact that you were a boy in their books. At the mill they gave young boys a new name, often the name of someone who'd been killed in the war, that was how they got round the rules. In the books I was down as David Morris, I found out later he'd been killed at the front when only seventeen.

You got tired working on the looms because it was long hours, six in the morning until six at night, five days a week and half a day on Saturday. It was non-stop work and you never got a second to rest. But the women would look after you, they knew you were just a kid.

The thing I abhorred most was when the jute got in your eyes, they would start watering, and your nose streamed and you felt sick. This particular jute was nicknamed salt and sugar and I remember looking out of the window over the beautiful loch and the burial ground and thinking, 'God, if I could just get a job with a farmer, with the fresh air and greenery.'

I would work at the jute mill for maybe six weeks at a time. I got away with it because there was only one school inspector for Dundee and you'd get a fair run before he came in. He just went round all the mills checking up, because boys were working every-where. The inspector would say, 'Oh, it's you again,' and he'd send me back to school. They'd be talking about verbs and nouns and semi-colons and I didn't know what they were speaking about.

In the evening I'd sit with Mum and she'd be worried about me working and she'd say, 'I hate it when you come home so sick, son,' and I'd say, 'Oh, it doesn't bother me,' and I stuck it for five years, going in and out of that factory, being sent back to school, then back to the mill; the school and the mill were only about 100 yards apart.

There was one girl whose formal education began only shortly before others', such as Dennis Gilfeather's, had partly ended. After Gertrude Farr's father had been shot for cowardice in 1916, her mother had been left to search desperately for employment that would give her and her daughter some semblance of security and they had found it in Hampstead at the home of Lord Arkwright. There, Gertrude had not gone to school but had been allowed to sit in and listen to the lessons given by a private tutor to the Arkwrights' three daughters, Margaret, Brigitte and Anne. Only years later, when her mother finally left the Arkwrights' employ-ment, did Gertrude attend school.

I had a wonderful upbringing as regards accommodation and surroundings. The three daughters were a little older than me but they treated me the same as them, they were really lovely. They played with me, but they told me what to do as regards games, I could never tell them what to do for I was still the daughter of a servant and they were above me. I also had lovely clothes because I was given all the girls' left offs and I used to play with their toys; there was a wonderful dolls house and dolls.

Yet my upbringing was unnatural. Whenever I hurt myself, Mother used to say, 'Now don't you cry. Don't you let cook hear you.' She was so afraid that if I made a fuss we'd have to go. If I was ill, I used to be isolated into the bedroom garret right at the top of the house. If I got mumps or measles I would be left up there with a sheet dipped in Lysol draped across the door to keep the germs away from the rest of the family. I would be shut away for hours and hours up there as Mum worked as a skivvy, carrying the coal, taking the water up, cleaning.

Gertrude's mother was immeasurably grateful for the job she had, because she was aware how precarious her employment was. Unless she admitted her circumstances, no one would offer her a position with a young daughter in tow, but by owning up to the execution of her husband, she might preclude herself from the job anyway. It was a very difficult situation and therefore she was tenacious in holding on to what she had, as her daughter remembers.

There was one instance which worried mother greatly. At the end of the kitchen on the stone quarry floor was a big round vat filled with isinglass, a gelatin that was used to preserve eggs. Well, cook had come down on two or three mornings and noticed that there was a trail of this isinglass, rather like a snail's trail, which indicated that some eggs had been taken. Then sugar went missing, then tea went, and then cigarettes, these were used to fill up Lord Arkwright's silver cigarette box everyday, and then some material went missing. This went on for some time and Mum said she knew the finger was pointing at her because she was the poorest one who was working there. She was the bottom of the pile.

One morning she was cleaning the bedroom of the seamstress, the lady who would repair the sheets and the pillowcases and make the dresses for the girls. Mum went to clean under the bed and saw there was a case underneath and she opened it and, to her horror and surprise, there were bundles of material and packets of sugar and tea and cigarettes and eggs all rolled up in paper. She told me later that she was so furious that she jumped on the case and smashed everything, smashed the eggs and the cigarettes and the tea.

The culprit had been very trusted; she had her own apartment there, and was held in high esteem. Well, she had to dispose of all this stuff, so she gradually wrapped the items up in newspaper and put them in the dustbin. When Mum realised what she was doing, she requested an audience with Lady Arkwright and apparently asked if she would come downstairs to the basement to the dustbins where Mum opened the lid and showed her the evidence. The seamstress was instantly dismissed, but Mum said she was so angry as the undercurrent had been there that it was her, and she felt intimidated.

Without the support of a husband, without, in the cases of Gertrude and Dennis, the support even of families, the burden on women was unrelenting: there was the unending fear of hearing that a spouse had been killed or seriously injured, and a terror of being left on one's own to cope. In a survey conducted after the war, it was found that 12 per cent of widows died within a year of their husbands and 14 per cent reported seeing his ghost. How many more went half mad with the pressure was not recorded although children recalled the occasional outbursts of anger at the sheer frustration of their mother's situation, as Donald Overall remembered.

'Mother had a vile temper at times and she liked tea like varnish. I had to make her a cup of tea one day and it was a little weak. Cecil was standing right behind me, she said, "What's this rubbish?" and slung the jug of tea at me, I ducked and my brother copped the lot which made it a bloody sight worse.' Cecil was his mother's favourite because he reminded her of his father, but looks such as these could cut both ways.

Lily Jones was very close to her mother, but, unlike her brother Wyndham, she did not look like her father.

Mother disciplined my brother very much, because Wyndham was exactly like my father, big brown eyes, dark brown hair, exactly like Daddy, and I think somehow or other, because it must have been in her mind, she could not help but be annoyed, I really do. He reminded her of her loss and she'd grumble at him like the dickens.

Even at the age of ten, Clara Whitefield had grown to be tough.

I never weakened. I always did my work as it should be done, God gave me strength and knowledge to do it. I did the washing in a dolly tub, rubbing board and a mangle. Mum used to come home and say, 'These aren't very clean.' Inside me I went up the wall but I did not say a dickie bird, I just put up with it. 'These hand-kerchiefs are filthy, you haven't washed them clean,' but I was washing for four of them! I got fagged out but I didn't complain. I had to do it.

The loss of precious love and comfort hardened many women not just to the outside world but at times to their own children. They identified that something had changed in Mother, too, that something had died with her husband or son, but such children could also recognise small gestures, signs of love and gratitude that no one else would pick up, and that gave them the fortitude to go on. The work of these children alleviated some of the intense strain their mothers were under, and there was a deepening bond between parent and child, as Dennis Gilfeather well knew.

My dad used to have a nickname for Mum, 'Trilby', and he used to say, pointing to me, 'Trilby, that one's like you.' A lot of people noticed it. She always knew I'd help her; run any message; go and do what she needed. Dad had been a miner when he was young and his lamps hung in the house and Mum would burnish them every Friday night, so I said that I could do that and took the job over. I would scrub the floors too. This was not just linoleum but inlaid linoleum which lasts longer but it was harder to scrub, and I'd be down on the floor, and she'd come in and say, 'Oh I wish you hadna done that,' and I'd say 'I wasna doing anything else.'

Children gained an enormous amount of pride and satisfaction from the feeling that family survival ultimately depended on their input. Clara Whitefield never forgot that feeling and the intense gratification it invoked.

My mother worshipped me and she never forgot it. She was so pleased that I was saving money and looking after the family but she would not show it, she was a very hard woman, hard as nails, but I knew her from old and she did appreciate it, you could tell the feelings. I was proud and I loved doing it, but it did make me old.

Donald Overall was equally proud of his contribution:

When we used to go out I would walk in front of Mum, open all the doors for her, be protective. I'd look after my brother Cecil and I'd look after my mother and she would say do this, do that and I'd do it. I would never argue about it, I accepted it all. Then now and again she would give me and my brother a halfpenny to go and buy some sweets as a treat. My brother would then stand behind me as he ate his as the other kids would try and knock them out of his hand. I would shield him.

Obviously I lost my childhood but I never felt that I had, because I had to look after my family, and I felt ten feet tall.

8

Anger Management

'Treasured thoughts
Of a husband so dear
Often recalled
By a silent tear'

224332 Private Arthur Leaity
272nd MT Company, Army Service Corps
Killed in action 21 April 1917, aged thirty-five
Buried Achiet-Le-Grand Communal Cemetery

The instant that the Armistice agreement came into legal force, the living parted company with the war dead. It is hard to overstate the impact of the moment when Death, the ever-present companion of the soldier of the line, suddenly took its leave as quickly as its malevolent presence had once arrived. That is not to say that many men did not succumb to their wounds in the weeks, months and years ahead: thousands did. Other men died in accidents while still serving overseas, clearing munitions, for example, and of course the flu pandemic that ripped through Europe that summer and autumn made no distinction between soldier and civilian. But as of eleven o'clock that November morning, a deep psychological rupture occurred: no longer were all men the same, fighting under a more or less equal threat of death; now there were survivors, survivors burdened with guilt. The dead would remain on the battlefield and the living were freed to return home to continue their lives.

The Armistice might have been only a cessation of hostilities but it was greeted by most as the end of the war. Overseas, raucous celebrations did not generally follow the announcement. Most men individually accepted the Armistice with a mixture of dull anger, sometimes resignation, frustration and even depression. They knew they had had the Germans on the run and the Armistice felt, in boxing terms, like a referee's technical stoppage and not the knock-out blow long fought for. Typically, men experienced a sense of bewilderment; for so long their lives had been forfeit; now their goal was won, but their objective lost. What would they do now?

Private Stephen Graham was incredulous at the news. It was common in the army that the objects of men's desires were manifest in rumour, and few men believed that this particular news could be true.

> Half an hour later most of the battalion was drilling, and the officers calmly and politely told the men the war had ended. Then men began to go about like owls disturbed at mid-day and kept saying to one another without any particular excitement, 'What do you think of it, eh?'

The men of the 6th Royal West Kent Regiment held a muted ceremony on news of the Armistice. Drawn up in a square, the battalion listened as a bugler sounded the ceasefire. Their Commanding Officer, Colonel William 'Bob' Dawson, was given three cheers in absentia, followed by the band playing the 'Marseillaise' and 'God Save the King'. It was all a bit half-hearted and lacklustre, for the popular CO who had led the men for much of the war had been wounded and his absence had considerably dampened interest. 'There was no sense of victory, much less any hatred of the enemy, only a strong desire to get home,' recalled one 6th Battalion officer, Captain Alan Thomas.

An eerie peace descended on the battlefield. In Frederick Voigt's unit there had been some excitement among the mostly conscripted soldiers, even odd scenes of wild exuberance, of singing and dancing. A bonfire was lit and signal rockets fired into the sky by men relieved that the threat of death had been irrevocably lifted. Such sights infuriated others. Voigt remembers one man 'glaring with fury', and shouting, 'Bloody lot of fools. They ought to have more respect for the dead! The war's over, and we're bloody lucky to get out of it unharmed, but it's nothing to shout about when there's hundreds of thousands of our mates dead or maimed for life.' The violence of the man's emotions was not exceptional; it was just that the expression of his anger had been triggered. It did not bode well for the future. 'I'll tell the civvies something about war when I get home,' he bellowed, 'I'll tell 'em we rob the dead, I'll tell 'em . . .' The man threw himself back into bed wrapping himself into a blanket and did not say another word.

Such anger was consistent with what became known as 'survivors' guilt'. It was an emotion that could manifest itself in different ways but the upshot was a psychological and emotional embrace that bound soldiers to their dead friends – their 'other' family – for life. It was not the same as the bond between bereaved wives and parents and their husbands and sons, and sometimes children and their fathers; theirs was a link based, rather, on life-long gratitude, veneration and love. How all these people, soldiers and civilians, would deal with their sense of separation and loss would vary wildly but would often boil down to one common denominator: anger management.

Almost without exception, no one could accept the news of a death with equanimity; it was how they coped with the news that would dictate both how their own lives would eventually be spent and also how 'coming to terms' would send further ripples down the generations. Today it is known erroneously as closure. It was not closure at all; it was simply a question of people finding their own way of coping with devastation. Some people managed better than others, some could not cope at all, but few found any resolution to their loss without dealing with issues of anger. It was a personal voyage that for many would begin again, and in earnest, the day the guns finally fell silent.

The fighting continued right up until 11 a.m., and even after that there were sporadic incidents of gunfire, as not everyone received the order to cease fire that morning. Raids of enemy positions had been undertaken that day, and up to a minute or two before 'peace', gunners blazed away, firing their shells in a final hurrah. One colonel, Walter Nicholson, recorded that in his sector the firing from the German lines was heavy all morning, including one particularly wearisome enemy machine gun. 'Just before 11am a thousand rounds were fired from it in a practically ceaseless burst. At five minutes to eleven the machine-gunner got up, took off his hat to us, and walked away.'

Those men who knew the war was almost over were anxious to keep their heads down. In some areas, rumours had been circulating the previous evening of an imminent Armistice. Grenadier Guardsman Norman Cliff recalled taking shelter in an isolated ruin just hours before peace, German snipers 'peppering' the walls. 'When two or three of our group stopped bullets, it seemed the bitterest tragedy that could befall them – to have survived so much, only to die in the last hours of the war.'

How difficult, then, would it be to celebrate peace when a comrade was killed in the last hours? In 377 Battery, Royal Field Artillery, there had been considerable excitement that morning until at 10 a.m. a single shell came over and killed one of the men. 'There was more grief over this casualty than anything I can remember,' wrote William Carr, a subaltern in the battery. 'It seemed so unfair.'

It was unfair, bloody unfair. Every death or serious injury in those last days and hours was no more tragic than any other during the war; it just felt as if it was. None was more bemoaned by serving soldiers than the life-threatening injuries suffered by Colonel Bob Dawson. He had been commissioned in 1914 and had served with his battalion for all three and a half years since it sailed for France in June 1915. Not only had he risen to become its Commanding Officer, he had won a reputation for wonderful leadership and exceptional bravery. He was wounded nine times and won the Distinguished Service Order, second only to the Victoria Cross, on no fewer than four occasions and was also four times Mentioned in Dispatches. Then, shortly before the Armistice, he was wounded again, and, in the context of the war, in the most ridiculously mundane circumstances, as Captain Alan Thomas recalled.

> He was going on his rounds and had just left B Company's head-quarters. On his way back he had seen some celery growing in the garden of an empty house and had gone to take some for tea. As he was picking the celery a stray shell came over and fell within a few feet of him, shattering his leg and wounding him in several other places. He managed to slither into a garden shed where he blew his whistle in order to attract attention. It was some time before two men who happened to be passing heard the whistle – and discovered their colonel.

The stray shell was the last 'ever fired' on the battalion. Colonel Dawson was taken to hospital; the battalion was robbed of its remarkable leader right at the end of the war. 'I never knew a man who had a stronger personality,' wrote Thomas. 'He was an inspiration to those who served with him and whenever men have spoken of the 6th West Kents they have thought of it as Dawson's battalion.'

Right across the Western Front, men slowly recovered from the shock that there would be no more bombs, no more shells, no more bullets, and their thoughts turned to home. 'We shall get back to our homes, to our wives, to mother and father, and all we love in Blighty,' wrote Stephen Graham. 'The pulse of some, even of the bravest, beat more freely,' he noted. 'They were spared. Their wives, mothers, children, and friends were reprieved. For

dying was not the hardest thing; the hardest thing was plunging
one's home into sorrow.'

Frederick Voigt was keen to get home; indeed, he had never
wanted to go abroad in the first place. He had done his duty but
never made any pretence that he was anything other than a civilian at heart. Peace was welcome, of course, but he felt trapped
between conflicting emotions.

> So the war was over! The fact was too big to grasp all at once, but
> nevertheless I felt an extraordinary serene satisfaction. Then some-
> one said: 'The people who've lost their sons and husbands – now's
> the time they'll feel it.' The truth of this remark struck me with
> sudden violence. My serenity was broken and I looked into the
> blackness of it. I knew what I was going to see, but, nevertheless,
> I looked, in spite of myself, and saw innumerable rotting dead
> that lay unburied in all postures on the bare, shell-tossed earth.

Whoever that 'someone' was, he had made a prescient comment.
That day, two hundred miles away in Paddington, London, eight-
year-old Doris Davies returned from school and was surprised to
find her mother visibly upset. Ever since her husband, Charlie,
had died of shrapnel wounds in February 1916 she had remained
stoic, if that was the right word. She had also lost two brothers in
the war, and had taken to dressing in dark clothes, though she had
retreated from the idea of wearing full widow's weeds. Since the
death of her husband, Daisy Davies had 'clammed up' as her
daughter witnessed; she had not shown much emotion to anyone,
not even the children. Now, on Armistice Day, she did 'feel it',
but in her case the emotional dam was breached only briefly and
never burst.

> I came home from school and mother was washing in the scul-
> lery and she was crying and I asked her why and she said, 'Well,
> I have no one to come home and love me.' I didn't really know

what she meant and I think that was the last time my father was mentioned. After then I can't recall my mother talking about him, ever. I can remember just standing there and watching her cry. It didn't really touch me. You are too young to realise sorrow or love.

Daisy had one small consolation at least, according to her daughter. Her husband had a grave and, although she never managed the trip to Belgium, the fact that he was buried by his comrades with prayers said over his grave was something. When their daughter visited the grave over eighty years later, it was her turn to cry.

I realised that I had a father now. I had always known he was buried in Belgium but he wasn't around so I didn't know him. But seeing a gravestone made a lot of difference, to know that he was there. It also hit me, perhaps even harder, that Mum was left alone with three young children.

For the bereaved, the Armistice, irrespective of when it came, would always have come 'too late'. Nurse Vera Brittain wondered if the war could have ended much earlier that year, before her brother died, or perhaps years before, if politicians had not demanded outright victory instead of a negotiated peace. Then perhaps her fiancé Roland Leighton might have been saved. 'If only.'

When Vera heard the maroons sounding, giving news of the Armistice, she did not stop work but automatically continued what she was doing as her subconscious stirred a deep-seated memory. She was taken back to an organ recital she had attended at Micklem Hall in Oxford. The music had been *An Occasional Oratorio* by Handel that described the mustering of troops preparing for battle, the expression of sorrow for the fallen and the triumphant return of the victors.

Vera had written to her fiancé and described how the organ had swelled

forth into a final triumphant burst in the song of victory, after the solemn and mournful dirge over the dead. I thought with what mockery and irony the jubilant celebrations which will hail the coming of peace will fall upon the ears of those to whom the best will never return, upon whose sorrow victory is built, who have paid with their mourning for the others' joy. I wonder if I shall be one of those who take a happy part in the triumph – or if I shall listen to the merriment with a heart that breaks and ears that try to keep out the mirthful sounds.

Norman Collins also heard the maroons, not in London but in Sheffield, where he was staying with relatives. An officer in the Seaforth Highlanders, he had been wounded twice. From his hospital bed he had tracked the fortunes of his battalion and noted in his letters how almost all the regimental officers he had known had been killed or invalided home, as, too, had the majority of the men under his command. He was shaving when he heard the noise outside. 'My one thought was 'It's too late – all my friends are gone – it's too late. It's no good having an Armistice now.'

As he stood there he suddenly had a vision. He was standing in a trench.

I could not put my head up because I was under fire, but above me, at eye level, walking past, were hundreds and hundreds of boots and puttees . . . They went on and on for hours, and I realised it was the dead all walking away and leaving me behind. I felt worried and frightened that they were leaving me by myself; that I had been left behind. They were marching away into the distance, where I would never follow.'

This vision returned to Norman on several occasions and he chose not to tell anyone until he was nearing the end of his life.

'I felt it was a private matter between my old comrades and myself.'

In London and in cities across the country, civilians went mad; crowds filled Whitehall and The Mall, while vast numbers paraded outside Buckingham Palace where the King and Queen stepped on to the balcony, to general delight. Nearby, medical students carried a skull impaled on a pole, shouting 'Hoch der Kaiser', and children swarmed over captured artillery that had been paraded for public inspection; bonfires were lit and fuelled with anything that came to hand, police constables judiciously turning a blind eye. The sights and sounds of extravagant celebration appalled some. Oswald Mosley, aged twenty-one, a former officer and a prospective MP for the Coalition Government, berated one girl as she climbed down from the back of one of the stone lions at the base of Nelson's Column. Swathed in the Union Jack, she had only just finished belting out 'Land of Hope and Glory'. 'Do any of you think for one moment of the loss of life, the devastation and misery?' he asked her. The poet and officer Siegfried Sassoon arrived in London only to see people making fools of themselves. He hated what he saw as 'mob patriotism' around him. 'It is a loathsome ending to the loathsome tragedy of the last four years,' he wrote in his diary that day.

Vera Brittain was persuaded by other nurses to go and see the fun in town and she 'mechanically' followed them, 'seeing the sights' half masochistically, scenes of joy and happiness that were all but alienating.

'I detached myself from the others and walked slowly up Whitehall, with heart sinking in a sudden cold dismay,' she wrote. 'Already this was a different world from the one that I had known during four life-long years.' Brittain predicted a brave new world of fun, amusements and forgetfulness, a world in which people would selfishly pursue their careers. This new world would be alien to her and she would take no part in it.

Walking among the crowds in London was Sir Arthur Conan Doyle. It was a little over two weeks since his officer son, Kingsley, had died of pneumonia and only days since he was buried. Conan Doyle was emotionally wrung out. He understood that people had the right to rejoice but he was nauseated when in the dense crowd he saw a man he described as 'hard-faced' hacking at the neck of a whisky bottle before swigging it back. It was a base and crude public display from a man destined to live, owing to the noble self-sacrifice of men like Kingsley who, in 1916, had been badly wounded on the Somme. Conan Doyle watched the 'hard-faced' man and violently wished that the crowd would lynch him. 'It was a moment for prayer, and this beast was a blot on the landscape,' he wrote. It was a bitter pill for the august writer to swallow. Over the course of the war, Conan Doyle had lost his son, while his wife had lost not only a son but also a brother and a nephew. His sister had lost her husband and a son. In February 1919 Conan Doyle was also to lose his brother, Brigadier General Innes Doyle, from influenza.

Back in France, Colonel Bob Dawson was lying in a hospital in Camiers, near Etaples. His wounds were critical and his parents were sent for. For weeks Dawson clung to life. Towards the end of November, Alan Thomas went to see his Commanding Officer.

> He was glad – and sorry – to see me. He took it kindly that I had come, but he hated anyone to see him in a helpless state. I stayed with him a little while. Then his lunch was brought. It was a herring and it had to be fed to him by a nurse: but before the meal began he turned me out. He could not have borne to be spoon-fed while I or anybody else (except the nurse) was watching him.

Two weeks later Colonel Bob Dawson died aged twenty-seven.

In order to be granted a ceasefire, the Germans had to acquiesce unconditionally to a host of demands made by the Allies. It was either an agreement or a resumption of hostilities, and the Germans were in no position to pick the latter. Defeat was inevitable. Better to sue for peace while the retreat on the Western

Front was still just about controlled than to do so when it became headlong. Better, too, perhaps, to call a halt while still on French and Belgian soil than to invite the fighting on to their own.

The Germans had to evacuate all occupied land within days; hand over huge quantities of weapons and ammunition, and release, with immediate effect, Allied prisoners of war. For this reason, prisoners were among the first men to return home and they attracted considerable press and civilian attention, though not always for the happiest of reasons.

Jack Rogers had been captured in March 1918. He was among the first batch of prisoners to sail up the Humber; from the ship's railings he could see hundreds of people waiting to welcome them back. After they disembarked, they boarded a train.

As we looked out of the carriage windows, up and down the plat-form were any number of women. These poor mothers were walking up and down the platform, each of them carrying a picture of a missing son or husband. They came up and showed you the image and asked, 'Did you know him? Have you seen him? Was he in your regiment?' You wanted to give them a little hope, to say we had seen them, but no, we hadn't, we couldn't tell them anything.

Since the disappearance of their son in 1916, the parents of Arthur Sherington had made exhaustive enquiries as to his where-abouts, but to no avail. Arthur's father, Robert, himself already sick, had expended much of his remaining energy in writing letters and visiting friends who worked for the press for help but no news had never been good news. Then Robert died, and Letitia was left to struggle on with four children. When the Armistice was signed, she felt relief that the slaughter was over.

Then the months of agonized waiting in the hope that among the prisoners of war, among the men in hospital who had lost their memory, Arthur might even yet come home . . . It would have been a merciful blow if we had heard that he was killed – but he was missing – and even after this lapse of time, those years of hopes that were deferred don't bear thinking of.

Six-year-old Mary Morton had given up all hope of seeing her father again. He had disappeared during fighting near Arras and any chance that he had been taken prisoner faded as the weeks, then months of silence turned to years. It was back in February 1916 that her mother had received notification that her husband had been reported missing, believed killed, and nothing had been heard of him since. If he had been a prisoner, then surely he would have written; surely the International Red Cross, long concerned with prisoner welfare, would have been aware of his name.

Because of the deafening silence, Mary's mother moved on with her life, accepting that her husband was dead. She met another man, Hugh Aird, a tailor by trade, and a year later he moved into the family home where the pair set up a cottage industry sewing garments. Mary's mother seemed happy again and Mary herself began to forget the soldier in the framed photograph that remained on display until her mother put it away in a drawer. 'Too many memories,' she had said, though her mother-in-law was not best pleased. The children accepted Hugh, who seemed nice enough and worked hard to win their trust and, latterly, affection.

Then, on 3 January 1919, everything changed. Kirsty, a neighbour and close friend of the family, came to the house with a newspaper. It was only 6 a.m. but she banged on the door in order to be let in. Her hands were visibly shaking as she showed them the news. 'The headlines stated that another hospital ship had docked at Southampton with three hundred prisoners-of-war,' recalled Mary.

Their names were printed in long columns in alphabetical order. Hughie ran his finger down, stopped, then read out in a hoarse voice: 'Morton, George, Sergeant of the 1st Battalion Royal Scots Regiment.' Mama stared at him, then slipped sideways in her chair. He gave her a little water, and when she spoke, she whispered, 'What shall we do?' over and over again.

There was only one thing to do and that was to leave. Hugh took Mary's now heavily pregnant mother away to his sister's house. Mary and her two sisters would remain with George's mother to meet their father when he came home.

For missing men to return after being accepted as dead by the authorities was rare but hardly unique. It was not unknown for memorial services to take place, obituaries to be published and for estates to be wound up, only for the missing man to reappear. The problem was that their miraculous appearance held out hope to other families, hope that was out of all proportion to the numbers. In January 1919, search parties were sent by the British into Germany's hinterland to visit all the outlying satellite camps that were affiliated to the larger and better-known POW camps, as well as visiting hospitals, prisons and even farms where a small number of long-term prisoners had been employed. However, the number of men reported to have been found did not exceed 120, and many of these were former prisoners who had decided to remain in Germany of their own free will.

In February 1919, the MP for Twickenham, William Joynson-Hicks, asked the Secretary of State for War how many servicemen were missing in all theatres of war; the answer was 359,800, of whom 198,000 were prisoners, and death had been presumed in another 97,000 cases, owing to the absence of any indication over a long period that they were alive; this left 64,800 whose fate remained 'undetermined'.

Of the estimated 198,000 prisoners held around the globe, something in the order of 140,000 were expected back from Germany, but the numbers returning were always going to be fewer, not greater, than expected. The Germans had never kept a consolidated nominal roll of prisoners so that no one could be sure precisely how many were alive. There was certainly a serious discrepancy between German and British estimates of how many men were still in captivity at the beginning of 1919. The Germans reported that they had fewer than 14,000 prisoners; the British expected more than 35,000. The difference, 22,000, was astonishing and while this figure was whittled down over time, thousands of prisoners believed at one time to be in German hands were never properly accounted for. During its answer to Joynson-Hicks' questions, the government did at least refute unspecified claims that any prisoners were being held in 'secret camps or asylums' after the Allies' searches were completed in March. A declaration was then made that all enemy districts were clear. 'There was no indication whatsoever that the Germans were keeping any prisoners in hiding,' reported the Controller of Officers Casualties Department.

Even so, six months after the war, a large but unspecified number of letters were still being addressed to the War Office and the Central Prisoners of War Committee concerning missing men. For thousands of families there would never be a satisfactory answer.

Most of the missing had died of illness or injuries and the Germans had simply failed to notify anyone, such as the International Red Cross in Geneva. The Germans had also grossly mistreated a small number of prisoners and by no means only those considered recalcitrant. Hundreds of prisoners had been chosen to work in salt mines in the Hertz Mountains from where contact with the outside world was sporadic, if it existed at all. Other prisoners laboured just behind the fighting line on the Western Front and Russian fronts where the danger of being killed or wounded by shellfire was intolerably high. It was in such conditions, beyond the reach of the International Red Cross, that men had disappeared from all view. A few, like George Morton, believed by the British to have been killed in action, managed to survive and now returned home.

'Arriving 3.30pm Central Station, Saturday 4th Jan. George.'

'Daddy came marching in, his face wreathed in smiles,' remembered Mary. He immediately hugged his mother then looked at his children.

Then with a great flourish, he threw off his top-coat and said, 'Where is she hiding?' and ran into the front room. Granny quickly followed, closed the room door, there was no sound. All the family left at this point, only Uncle Johnny was left with us, listening intently should Granny need him.

When they both came into the kitchen, Daddy's face looked grim, he said, 'It's happened to a lot of men. I never thought it would happen to me. Why couldn't she have waited?' He was so angry about her being pregnant. I think that was the worst bit for him to swallow.

Mary's grandmother asked why he had not written, as they had all assumed he was dead. George had been very seriously wounded; most of his right hand had been blown off and he had scars down his right side from head to foot from a bomb explosion. He was explaining his plight when his mother, perhaps not wanting him to talk about such things in front of the children, cut him short.

The next morning, George announced that he was going to apply for a divorce immediately, selling the family home and all the furniture. He would still have to return to hospital for treatment, and then he would attempt to get a job in the Civil Service. In the meantime, as his mother was too old to look after the children, they would have to go into an orphanage run by nuns for ex-servicemen. In due course he would set up a new home and then come for them. For Mary Morton and her sisters, life had been irrevocably turned inside out because, in this case, the dead had returned.

The halt to hostilities on the Western Front did not mean a cessation in anti-German rhetoric, a feature of that other war, propaganda. Publicly, politicians tumbled over each other to spout ire at the enemy, a necessary and invariably popular stance after such an exhausting and emotionally draining war. Those few MPs who displayed any hint of sympathy towards Germany were booted out of office at the hastily organised General Election of December 1918.

Ever the opportunist, Lloyd George led the way, promising to squeeze the Germans 'till the pips squeaked', but for all the speeches and the promises to hang the Kaiser, senior politicians knew that Germany was a vital trading nation and a bulwark against the threat of the Bolshevik virus then spreading from the east. After the Armistice, Bolshevism not German militarism was considered the greatest future threat to European stability.

The British public could be forgiven for not noticing this new threat. Hatred of the Germans had been raised to fever pitch with the stories of atrocities published in newspapers and pamphlets. The ceasefire was not the time to deflate that animosity by appearing conciliatory, yet talking tough and being tough were two different things. The Allies' list of chronicled atrocities was long and so, therefore, was the list of war criminals to be prosecuted, beginning with the Kaiser and flowing down the chain of command: 1,580 names in all.

Of course the Kaiser did not hang; he was not even tried. The political will to have him removed from Holland, where he was in exile, was not forthcoming. Indeed, the Germans were allowed to conduct the war crimes trials themselves in Leipzig, a town about as far away from Allied control and influence as it was possible to get. The only people convicted were lowly ranked officers, NCOs, and privates, and even those who were found guilty received sentences which were paltry in length. When it came to actually squeezing pips, the British government showed precious little interest.

Anti-German propaganda had been a useful tool to keep the public motivated, though it came at an unforeseen cost. The rising number of battlefield casualties had stoked the deepest fears of families back home and the reports of terrible German treachery only heightened the anxiety. In the last weeks of the war, Captain Arthur Prosser disappeared during one of the final spasms of fighting. When news reached his parents that he was missing, the initial statements, like those concerning Angus Macnaghten, were very good. In a letter dated 28 October, Prosser's battalion chaplain reported that the area where Prosser had fought had been carefully examined and there 'were no signs of foul play'.

> In one village they told us they saw three officers, two wounded and one not wounded (Prosser we think) go through in a car the day after. As they (the Huns) buried one boy, who died of wounds about 2 kilometres beyond the canal, and took the trouble to see all his papers together and put them on the top of the grave, I think there is every hope that the prisoners are all right . . .

But nothing definite was heard of Captain Prosser before or after the Armistice. It must have been especially agonising for a mother to lose her son so tantalisingly close to the end of the war. Captain Prosser had led a charmed life. Although he had been wounded and gassed, he had survived nearly four years in France, so long, indeed, that it seemed impossible he could now disappear. There must also have been a gnawing fear for his parents that, as the world's attention turned from the battlefields towards the Palace of Versailles and the peace negotiations, somehow their son might be forgotten.

It was not long before Rosina Prosser's almost uncontrollable anxiety spilled over. She hated the Germans and had been inclined to believe everything government propaganda told her. Then a report was received that the Germans had informed a *Burgomeister* of a village close to where Prosser had last been seen that the young captain had died of his injuries. After the news, the War Office, in writing to the parents, was 'constrained to conclude' the worst. Rosina Prosser quickly replied:

> Knowing the fiendish devilry of the enemy could it be possible that they, during the latter days of their occupation, purposely informed the *Burgomeister* of the death of a different man and are perhaps at this moment wreaking their evil genius on my poor

boy? Can three officers of His Majesty's army having served him well and faithfully for four years (in my son's case) disappear in the manner aforesaid with no further notice on the part of the War Office than a mere regret at being constrained to conclude?! I remain resentfully, indignantly and heartbrokenly his mother.

Just like Hazel Macnaghten, Rosina Prosser believed the silence from her son was down to the enemy. If he had been alive,

he would not have refrained from writing home unless compulsorily prevented . . . Therefore he must either be under lock and key starving and slowly perishing in some German prison or have been laid low and died of pneumonia. He spoke German and French fluently, was an athlete but handicapped by indifferent sight – unless stricken by illness he could not disappear in this dreadful heartbreaking manner.

The propaganda that had induced so many to go to war, and others to support it at home, wreaked a Faustian revenge. While there was any chance Mrs Prosser's boy could be 'perishing' in a German prison, her search would go on and so, like Hazel Macnaghten's, Rosina's enquiries into her son's disappearance continued while the politicians squabbled over a peace treaty and the priorities of a nation moved towards commemorating the glorious and definitely dead.

Although Mrs Prosser held on to the hope that her son might still be alive, her husband was preparing himself for 'the worst'. If, as he seemed inclined to believe, his son was dead, would the War Office, he asked, make sure of one point?

I hope to receive your assurance that the fact that Captain Prosser died of wounds received in action will be recorded and not simply that he died an ordinary death in a Belgian town.

Did it really make any difference whether a death was either ordinary or extraordinary? It certainly did, and never more so than to a father who was himself an army officer. Major General Walter Braithwaite, Commanding Officer of 62nd Division, lost his son in July 1916. Lieutenant Valentine Braithwaite was reported 'missing'. Nothing further was heard of him and in April 1917 the Army Council was forced 'regretfully to conclude' that he had 'died on or since 2nd July 1916'.

Weeks later the War Office received a letter from Major General Braithwaite.

> I beg most respectfully to request that seeing that my son – when last seen – was charging a German trench at the head of his platoon, the word 'died', in reference to the manner of his death, may be altered to 'killed in action'. I am aware that the expression 'died' is used officially where there is no clear ocular evidence of death to be produced. I very much hope, however, that considering the circumstances in which my son was last seen, i.e., charging an enemy trench at the head of his men in the middle of a Battle, his mother and I may have the, at least melancholy, satisfaction of having our son returned as (presumed) 'killed in action' . . . I think perhaps, it is not too much for a soldier to ask the War Office to do for a soldier's son.

The War Office acceded to his wishes. For posterity, both Major General Braithwaite and Arthur Prosser wanted it to be 'clearly known' that their sons had played their part and made the ultimate sacrifice in the nation's greatest and darkest hour of need.

Given the enormous challenges the war had presented, the great moral questions it had posed and the colossal stakes wagered by all sides in life, liberty and prosperity, could there be anything more utterly futile than a death that was in no way heroic but ultimately mundane?

The cessation of hostilities may have abruptly halted the

Charles Chilton, aged around eighteen months, pictured shortly after the death of his father in 1917. His mother, Gladys, died in 1923 leaving Charles to be brought up by his grandmother. Charles went on to co-write the screenplay of *Oh What A Lovely War* with Joan Littlewood.

Boys seemingly aged between twelve and fourteen work in a factory in 1917. The legal employment of school-aged children was accepted by the government but many more worked illegally, such as Dennis Gilfeather who was employed in a jute mill aged nine after his father was killed in 1915.

'Every little helps' says the caption. However, after the death of a father forced mothers back to work, many eldest children such as ten-year-old Clara Whitefield became 'mother' to younger siblings, washing, cleaning and cooking at home while education was abandoned.

A boy hoes the drive to a large house. Len Whitehead was sent to work at the local vicarage before and after school to bring in extra money after his brother was killed at the battle of Loos in 1915. Len also took days off school to help with the harvest on his father's farm.

Children of Gibbons Road School in Willesden, London, making clothing for soldiers at the front. Children were widely encouraged to provide comforts for the men in the trenches.

A boot repair factory on the Old Kent Road, November 1917. Widowed women could not survive on the allowances paid by the government and returned to work to make ends meet, leaving their elder children to look after siblings.

Emily Sutton with her two surviving sons: Isaac, serving with the Army Service Corps, and Ernest Sutton.

Private George Sutton, aged nineteen, prior to his departure overseas where he would serve with the 2/6th West Yorkshire Regiment. He was killed in May 1917.

Her family reunited again, at least in spirit. George's picture is superimposed on the original image in an act of remembrance for a dead son. George is buried in Achiet-Le-Grand Communal Cemetery Extension.

Private Ernest Naylor (*far left*) aged thirty-two and married. He was killed in action just three weeks before the end of the war.

The personal inscription to be placed at the base of Ernest Naylor's grave. His widow Alice would have had to pay over fourteen shillings for the work on her husband's grave.

No. 10411

IMPERIAL WAR GRAVES COMMISSION.

Dear Sir (Madam),   Date......16 JUL 1924......19

I am directed by the Imperial War Graves Commission to ask you to be so good as to forward to the
FINANCE DEPARTMENT, Imperial War Graves Commission, Wimbledon House, 82, BAKER STREET, LONDON, W.1.

the sum of ......14/2 ...... in payment of the following personal inscription :—

In memory of my dear Husband
The Lord giveth
And taketh away

consisting of 49 ......letters at......3½ᵈ......per letter, which will be engraved at your
request on the headstone of......Pte E Naylor

Regiment......York and Lanc Regt......age 32 in Cemetery......ROMERIES C.C. "O"

Cheques, Postal and Money Orders should be crossed and made payable to the Imperial War Graves Commission.

You are particularly requested to return this
Form with remittance, on receipt of which a
formal acknowledgment will be sent to you.

I am,
Your obedient Servant,
FABIAN WARE,
Major-General, Vice-Chairman.

Mrs A G Naylor Rotherham Yorks

The Vice-Chairman
Imperial War Graves Commission

Begs to forward as requested a Photograph, taken by
the Director-General of Graves Registration and
Enquiries, of the Grave of :—

Name......Overall

Rank and Initials......Pte H

Regiment......London Regt

Position of Grave......Croisilles
Railway Military Cemetery

The grave of Donald Overall's father, photographed by one of the Graves Registration Units working on the Western Front. Pictures were supplied for free to those families who applied to the IWGC.

One of the typical memorial cards printed and sent to families and friends. Donald Overall was aged just five when his father was killed and naturally he assumed the role of looking after his younger brother Cecil.

In Affectionate Remembrance
of

HARRY,

DEARLY LOVED HUSBAND OF
MABEL OVERALL.

Who was Killed in Action, June 15th, 1917.

A view across the cemetery at Aveluy on the Somme. The party of grieving relatives are talking to their guide, supplied by the IWGC to take them around the battlefield. Guides, almost without exception, were drawn from amongst men demobbed from the army. Peter Miller's cousin, Harry Keeling, lies in this cemetery.

An unknown three-year-old stands in front of the grave of Second Lieutenant Ernest Taylor, Varennes Military Cemetery. Some 360,000 children lost their fathers during the Great War.

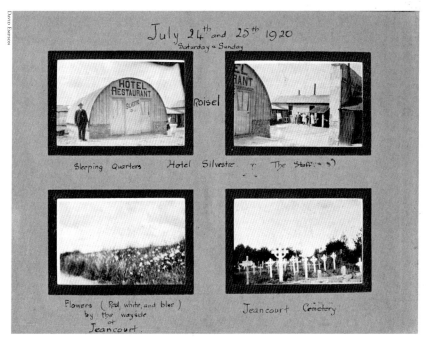

July 24th and 25th 1920
Saturday & Sunday

Roisel

Sleeping Quarters   Hotel Silvestre   The Staff (= 3)

Flowers (Red, white, and blue) by the wayside at Jeancourt.

Jeancourt Cemetery

Four photographs from an album showing the battlefields of the Somme within a year or two of the cessation of hostilities. The number of civilians undertaking pilgrimages to the Western Front grew exponentially in the early 1920s.

A private memorial card made by J. D. Pritchard's grieving mother, Elizabeth. Curiously, she refers to the agony of the 'unknown grave' and yet his body lies in an identified plot at Bailleul Communal Cemetery Extension.

Never forget: Frank and Emily Prestidge's drawing room, Llandudno, in part dedicated to the memory of their son Lieutenant John Prestidge, killed in May 1917.

A private shrine in what appears to be a family living room
to a son who fell while serving in the Middlesex Regiment.
After the death of Ellen Elston's father, her mother turned the
portrait of her husband to face the wall, no longer willing to
be reminded of her loss every time she entered the room.

The King prepares to unveil the Cenotaph. Behind him stands the gun carriage carrying the body of the body of the Unknown Warrior. Eight-year-old Donald Overall was present with his mother and felt the supremely charged atmosphere of the day.

The Unknown Warrior lies in State in Westminster Abbey prior to his burial.

Programme Memoir.

"THEY DIED THAT WE MIGHT LIVE."

Unveiling of the Cenotaph
AND
The Unknown Warrior's Funeral.

Thursday, November 11th, 1920.

The programme of the day's epic events, as carried by Donald Overall's mother. Such was the profound hush that greeted the two-minute silence that Donald recalled that the rustle of autumn leaves was the only audible sound.

One of the four nameless bodies chosen from different areas of the Western Front, from among whom the body of the Unknown Warrior was selected.

The sea of flowers and wreaths laid at the base of the Cenotaph. A young mother with her daughter adds her tribute to a lost love.

The crowds file past the Cenotaph. Any civilian joining the queue could expect to wait between five and seven hours to pass by the memorial to pay their respects.

November 1918: after one week in which over a million civilians filed past the coffin of the Unknown Warrior, the ceremony to seal the grave was about to start.

In Pwllheli in North Wales, the wartime Prime Minister Lloyd George gives an address to local people after unveiling the town's monument to its lost sons. In Newport-on-Tay in Scotland the unveiling of its war memorial caused outrage when local dignitaries sought to omit the name of a local man shot for cowardice.

This plaque, designed by Edward Cater-Preston after a Government-sponsored competition, was sent to the parents of Ernest Wilson, killed in the fighting at Ypres in August 1917.

Second Lieutenant Ernest Wilson: Emil Loose found the young officer's address on his body and, through a British Sergeant serving with the Army of Occupation in Germany, contacted Wilson's family in 1919.

Emil Loose, the German soldier of the 239 Badische Infantry Regiment who held Ernest Wilson as he died, while the fighting raged around him near Polygon Wood. Loose was in regular contact with the Wilson family after the war.

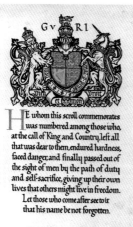

Gᵥ R I

HE whom this scroll commemorates was numbered among those who, at the call of King and Country, left all that was dear to them, endured hardness, faced danger and finally passed out of the sight of men by the path of duty and self-sacrifice, giving up their own lives that others might live in freedom. Let those who come after see to it that his name be not forgotten.

2/Lieut. Raymond Ernest Wilson
Royal West Surrey Regt.

The scroll accompanying the plaque.

A map drawn by Emil Loose to show the approximate position where Ernest Wilson was buried. The map encouraged Wilson's parents to fund a search of the land inside the edge of Polygon Wood but their son's body was never identified.

I think that in this case I have done my duty as a soldier towards a wounded and dead adversary. The spot where your son fell I have marked in the sketch.

In the hope that this will reach you safely and that I shall soon hear from you again, I am with best wishes,

Yours,

(signed) Emil Loose.

Donald Overall and his brother Cecil shortly after the death of their father: although aged just five, Donald became the man of the house and helped his mother in any way that he could, running errands, shopping and looking after his brother.

Donald Overall as a Flight Engineer in the RAF during the Second World War. He was acutely aware that he might leave his two sons to be brought up without a father figure in just the way that he and his brother Cecil were.

2007, south of Arras: Donald visits the grave of his father for the first time in ninety years.

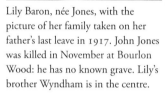

Lily Baron, née Jones, with the picture of her family taken on her father's last leave in 1917. John Jones was killed in November at Bourlon Wood: he has no known grave. Lily's brother Wyndham is in the centre.

July 2010: Lily enters Bourlon Wood for the one and only time, leaving a wreath of lilies and a note: 'Thank you for five years of real happiness – I've missed you all my life.' Lily died in December 2010 aged ninety-eight.

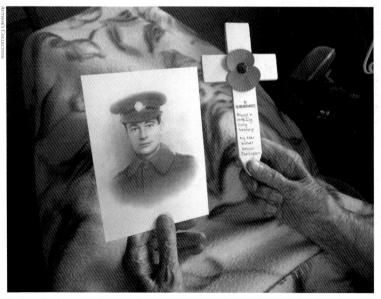

Arthur Sherington and a cross that was to be taken the next day and placed on the Thiepval Memorial to the Missing on the Somme. Both picture and cross are held by Arthur's sister, Joyce Crow, née Sherington.

A battlefield visit in the early 1920s made by Mrs Simpson. The strain on her face is obvious. Her son, Private Frederick J. Simpson, killed on the eve of the Somme battle, lies in Carnoy Cemetery.

addition of new names to the lists of those killed in action, but it did not halt a flood of names that would appear in the press as killed by something as lethal as any German gunner: influenza, the strain of which was so virulent that a victim could die sometimes within hours of appearing hale and hearty.

It was hard to square the deaths of those soldiers who succumbed to the influenza pandemic in France or Belgium with the epic idea of the 'Glorious Dead'. Influenza killed heroes, but there was nothing heroic about being laid low by such a virus. In November 1918, Bevil Quiller-Couch was a twenty-eight-year-old major in the artillery. A regular soldier, he had embarked for France on 17 August 1914. He had been wounded more than once and had won the Military Cross in 1916, 'for exceptional ability and energy'. He survived the war but not the pandemic. On 2 February 1919, Bevil had written to his fiancée that he was lying in bed with a small chill, '. . . when one lived in holes in the ground I never caught chills which seems rather silly . . .'; by the 5th he was in hospital dangerously ill and delirious; by the morning of 6 February he was dead. That day a nursing sister on Bevil's ward penned a note to his family: 'It is so awfully sad to think that a big strong cheery man, as he seems to be, should go so quickly, especially as he had gone through the war so successfully.'

In a terrible twist of irony, Bevil had chosen not to propose to his long-time girlfriend May on the outbreak of war for fear of leaving her a widow. In the days after the ceasefire, he had asked May to be his wife. She accepted and then, before they met again, he died. 'There are few households in this land that this war has left without a domestic sorrow far more real, more natural, more abiding than any exultation over victory,' wrote Bevil's father, Sir Arthur Quiller-Couch.

All the old statues of victory have wings: but Grief has no wings. She is the unwelcome lodger that squats on the hearth-stone between us and the fire and will not move or be dislodged.

On Armistice afternoon a funeral took place in Walthamstow Cemetery of a young victim of the epidemic, Gladys Stevens. She was thirteen and the half-sister of Private Ernie Stevens, a nine-teen-year-old soldier with the Middlesex Regiment and prisoner of war. He had survived nine months in captivity and he was one of the first to get back to Britain. As he approached his home he decided to make an impromptu stop at a café.

It is very difficult to explain just how much you miss the love of your people and I wanted to collect my thoughts. The lady there welcomed me home and I sat down and had a drink. When I went up to pay, she took the money, then said to me, 'By the way, Ernie, when you get indoors you are going to hear some bad news.'

It was my step-father who opened the door and he shouted to Mum, 'It's Ernie.' I'll never forget that, 'It's Ernie.' So Mum came out and of course there was hugging and kissing and then they helped me into the dining room and sat me down and took off my overcoat and my cap, hung them up, and then my mum told me about Gladys. That was a blow that really hit very, very hard. I loved that little girl. She was such a wonderful child.

I asked my mum if she minded if I went out. She was a little reluctant but she nodded and I think she realized that I was not in a fit state to sit there and almost say nothing. It was a very trying time. I had to control myself as much as I could and so one of the best ways was to go out and take a walk up the high street and try and think things over.

On the day Gladys was buried, around a thousand Londoners succumbed to influenza. The same day in *The Times*, sixteen of the fifty public announcements of death cited pneumonia following influenza as the cause, while across Britain as a whole between 250,000 and 280,000 additional lives were lost. People believed at the time that the country was more susceptible to illness because they had been weakened by the strain of war and rationing. On the contrary, influenza had taken many more of the healthiest than of the elderly and infirm.

It was extraordinarily cruel for soldiers who had fought in the belief that they were protecting their homes and families now, on their return, to discover that their loved ones had been taken, regardless of all their efforts. This was not the way it was supposed to be.

No sooner had the war ended than enquiries began into the possible exhumation and repatriation to Britain of soldiers' remains. Since the disquiet over the homecoming of Lieutenant William Gladstone's body in April 1915, the Adjutant General had issued a blanket ban on the return of the remains of any soldier. This ban was reconfirmed in December 1917 by the Commander in Chief in a General Routine Order, No. 3055. Haig's decision was taken in light of the stated views of the Directorate of Graves Registration and Enquiries, to refuse repatriation of bodies. His stance was also taken in sympathy with the broad sentiments of serving officers and men, in as much as they could be ascertained in wartime. The authority of Haig's Routine Order ended with the close of hostilities, at which time different views emerged over the rights of the family to the dead body and the rights of the army to withhold access.

The Imperial War Graves Commission (IWGC) had already received letters from families requesting the right to exhume bodies once the fighting ended. The number seeking permission was small, around a hundred, but that did not mean there would be little or no demand if rights were once granted.

The Commission consulted the government, voicing its concern over its legal and moral authority to refuse relatives the right to bring bodies home. In reply, the government suggested that a final decision could be postponed in the hope that when the public saw for themselves the proposed war cemeteries, they would become more accustomed to the idea of leaving their loved ones with comrades overseas. However, that idea was rejected. Without a definite ruling, wealthier relatives might begin exhumations. There was no question that the government would fund such activity but almost certainly any reports of bodies being brought back to Britain would lead to 'agitation' for government support for those who could not afford to undertake the removal themselves. If permission was going to be refused, it should be done publicly and at once.

The IWGC and the government decided that the finest memorial to the dead would be that they be left together, regardless of rank and class, in the country where they fell. If bodies were brought home at an individual's expense, it had the potential to ruin the parade-ground look of cemeteries. Furthermore, if cost became an issue and officers were removed in great numbers, there would be a negative and lasting impression left on the Western Front that the sacrifice had not been evenly shared.

So an announcement was made in the press that exhumations would not be allowed. 'Comradeship in Death, Soldiers' Bodies not to be Brought Home,' announced *The Times* on 29 November 1918.

> The removal of bodies to their native countries is strongly desired by the relatives in a small number of cases but the reasons against this course appeared to the Commission overwhelming. To allow removal by a few individuals (of necessity only those who could afford the cost) would be contrary to the principle of equality of treatment; to empty some 400,000 identified graves would be a colossal work and would be opposed to the spirit in which the Empire gratefully accepted the offers made by the Governments of France, Belgium, Italy and Greece to provide land in perpetuity for our cemeteries and to 'adopt' our dead . . . The evidence available to them [the Commission]

confirmed their conviction that the dead themselves in whom the sense of comradeship was so strong, would have preferred to lie with their comrades.

There may have been other reasons that were better not mentioned. The stories of bodies gathered up in sandbags, bits of bodies buried when the rest could not be found: this was not how relatives would assume their loved ones to be. What would happen were they to be in attendance during exhumation? Furthermore, to whom did the body belong? In family disputes, would parents take precedence over a wife when it came to ownership? These were headaches that might well have been foreseen and influenced the decisions taken.

Mrs Ruth Jervis was one of those parents anxious to read the Commission's decision and her response to the news that she could not bring her son home was withering. On 1 December she wrote to the Commission.

Sirs

I was shocked beyond words and grieved more than I can say, as I read the decision of the Imperial War Graves Commission (in the daily papers for Friday the 29th alto.) . . .

First of all, let me say here that I protest most emphatically against that decision, as I consider the parents at least might have been consulted before you sat in council to discuss what shall be done with the remains of our sons. I speak plainly (as I have a right to), being one of many mothers whom have been called upon to sacrifice an only child, in the defence of our country. Is there no limit to the suffering imposed upon us, is it not enough to have our boys dragged from us and butchered (and not allowed to say 'nay') without being deprived of their poor remains? . . . The country took him, and the country should bring him back.

Gunner Harry Jervis was twenty-two when he died of a shell wound to his chest. He had joined under the Derby Scheme in late 1915 and been sent to France, after a short period of training, in February 1916. He served for over a year before being killed, his small collection of personal possessions, including some coins, a wallet, letters and a broken wristwatch, being returned to his parents. His body was buried close to the 3rd Canadian Field Ambulance where he was taken after being hit.

The IWGC replied by letter to Ruth Jervis, although the response they gave was not satisfactory, according to Ruth, who wrote again with passion and deep-seated anger. Not only was she furious at the refusal to bring her son home but she was livid that she had read in the newspaper that she could not erect a cross for her son and that a military headstone would be placed over him. Furthermore, any inscription she might leave would be limited to three lines. 'What next?' she asked bitterly. 'May I ask how long we may remain at the graveside when we get there?'

I wonder you have the decency to refer to him as being my son at all since you consider you have the right to withhold his remains from me. Militarism has destroyed his body and it seems to me if some people in this country had the power they would deal with his soul also, but thank heaven that at least is beyond you. If we mothers of England marched on Downing Street in thousands, like the munition workers and suffragettes, then we might receive some justice . . .

I think we've come to a pretty state of things when a mother has to beg for the remains of her own boy. I want my boy home and I shall be satisfied with nothing less, and who has the right to deny me more under heaven?

Placed next to this letter in an IWGC file is an internal memo: 'I don't think it is any use attempting an answer to Mrs Jervis's

last letter – it will only irate her further.' No further correspondence from Ruth Jervis, if it was ever received, survives.

Ruth Jervis's impassioned letter survives as an example of the
powerful emotional demands that could be made on the
Commission to return soldiers' remains to Britain. Other surviving letters were less emotional but instead carefully noted apparent
loopholes in the authorities' case. The Commission's assertion, for
example, that 'the dead themselves . . . would have preferred to
lie with their comrades', was challenged, though not head-on, by
William Dawson, father of the erstwhile Commanding Officer of
the 6th Royal West Kent Regiment, Colonel Bob Dawson.

His son had specifically asked that his body be returned to
Britain in the event of his death. This request was probably made
when the colonel's parents had been permitted to visit their son
while he was lying critically wounded in a French hospital. The
father respectfully asked, therefore, by what authority could the
right vested in him, not only as a parent 'but by law as the Legal
Personal Representative of my deceased son', be superseded?

The Commission turned to government lawyers for advice and
was told that the body was not the 'legal property' of his father
and therefore he could not claim any rights. As to his appeal that
his son specifically requested burial in Britain, the Commission
merely restated its known position on repatriation.

If William Dawson was rebuffed on this occasion, he returned
to the issue shortly after the Versailles Peace Treaty was signed
and the text of the Treaty released. He noted that Section II of
Article 225 (3rd Paragraph) stipulated that all countries party to
the peace agreement would offer 'every facility for giving effect to
requests that the bodies of their soldiers and sailors may be transferred to their own country'. Therefore, he asked, 'Will you please
inform me why this clause of a Solemn Treaty is repudiated "until
further notice"?' The Commission's reply is not recorded.

To be fair, the majority, possibly the vast majority, of civilians
accepted and even preferred (as was the case with Sir Harry Lauder)

that their loved ones' remains stayed where they were, an impression often confirmed by families on post-war battlefield visits. 'The well-kept cemetery with its neat flower beds was all that we could have desired for a last resting-place for him,' wrote one family member visiting the Somme. Commission files contain letters in which families who had at first asked for exhumation later appeared mollified by the Commission's stated endeavours and ideals. Henry Cook, a widower who lost his two sons within three months of each other in 1917, was one of those who confirmed that, while he would prefer his boys to be buried together in his parish cemetery in Guildford, it was also entirely fitting that all 'brave lads' who fell together should remain together.

Although the issue of exhumations appeared to have been dealt with, the matter would not simply fade away. 'I am afraid,' wrote William Dawson slightly menacingly, 'there is going to be great and grave trouble over this question unless your Commission, instead of thwarting, endeavour to assist me to carry out my son's expressed wish. And there must be hundreds of similar cases.' Later there would be a more considered and organised demand for the repatriation of bodies and Dawson's prediction that there would be 'grave trouble' turned out to be prophetic.

Manchester businessman Harry Wakeman was one of those 'hundreds'. He enquired twice whether his nineteen-year-old son Malcolm could be returned to his home. Malcolm had died of his wounds three weeks before the Armistice, after he was shot in the head while in aerial combat above the trenches in France. After the second request for repatriation, Harry Wakeman was sent the government's detailed view on the subject and the reasons for its policy: it appears that, unlike William Dawson, he accepted the decision, but it was about the only thing he would accept with such equanimity.

Back in October, both he and his wife, Clara, had been given special leave to visit their dying son in France and they had caught a train from their home town just two hours after receiving the

telegram giving them permission to go. After his return, he wrote
to the Air Ministry requesting payment for the two train tickets
he had purchased. Payment, though, was not as simple as he
expected. It was the first of several run-ins he had with officialdom
over the next few months that suggested more was going on in
Harry Wakeman's head than simply getting facts correct and
finances straight.

The Air Ministry had not rejected his claim for reimbursement
but there were qualifications. On 30 December 1918 the Ministry
detailed its position.

Sir, with reference to your letter of the 16th instant, I am directed
to point out that the telegram sent to you on the 5th October
stated, as is usual in such cases, that if you were unable to bear the
expenses of your journey to France, the telegram should be taken
to the police station. The police would then have issued to you
two free warrants (3rd class only). If, however, you can state that it
was lack of time that prevented you from applying for warrants,
and that you are not in a financial position to bear the expense, a
refund of your fare and Mrs Wakeman's will at once be made.

Assistant Financial Secretary [AFS].

The problem was that Harry Wakeman was not poor, not as
some people in that society were poor. He had a small business
that had not fared well during the war years, with a turnover
roughly half of that during peacetime. Nevertheless, bearing the
cost of the journey, nearly £9 excluding other ancillary expenses,
was not easy. The real question was why he should pay at all. He
pointed out the speed at which he and his wife had left Manchester,
that he lived several miles from a police station and that he had
only travelled third class when, as the father of an officer, he
believed he was entitled to first class travel. 'I am surprised at the
Air Ministry trying to treat anyone in such a shabby and what I
may say rather brutal manner,' he wrote indignantly. 'I should

like to state that I am not one of those fortunate individuals who are highly paid for doing a little work in many of the Government offices.'

A week later the AFS replied.

I am directed to explain that this department is only empowered to make refunds of fares from public funds in such cases if the relatives are not in a position themselves to bear the cost . . . It is regretted, therefore, that under the rules by which the Air Ministry is bound, it is necessary before payment can be made to obtain from you, if you will be so good, an explicit statement that your financial circumstances are such that you cannot afford to pay the sum of £8 12s. 8d. which you claim.

The incident gives a fascinating insight into the time. When paperwork was king and rules hidebound, there was simply not the flexibility in the system to take into account anything that stepped outside restrictive guidelines, no one higher up the administrative chain who could simply sign off this particular case. Given that Harry Wakeman had lost his son only weeks before, and in the service of his country, one can understand how irritated he would be with so much bureaucracy. Yet he was just one of millions of families all making claims on the public purse for various reasons and 'flexibility' could throw a system of vast administration into chaos. The right box had to be ticked for a refund and the implied heavy hint was there to make the statement that he was too poor to bear the financial burden.

After threatening to write to his MP and to contact the press, Harry Wakeman reluctantly agreed to tick the box. 'In answer to your letter of 11th January I suppose I may reply in the affirmative,' he wrote rather awkwardly. Within five days he received a reply that the money would be paid immediately. Interestingly, even before he received the settlement, Harry Wakeman had sent several pounds in donations to the nurses and doctors of the hospital for gifts in recognition of the care they had given to his son.

Wakeman's appreciation of the vagaries of war was very evident. He accepted that his son's body would not be returned and, when he received his son's personal possessions from Cox and Co.'s Shipping Agency, he did not even get irate that they had been badly damaged in transit. 'The goods were received in bad condition but for this I do not attribute any blame to you – the clothing had no doubt been in a sack for nearly two months and it seems a shame that what had once been a beautiful uniform should have been put into a sack along with boots and other things . . . the sack contents had been subjected to great pressure,' he wrote, noting that his son's suitcase had been 'crushed flat almost like a book'.

This was not a problem. However, when the packages arrived they had been subject to a 1s. 10d. surcharge. Delivery of officers' effects was supposed to be free and Harry Wakeman went to considerable trouble to be recompensed; he had given his son to the country's cause, he could accept that, but not for a moment was he about to let his family be short-changed by a penny-pinching and ungrateful government. In February 1919, he pursued successfully 10s. taken erroneously in income tax from his son's salary before he finally collected all the material relating to his dead son and closed the file for good.

9

A Nation as One?

'There's a cottage home
In England
Where his mother sits and
Weeps'

652025 Rifleman Peter Redmond
21st Battalion London Regiment
Killed in action 3 May 1917, aged twenty-four
Buried Bedford House Cemetery, Ypres

After the conclusion of the Versailles Peace Treaty in June 1919, the British government's attention turned to the idea of a Victory Parade. As well as a traditional march past, the Prime Minister, Lloyd George, decided that the day of celebration required a focal point upon which all those who came to watch, or who took part in the parade, could direct their attention. It made sense, therefore, to turn to the foremost architect of the day, fifty-two-year-old Sir Edwin Lutyens, widely admired for his skill in bringing together traditional architectural styles with the fashions and sentiments of the new era.

In early July, Lutyens was invited to Downing Street, where Lloyd George proposed the creation of a point of homage, a memorial, 'to stand as a symbol of remembrance worthy of the reverent salute of an Empire mourning for its million dead'. This memorial had to be ready in just two weeks, the architect was told, an extraordinary deadline given its strategic importance to the parade. Fortunately, Lutyens had already been sketching out ideas after a meeting he had had with the Commissioner of the Board of Works charged with building monuments to commemorate the war dead. Lutyens was able to deliver more than just the genesis of an idea: he brought a design to the Prime Minister that afternoon. His plan was to construct a monument he would call the Cenotaph, from the Greek words *kenos* and *taphos*, meaning 'empty' and 'tomb'.

As the Cenotaph was to be a temporary structure, a key prop for the day's events, wood could be used in its construction, dressed up to look like stone. However, on the day, the Cenotaph more than fulfilled its transitory purpose, indeed it was widely considered the outstanding feature of the parade. Suddenly the wooden edifice assumed a national significance that went far beyond both Lutyens' and Lloyd George's expectations. It was no surprise, then, that in the days following the Victory Parade letters began appearing in the national newspapers pressing the government to make the Cenotaph a permanent memorial.

'Sir,' wrote one reader to *The Times*,

> The Cenotaph in Whitehall is so simple and dignified that it would be a pity to consider it merely an ephemeral erection. It appears to be of a more lasting material than the other decorative efforts, and I suggest that it should be retained either in its present form or rendered in granite or stone . . .

The number of wreaths and bouquets placed by civilians on the steps of the Cenotaph continued to grow, as did the public clamour for a lasting memorial. Backbench MPs, never shy of climbing on board a popular bandwagon, at first asked questions, then called for a positive decision. It came. Less than two weeks after the Victory Parade, the Cabinet met. The discussions were upbeat: Lutyens' Cenotaph was to be made permanent.

*   *   *

On 11 November 1920, the Cenotaph was finally shorn of the ugly scaffolding and tarpaulins that had enveloped the new stone structure for months since the removal of the wooden memorial to the Crystal Palace. The new Cenotaph, described by a journalist later that day as 'grave, severe, and beautiful', was, in its concept, a tomb into which could be poured all the thoughts and emotions of every mourner. In its serenity and simplicity, it belonged to everyone and at the same time to no one: no grandiose design, no intricate carving or sculpture, nothing that might alienate anyone who stood there to be humbled by its majesty. Although devoid of any religious trappings, so as not to distress soldiers of other faiths, the Cenotaph had for a Christian nation a symbolism that spoke to many of the cave where Jesus' body had once lain but which, after the resurrection, had been found empty. With the decision to leave the remains of all those who had died where they lay overseas, the Cenotaph was carefully representative of the nation's acceptance that there would be no bodies to bury at home and, by its design, held out the implied suggestion of a life after death.

Shortly before the unveiling at eleven o'clock that morning, the vast crowds fell eerily silent. An eight-year-old boy, Donald Overall, was there. He stood side by side with his mother and younger brother, Cyril.

We got there very early and got quite close to the Cenotaph. Almost opposite it, and there we saw all the proceedings. There was the normal hubbub but when the service started even the wind made a noise, even the wind in the trees made a noise, I remember that, as King George V stepped forward.

Nobody dared move; nobody wanted to move. There was a small service and he pulled the string [he actually pressed a button] and the Union Jack flags that had draped the memorial dropped. And there was the Cenotaph resplendent, far better than it is today because it was brand new, spotlessly clean. My mother stood there with her arms round us two kids and she cried and I just stood there dumbfounded.

That morning we saw the unknown warrior come through on his gun carriage – we saw that, and the escort. Then later on we went to St Bride's church on Fleet Street where Dad's regiment, the London Rifle Brigade, held a service. The congregation consisted of ex-servicemen, widows and orphans, fathers and mothers. The organ was playing with the regimental band in accompaniment and the one hymn they played was 'Oh Valiant Hearts', and my mother was in tears once more. I can't forget that day. I was feeling for my mum and I'd never had to confront those feelings before.

After the service at the Cenotaph, the nation's attention turned to Westminster Abbey and the interment of the Unknown Warrior. The soldier, whoever he was, had been chosen under the cloak of the greatest secrecy, chosen in such a way that no one could ever put a name to the individual who had died in the service of his country. He would now be representative of all those who had left Britain's shores, never to return.

Originally, four bodies had been disinterred, each grave chosen at random, one from each of the four principal areas in which the British Army had been engaged: the battlefields of the Aisne, the Somme, of Ypres and Arras. The one consistent and distinctive feature was that the graves from which the bodies were taken had all been marked by a cross and the words 'Unknown British Soldier'.

Once the four bodies were brought together, one was chosen at midnight on the night of 7/8 November, again in total secrecy. That body was then transferred to a pine coffin and the other three removed for reburial. Three days later, after a voyage of great brooding pageant, the soldier arrived in London. By this time the pine coffin had been placed unopened inside a heavy casket made of English oak and sealed. On top, in the shape of a sixteenth-century shield, was an iron plate and the inscription: 'A British Warrior who fell in the Great War 1914–18 for King and Country.'

It was this casket that was now carried upon a gun carriage, and as the funeral cortège wended its slow way through the streets of London, it was followed on foot by the King. At the Abbey, the soldier was reinterred after a short service, and his grave filled with sixteen barrels of French soil. For the vast crowds that filled the pavements, and for those widows and bereaved mothers fortunate enough to be given tickets inside the Abbey, the ceremony had been full of emotion.

And then the public paid their respects. The queue was enormous, four deep, stretching from the North Door of the Abbey to the Cenotaph itself and, from the time the door opened shortly before one o'clock that afternoon, a ceaseless stream of people passed the grave at a rate estimated at seventy per minute. A programme of music was played on the organ throughout the whole of the pilgrimage, the Abbey organist, Mr Nicholson, having the help of four others, each of whom took his turn.

The vast numbers accentuated the impression that, if in nothing else, the country was at that moment united in honouring the fallen. Everyone understood the messages conveyed by the Cenotaph and the Unknown Warrior even if the public nature of the commemorations was not to the taste of everyone.

The need for people to pay tribute, if only for seconds, put a heavy strain on the day's organisation which, despite the pathos of the occasion, was noted, not uncritically, by one *Times* correspondent and printed the next day.

The Great Pilgrimage was transformed into a great test of endurance. Packed together in a dense mass extending half way across the broad thoroughfare, they were left standing there without movement for an hour and a half, and when a move was at length made, the scene at times bore more resemblance to a football scrummage than to a procession of mourners honouring the fallen. To many, after long railway journeys, upset by the sorrows of the day, and hours of waiting in the queues, the strain was too severe.

It was a real test of endurance, and many hundreds gave it up, while of those who refused to give in a large proportion passed the Cenotaph, and, having reverently laid their flowers on the growing pile which obscured its base, fell out, physically unable to face the strain of a further probable long wait in the queue leading to the Abbey. One white-haired old woman who joined the queue in Northumberland Avenue at noon did not reach the Cenotaph until half-past five.

The queues continued long into the night and all the following day. 'Women,' wrote one observer,

formed the nucleus of every queue, and of the women most were in black. They seemed to feel that it was at last possible to give some expression to the feelings that they were compelled to subdue while the war continued. Many of them carried wreaths, and there were few who had not brought some simple token to place by the Cenotaph.

The nation's wreaths lay side by side, irrespective of their donors. One bore the inscription 'From the Commander-in-chief, Atlantic Fleet, Flag Captain, Officers and Ship's Company. H.M.S. *Queen Elizabeth.*' Next to it lay a tiny bunch of lilies with a card attached: 'In loving memory of Tom, From Dad and Mum.'

At Westminster Abbey, an estimated 1,250,000 people were to file past the Unknown Warrior in the week before the grave was sealed. The importance of this unknown man was more than symbolic; it was enormously cathartic for those hundreds of thousands of people who had never found their missing relatives. The soldier brought back from France, whoever he was, became the son, brother, husband of everyone, not just collectively but individually, too, and that was what was so significant. Yes, it was remarkable that this ordinary man should be buried among the greatest in the land. It was an exceptional honour for a society that had been so steeped in hierarchy and status and was only now beginning to change, but these were footnotes to the story. The real significance lay in the opportunity for every individual to identify directly with the soldier lying in Westminster Abbey; that proved compelling. A steel helmet, web belt and bayonet being laid on the coffin drew attention to the fact that here was an ordinary man, as the war reporter Philip Gibbs pointed out in an article for the *Daily Chronicle* on 12 November.

> It was the steel helmet – the old tin hat – lying there on the crimson of the flag, which revealed him instantly, not as a mythical warrior, aloof from common humanity, a shadowy type of national pride and martial glory, but as one of those fellows dressed in the drab of khaki, stained by mud and grease, who went into the dirty ditches with this steel hat on his head.

One man, known to posterity only as Mr Chandler, stood outside the Abbey and in the aftermath of the ceremonies, picked up a rose that had fallen from one of the many wreaths. At home he bought or made a small wooden box into which he placed the rose, along with a note for his nephew. It read:

> In loving memory of your dear dad who arrived at Dover Nov. 10th 1920 in the destroyer *Verdun*. Buried in Westminster Abbey Nov. 11th 1920. The Unknown Warrior. The enclosed is a part of a rose which fell from a large wreath given by the British Army. I hope you will keep it and in years to come, you will be able to show it, in remembrance of your dad.

Another person whose identity remains unknown wrote at length in the style of a monologue with her dead husband. Her words were published in a small book, thirty-five pages in length, and with an extremely limited circulation. She had attended the ceremonies with her parents-in-law and her subsequent feelings typified the emotions of a great many grieving relatives. They are quoted here at length.

To My Unknown Warrior

The Evening of November 11 1920

Boy dear, I am so happy I have found you at last. I am sure the authorities did all they could, but oh, I am so thankful that the long and bitter disappointment of opening official envelopes is ended. I am so thankful that I shall never again have to read those cruel words, 'Regret – No Trace' . . .

I have found you at last. Today I stood by your grave. It seemed such a little grave for your great heart. The King and all the mighty of the land were about us, but it was my arms you felt around you as you sank to sleep. When the bugles blew the Reveille, I almost cried 'Hush!' for I had just heard your drowsy sigh of content. Sleep well; it has been such a long and tiring day. You will be rested when morning breaks.

Your father was the proudest man in all Britain today. His eyes were sparkling gems, almost too vividly bright in his statuesque face as he stood like a Guardsman on parade. I wonder how many times he changed his clothes before starting for the Abbey. It took the unified efforts of the whole family to get him ready in time this morning, though he was up before daylight. Can't you hear him? – 'It's a most extraordinary thing, my dear, that people in this house won't leave things in their proper places. I remember most distinctly that last night I put my . . .' And your mother, as ever, understanding everything, finding, arranging everything for him. 'We must take care not to be late, my dear. This is a great day, we must be off in good time.' . . .

I never understood what 'Death swallowed up in victory" meant until I watched your father by your grave. The honour, glory, splendour of your funeral made all memories golden for him, and, for the time at any rate, took all the sting from death. He had been so ambitious for you. He had sacrificed so much for you. You realized for him today the best of all his dreams – and so much more. For even he had never pictured you lying among the greatest of his people's heroes, beside Royal bones, taking your own proud place in his country's history, yourself history too. 'Buried in Westminster Abbey – my son John.' The words throbbed through him ceaselessly deafening him to all sound of the service . . .

Your mother? How can I hope to tell you of her thoughts in the Abbey? You know the twisted smile on her lips when she is greatly moved, the little bubbling laugh with which she smothers emotion. Your mother was very silent this evening. Her lips were still pursed though the smile had gone – the smile that puzzles those who do not know her and draws tears from those who do. Does anyone really know what any mother thinks on such a day as this? If I had been the mother of your son, boy dear, then perhaps.

Once I was taken right behind the scenes of your mother's mind and heart. It was on last Good Friday. After church I found her crying quietly. 'It is strange,' she said in that matter-of-fact way of hers, 'how sometimes, without warning, something quite unexpected gets past one's guard and cuts through all one's defences . . .'

Of myself I do not write, boy dear. You know without my telling you I was always proud of you and I am prouder than ever today. But as always, still a little jealous for you too. I hate to share you with anyone, even the greatest in the land. I cannot yield my place as mourner even to the King. I loved the crowds for the homage they paid you, but you are mine and mine alone.

Tonight when it is very dark, when all the statues are asleep and the Abbey silent as the grave, I shall steal through the portal of the mansion of the Dead, past the rows of famous warriors, and I will whisper to you words that no one else shall ever hear.

And kiss you good-night.

*   *   *

The proliferation of communal war memorials in every village, town and city, as well as the thousands of private memorials in churches, parks and buildings, underlined the need for people to commemorate their loved ones when all traditional rituals of burial and commemoration were denied. Up and down the country, the desire to design a fitting memorial for the war dead took up countless hours of discussion, debate and, no doubt, much heated argument; emotions could not help but run high on occasion.

Everyone had an opinion, some decidedly more coherent than others, some frankly bizarre. Indicative of how personal those views could be are the contents of the following letter, one of several that survive in the archives of the Commonwealth War Graves Commission. This particular letter was written by a bereaved mother in response to a public announcement made by the IWGC for suggestions as to how a memorial to the missing might look. Although this letter refers to a proposed British memorial in France, the sentiments give some impression of how very specific personal views sometimes were and how easy it might be to come to verbal blows when final designs were being chosen by a committee.

The monument should be in granite or marble of a soldier lying dead, with a half circle of angels standing around him with bent heads – and the text beneath 'He shall give his angels charge over thee' – Ps XCI. 11. I might tell you that I had a vision of my son, the late Captain N. D. R. Hunter, climbing a hill with determined face, with a half circle of five angels behind him; and he met his death, when climbing an embankment to locate the enemy's machine gun, which was enfilading his men . . . his body could not be recovered.

Should the suggestion be adopted I would ask that the monument might be erected in the cemetery nearest Bapaume, where my son fell.

Yours truly

Lena Hunter

Granite or marble: both expensive choices but, then, what did cost matter when it came to honouring those who had given their all? But money did matter, and not least to the recently demobbed soldiers, sailors and airmen. The memorials would cost countless millions of pounds sterling, just at a time when the economy was sinking into depression. Some servicemen felt that the public's demand to commemorate the dead was at the expense of the survivors who were being left without support of any kind. Frederick Young, a former serviceman and active member of the Comrades of the Great War, was frustrated that he was meeting, on a daily basis, former 'non-commissioned officers and men, who, having lost all they possessed, are at their wits' end to find employment, and in many cases are actually in want of food'. The voice of the 'Comrades' was different from the left-leaning former veterans organisations, groups that eschewed officer members for example. The Comrades of the Great War were, by contrast, a conservative organisation and loyalist and therefore criticism of the government was more studied.

The problem was that public consultation over war memorials, even commemoration as a whole, could all too easily be nullified by normally well-intentioned civilian dignitaries and town councillors, who habitually assumed they knew best. With little or no invited input from ex-servicemen, decisions were taken to spend money to commemorate the dead in a way that was directly or indirectly to the financial detriment of the men who had fought and survived. If questioning the design of a memorial was frowned upon, then what would be the reaction should someone wish to query its actual merit? 'Anything in the form of a cross is so sacred that comment and criticism can only be made in whispers,' wrote Young in August 1919,

> but people appear to forget that, whilst all honour is due to the fallen, yet a vast number of the survivors have run the same risk, and are equally entitled to their gratitude. Indeed, what is wanted is not

so much a monument to the dead, who are at rest in the hands of the
Almighty, as a memorial to the living . . . Surely if a war memorial
is required, the first to be considered should be those who have
taken part in the war and brought it to a successful issue.

Even former officers bemoaned their loss of voice. 'The do-good-
ers captured the Armistice,' wrote Charles Carrington, a former
officer in the Royal Warwickshire Regiment. For some years, he
and his former comrades met at the Café Royal in London for 'no
end of a party', on Armistice Day in celebration of their fallen
comrades but as time passed they found that their parties were out
of tune with public sentiments and they ended. 'To march to the
Cenotaph was too much like attending one's own funeral, and I
know many old soldiers who found it increasingly discomforting,
year by year. We preferred our reunions in private.'

The schism between civilians in public office and former servicemen was nowhere better illustrated than in the Scottish town
of Newport-on-Tay and the proposed commemoration to the
district's eighty-four lost sons.

The design of Newport-on-Tay's war memorial had been
entrusted to the famous Edinburgh architect Sir Robert Lorimer,
responsible for the Scottish National War Memorial at Edinburgh
Castle. His drawing consisted of a granite pillar surmounted by a
cross set upon a base, on three sides of which the names of the fallen
would be commemorated on bronze panels. The concept was not in
dispute but one of the names to be included was. Peter Black, a
private in the 1/4th Black Watch, had been executed for desertion
in September 1916 while attached to the 1/7th Black Watch.

According to Sir Robert, a number of bereaved parents were
refusing to submit their sons' names for commemoration if that of
Peter Black was also included on the memorial. In a letter to the
Works Department of the Imperial War Graves Commission, Sir
Robert outlined the position, noting that the local proposal had
been to omit the name as being 'unsuitable for a Roll of Honour'.

There had been vociferous objection to this, not from the executed man's family but from ex-servicemen who were insisting his name was included 'otherwise,' wrote Sir Robert,

> they say they will wreck the memorial . . . So there you are, a fine kettle of fish you will agree! I of course am strongly of the opinion that the man's name should not go on. If you could give me a ruling on the subject it would be extremely useful and might enable the committee to shut the mouths of the ex-servicemen.

Colonel Durham, replying on behalf of the IWGC, could give no such ruling as it had no jurisdiction over the erection of local war memorials, nor could they suggest a resolution based on previous cases as none had arisen, 'fortunately'. He could only suggest that, as the memorial was being paid for out of public subscriptions, the ex-servicemen could not insist that the executed man's name be placed on one of the bronze plaques, and if they carried out their threat to demolish the memorial, the matter would be one for the police. It was hardly a satisfactory answer but there was little else Colonel Durham could suggest.

Sir Robert Lorimer's robust views on the controversy were very evident and also wholly misleading. He was entirely incorrect in his assessment of the strife in Newport-on-Tay, for it transpired that the dispute was not really a case of civilians at loggerheads with ex-servicemen at all. A panel of the town's civil dignitaries, acting as the Newport War Memorial Committee, had met and made the decision to omit Private Black's name without consultation with anyone else.

The threat against the memorial was no idle one. Two men had stolen gelignite from a local quarry and they let it be known that unless their demands were met they would have the 'whole lot', meaning the monument, in the River Tay. These two men were later identified as John Spark and John Squibb. Both men had played with Peter Black as children, and Spark and Black, both pre-war Territorials, had.pledged to serve overseas on the outbreak of war. They had been given the regimental numbers of 2123 and 2120 respectively, indicating that they had probably enlisted together.

In late February 1915 both lads embarked for France with the 1/4th Black Watch, Spark being badly wounded in May and later transferring to the Royal Flying Corps. John Spark later claimed that Black had had a history of going absent even during training days (according to Black's Service Records on no fewer than twelve occasions) and that he had been mentally ill. Whatever his actual medical condition and his later behaviour, local opinion was far from being hostile to Peter Black, in fact the general view was overwhelmingly in favour of including Black's name. One lady was reported in the local press as requesting that if his name was omitted then they may as well leave her laddie's off, too.

Everyone knew that the missing gelignite was highly volatile and had to be kept in a cool place, but no one knew where it had been hidden. In fact John Spark, the son of a retired local police sergeant, James Spark, had secreted it in the last place anyone would think of looking. He had taken the gelignite, wrapped it in oilcloth and strapped it under the U-bend of his parents' toilet in Newport.

Given the delicate circumstances, a community meeting was called to resolve the issue at the town's Blyth Hall in May 1922. So controversial had the case become that the hall was packed out with three hundred local people, including three men who had served with Private Black. The local vicar, Reverend Frame, presided over the meeting while a journalist from the local paper, the *People's Journal*, reported the discussions.

The local ex-servicemen had expressed determination to oppose the decision [of the Memorial Committee], but efforts which had been made to reach an amicable settlement had failed. The meeting unanimously resolved that the name should be inscribed on the memorial . . .

Captain James L. Cumming, Chairman of the Dundee Area Council of the British Legion, said that they deplored that there had been any necessity for a public meeting of protest over such a question. The man had voluntarily joined the colours when sixteen years of age and had served for over two years in France.

Mr C. N. Craig, Dundee [2224, 1/4th Black Watch], one of the men who had served with the young man in France, said looking over the list of names of the gentlemen who composed the War Memorial Committee, there was not a single one of them competent to judge in this matter (Applause) . . . If the memorial tablets were already made, they should be scrapped and the lad's name added (Loud applause).

Craig's assertion that none of the Committee was 'competent' was based on the fact that not one of those making the decisions had served abroad during the war. It was not noted at the time, that Black, despite his very poor disciplinary record, had at least fought at the battles of Neuve Chapelle, Aubers Ridge, Loos and the Somme. In the end the meeting agreed that a committee of Newport citizens be appointed to act with the former servicemen and approach the Memorial Committee to insist that Black's name be added or that the Committee should resign. The Committee resigned.

In September that year, the memorial was unveiled bearing the names of all the local men who fell, including that of Private Peter Black. During the dedication, four local men stood in uniform at each corner of the memorial, in the traditional stance of respect: rifles upturned, hands crossed over the rifle butt, heads bowed. One of the four was John Spark, who had long since quietly – and carefully – returned the gelignite from the toilet U-bend to the quarry. Neither he nor John Squibb faced any sanction for the theft.

The case concerning Newport-on-Tay's war memorial may have been unique as far as the IWGC was concerned, but the issue of whether the names of executed men should or should not be included on memorials was not. Such were the disagreements in the village of Fulstow in Lincolnshire over whether an executed son of their village should appear on the memorial that none was constructed in remembrance of the ten local men who died. It was a situation not rectified until ninety years later, when a plaque, with all the names, was finally unveiled on the wall of the village hall. Nevertheless, the shame that attached itself to the families of those executed for cowardice or desertion was very real and had long-term effects on surviving relations.

For all their symbolic brilliance, the Cenotaph and tomb of the Unknown Warrior could not assuage everyone's feelings of loss. The refusal to return bodies of fallen soldiers to Britain had caused deep pain to many families, some of whom, rightly or wrongly, became fixated with the issue.

In 1919 a group of parents got together to form the British War Graves Association, led by its Honorary Secretary and Treasurer, Sarah Ann Smith. Her son, Frederick Smith, serving with the 2/4th York and Lancashire Regiment, had died of gunshot wounds at the end of September 1918. He had been buried in Grevillers Cemetery on the Somme and Mrs Smith, like many others, wished to see the return of her son's remains to Britain. After the press had highlighted the decision to refuse exhumation, she helped form a pressure group that even by government estimates had somewhere between 10,000 and 15,000 members.

For the next six years the Association repeatedly requested that senior politicians readdress the issue of exhumation, calling on the help of influential support including its President, the Leeds Central MP and racehorse owner Sir Arthur Willey. He had lost his son Tom, killed serving with the Leeds Pals on the first day of the Battle of the Somme. The Association's most high-profile supporter was Lady Maud Selborne, who agreed to be a patron. She was the eldest daughter of the three-times Prime Minister Robert Cecil, Marquess of Salisbury, and wife of the 2nd Earl of

Selborne and former First Lord of the Admiralty who had also served in Asquith's government during the Great War. Her son, Captain Robert Palmer, had been killed in the Middle East in 1916. Interestingly, neither Sir Arthur's nor Lady Selborne's son had an identifiable grave, yet they still chose to support those families whose loved ones did.

The Association, made up of branches established in the heartlands of the North and north Midlands, did not get off to the best of starts when a petition signed by 1,400 relatives of the fallen was sent to the Imperial War Graves Commission. The IWGC noted the petition but then cast doubt on the authenticity of many of the signatories; a number appeared to be in the same hand. It was a setback and for a year the Association campaigned for a change in policy but received little wider encouragement. Meanwhile, its membership continued to grow, the *Yorkshire Evening News* reporting in June 1920 that there were 2,000 members of the Leeds and District Branch alone.

Having made little headway, the Association held its first mass meeting on the evening of Armistice Day 1920, at which a resolution was passed unanimously that British relatives should have the same rights as those afforded by the United States to its subjects to bring, as the Association put it, 'their dear ones to be buried in Home Countries'. Details of the resolution were forwarded to Queen Mary in the hope that she might be able to exert some pressure over her son, the Prince of Wales, then President of the IWGC. In a letter, the Association appealed for Her Majesty's help:

Many thousands of Mothers and Wives are slowly dying for the want of the Grave of their loved ones to visit and tend themselves, and we feel deeply hurt that the right granted to other countries is denied us.

Queen Mary was urged to give the resolution her 'kind consideration' in the hope that some indirect pressure might be placed upon the Commission. Unfortunately for the Association, the Queen merely asked her Private Secretary to pass on the letter and resolution to the IWGC for consideration at their next meeting. There would be no change in policy.

The Association then petitioned the Coalition Government, but to little avail. In one note dated January 1922, the Secretary of State for War, Worthington-Evans, wrote that he was 'not interested in this Association or in the writer [Mrs Smith]' while a note attached to the Secretary's views asked his Principal Assistant Secretary (PAS): 'Do you think you could draft a letter which will stop Mrs Smith writing any more?' The reply was pessimistic. 'I am quite incapable of writing a letter that would stop any woman from writing any more if she is determined to do so,' the PAS wrote, 'but I attach a draft which may be useful.'

Madam

I am directed by the Imperial War Graves Commission to inform you that your letter of January 10th addressed to His Majesty's Secretary of State for War has been referred to them . . .

The Commission regret to have to inform you that they see no good purpose in further discussion of principles that, in the House of Commons and elsewhere, have long met with general acceptance.

The IWGC's policy was not going to change, especially when large sums of public money were being spent on beautiful cemeteries abroad, as well as great monuments to the missing. A line had been drawn and thereafter the Association's hopes of success ebbed away. On 2 July 1923 its President, Sir Arthur Willey, died after collapsing the previous day. He had been preparing to go to church on the seventh anniversary of the death of his son but had a seizure and never regained consciousness. Even the Association's energetic Secretary Sarah Smith was failing. 'I find the work of the Association almost too much,' she wrote to Lady Selborne in June

1924, 'but nobody will take my place and I feel I must carry on.'
Mrs Smith then confided to Lady Selborne: 'It seems we cannot
have our first object [returning the bodies of the fallen] and all we
can do is try and give help and comfort and band ourselves
together', adding, 'Our new President promised a good deal but
he has done nothing yet, and indeed he will not answer our letters,
I don't know why.' Mrs Smith's air of resignation was palpable.

In March that year Sarah Smith had written to the new Prime
Minister, Ramsay MacDonald. As he was the country's first ever
Labour Prime Minister, she may have felt that a little encouragement might be forthcoming, but his reply referred only to the fact
that it would be impossible to remove 800,000 bodies 'scattered
all over the world'. Therein lay the dilemma for a cash-strapped
nation. If exhumation was ever allowed, just how many would
actually request the return of a dead son, husband or father?

To be fair, the Association had never claimed to represent a
majority view in the country and Sarah Smith, when writing to
the Prime Minister, was keen to underline the fact: 'We who
wish for removal are really a minority and it is difficult for a
minority to get justice.' How small or how large a minority it
was in reality was an unfathomable question. How many parents
who would not have campaigned for a change in policy might
have accepted the opportunity to bring back their loved ones to
Britain had an open offer been made? In such circumstances the
only possible comparison is with the United States. Its decision
to allow repatriation eventually saw around half of its total war
dead of 116,000 returned to America, the last being repatriated
in the late 1940s.

The Association did not entirely fold, but letters to the IWGC
concerning repatriation of the dead ceased in 1925. It had failed
in its primary objective to return home the remains of soldiers,
although not without five years of agitation and flashes of considerable guile. Midway through the Association's existence, it
seemed to touch briefly on a subject that the IWGC had feared,

and not without good reason: the spectre of clandestine and wholly illegal private exhumation.

In November 1922 the Association had decided on a direct approach to the Belgian Defence Ministry with a request to exhume the remains of number 41985 Private Arnold Dyson of the Lincolnshire Regiment, buried in Roisin Military Cemetery. The request was made on behalf of the boy's mother, Ada Dyson, and ended with the words 'Perhaps you would also give me some idea of the cost of removal and transport'. The tone of the request made it clear that permission was being taken for granted and that, perhaps, was the point: it was in essence a bluff but with significant ramifications. If the Belgian authorities, signatories to the Peace Treaty's Article 225 (the facility to return the fallen to their own countries), could be persuaded to release the remains of British soldiers without the British government's approval, then a precedent might be set that could prove difficult to reverse.

The Belgians did not fall for the ruse and immediately informed the IWGC of the request, triggering a sternly worded message sent by the IWGC to the Association. 'The Communal Authorities at Roisin have been specially warned in case an effort should be made to exhume and remove the body.'

As far as it is possible to tell, the Association had not actually threatened to exhume the body themselves but was seen to act in an apparently underhand manner. The IWGC had misinterpreted the Association's move. Recent incidents involving families' attempts privately to recover remains from War Graves cemeteries had made the IWGC especially sensitive to any perceived threat, however oblique. The IWGC's understandably blanket refusal to sanction exhumations had driven a few families to take the law into their hands and bodies had gone missing.

It was not until May 1931 that the details of secret exhumations came to public attention. The *Sunday Express* broke the story, but it was already twelve years old. The events had been kept quiet by the IWGC for obvious reasons. Between 1919 and 1922 there had been a small number of attempts to smuggle bodies, not only to Great Britain but to Canada as well; some were successful, others were thwarted.

One of those returned to Britain was Major Norman McLeod Adam of the Royal Field Artillery, son of Major General McLeod Adam. He was killed in August 1918 and buried in an isolated grave near Fontaine-lès-Croisilles, near Arras. It was probably because of its isolation – it had apparently not been brought into an IWGC cemetery – that the major general was able to enlist the help of the local mayor. Under police questioning, the mayor later claimed ignorance of the law forbidding exhumation. The body was successfully removed in June 1922 and taken to Glasgow where it was reburied the following month.

It was also with inadvertent French cooperation that the body of Corporal James Burgess was smuggled back to Britain. Burgess had served on the Western Front for the entire duration of the war and, during the latter part of his service overseas, he met a French woman, Germaine Marie Victorine. In June 1918 Private Burgess was given fourteen days leave to marry and might have settled permanently in the French capital had he not tragically succumbed to influenza in February 1919. He was buried in Levallois-Perret Cemetery in Paris. Just three months later, and for reasons that are now opaque, Germaine Burgess obtained authority from the Prefecture of Police to exhume Corporal Burgess, his body being returned to Britain in secrecy and buried in Englefield Green close to the home of his mother.

Other attempts to exhume bodies were more cloak-and-dagger. Gunner Frank Baron had been killed serving with the artillery in September 1918. Twenty months later, his brother Herbert travelled from Hull with the intention of retrieving Frank's body from Westoutre Military Cemetery in Belgium. He visited the British Consul at Antwerp, claiming he had permission to exhume his sibling, and asked for a letter with details as to the normal procedure for removing a body to Britain. With this information, he hired a hearse and civilian labour and went straight to the cemetery, exhuming his brother and placing him in a coffin. It was only by chance that some passing Belgian gendarmes prevented the body being taken away. Herbert Baron and his assistants were prosecuted and fined.

It is noteworthy that most of those who led the British War Graves Association, as well as those families who took it upon themselves to recover remains, lost relatives in the last year of the war or after the cessation of hostilities. The only logical explanation is that in these cases the raw pain of bereavement had not had time to abate and so clouded judgement. It may also help to explain why the British War Graves Association gradually declined in strength and significance a few years later. Time, the great healer, had begun to mend even the freshest wounds.

There were exhumations after the war – legal ones – but only to bring together isolated graves into larger permanent cemeteries where they could be looked after. There had been emotionally charged and clearly knee-jerk suggestions at the termination of fighting that all bodies should be left where they were. But as the land was to be restored to agriculture, this was hardly practical and would, as the IWGC suggested, 'place the cultivators of the land in a most unfair position'. Applications were therefore made by the British authorities to the French and Belgian governments to exhume those lying in scattered graves and this was accepted. This concentration was to include all smaller cemeteries (fewer than forty graves) and, if necessary, larger cemeteries which were sited in untenable locations. Ruth Jervis's son Harry was exhumed in August 1920 and reburied in Roclincourt Highland Cemetery, close to Arras. Sir Oliver Lodge's son Raymond was also disinterred and, along with the remains of eighteen other soldiers, taken to Birr Cross Road Cemetery to the north-east of the village of Zillebeke. This cemetery had been started in August 1917 during that summer's offensive and originally included those who had succumbed to their wounds at the neighbouring Dressing

Station. It was enlarged by post-war additions so that, in the end, 833 men were buried there, of whom just under 500 were identified. As a matter of course, relatives were reassured that the work had been carried out with the utmost reverence after which 'the appropriate religious service' was held, usually in the presence of a military chaplain.

The desire by some families to leave bodies where they had fallen had been largely in vain: largely, but not entirely. A very few people had been able to purchase the land on which their son or husband had died and by doing so could rightfully argue that the remains would not disturb agriculture and therefore they, too, should stay undisturbed. The parents of Captain Pulteney Malcolm, killed in August 1918, had first fought to bring the body of their son home but, when this failed, they fought every attempt to have him disinterred and moved to a cemetery. His body lay with twelve others where they had been buried by the Germans, and the landowner, in sympathy with the Malcolm family, agreed that the soldiers could remain where they were. Eventually the IWGC abandoned its current proposal in order to use a site which could encompass the thirteen dead, building the walls of the cemetery in such a way as to include the existing graves, bringing a further 150 bodies into the site. A memorial to Captain Malcolm stands today just outside the boundary wall.

The mother of Captain Francis Dodgson, killed in July 1916, was equally adamant that her son should not be moved. She had told the IWGC that she hoped to purchase the land where her son lay but when she visited France she was shocked to discover his grave had already been relocated to a cemetery. Without hesitating, she left for Amiens where she found a granite post, war rubble from the town of Albert. One side of the round post was flattened by a local stonemason and inscribed to the memory of her son. She returned and placed it where his grave had been. The post survives, although it has been moved a short distance after the field on which it stood was sold.

This desire to erect memorials to the memory of sons was almost always secondary to the wish to preserve, through acquisition, the land on which sons and husbands died. Sometimes the purchase was about the preservation of a specific grave; sometimes it was to keep the ground, as they would see it, as sacrosanct. Lieutenant Keith Rae, killed at Hooge in July 1915, had never been found and his father, Edward Rae, bought the land where Keith died, just as Major General Walter Braithwaite did for his son Valentine, who had disappeared at the head of his troops on the Somme. The memorials, and the land upon which they stood, could be purchased only by those with the wherewithal to do so; in Braithwaite's case over 1,000 square metres of land where he believed his son fell.

One further case concerns the body of Lieutenant Henry Isaacs of the 7th Suffolk Regiment, killed at Arras in April 1917. His father had made exhaustive efforts to discover the whereabouts of his son's grave that had at one time been identified but lost in later fighting. Failing to find his son, he bought three-quarters of an acre of land where Henry had fallen and built a large and ornate calvary on the site. Neither he nor his wife wished to be parted from their son and in an extraordinary act of devotion they bought a house, 11 rue de Beaufort, in Arras, moving to France so as to be able to visit their son as often as they wished. They remained there until the Second World War when they were forced to return home; Mr Isaacs died in 1942, his wife twelve years later.

By and large, congregating bodies into larger military cemeteries helped facilitate visits by families who wished to travel abroad. Most visitors to the battlefields of France and Flanders would have been very anxious to be regarded as battlefield pilgrims rather than as tourists, although the notion of visiting a battlefield out of interest, as tourism, was nothing new. There had been a steady procession of visitors to the site of Wellington's victory at Waterloo for decades. Even during the Great War, a number of serving soldiers such as Second Lieutenant John Gamble predicted in their letters home that there would be a post-war influx of 'sightseers' and 'tourists', and this was long before the great attritional battles of the Somme, Arras and Passchendaele seared these place names on to the British consciousness.

Incredibly, there had been a small number of enquiries from inquisitive tourists to visit France even as the battles raged. In March 1915, *The Times* ran a short article entitled 'Trips To Battlefields. No "Conducted Tours" Till The War Is Over'. Thomas Cook, it turned out, along with two other travel agencies, felt it worthwhile and indeed necessary to announce that they had not the 'slightest intention' of running tours while the fighting was still in progress.

After the war, all this changed. From the earliest days, an increasing number of people crossed the Channel to visit the hallowed ground around Ypres and on the Somme. Accommodation was then at a premium. In 1919 the YMCA, for example, had a seventeen-bed hostel near Ypres providing bed and breakfast, but it was fairly primitive and there was little available for another year or more. As for travel, the roads were still very difficult by car and the chance of regular punctures appreciably high. Even so, advertisements began to appear daily in the press. In June 1920, Thomas Cook offered tours on the Western Front starting at £8 11s., and the South Eastern and Chatham Railway Company a two-night stay with travel and food included from an impressive £15 15s., prices well out of the reach of poorer families.

Offering tours did not necessarily denote that the takers were tourists: far from it. Tens of thousands of people who took the opportunity to visit the Western Front in the 1920s were those who had lost relatives. Whether they crossed the Channel with a more commercial firm or with charitable organisations such as the Church Army, Ypres League, or Salvation Army, their trip was to visit what was in their eyes holy ground. This was their opportunity to see where loved ones had fought and to pay homage to those who had fallen. It was reported that one elderly gentleman, a father, insisted on walking several miles to a cemetery near Ypres not only to visit the grave of his son but because 'he would never pass that way again and he wanted to feel that he had traversed the same road that his son had traversed on his last journey on earth'.

Those early trips were not for the faint-hearted and it is hard to imagine that these first pilgrims understood what they were going to see. Ethel Healey had been keen to travel as soon as she knew where her husband Albert had been buried and saved hard for the trip. He had been killed in late March 1918 and his belongings, including bloodstained photographs, returned to her by the Germans through the Red Cross. Ethel's sister Bertha was married to a former officer and wounded veteran of the Western Front, Samuel Braggins. After the war he began working for the IWGC and he specifically warned her against going because of the sights she would encounter. It was better to wait a while and then she could take her young daughter Joan, too.

Sir Edward Poulton was not one to be put off. In December 1918 he was among the very first visitors to the battlefield to visit his son Ronald. He knew the location of the cemetery near Armentières and he also knew that the fighting earlier that year had ebbed and flowed over the area and that his son's grave might now be destroyed. Five days before Christmas he arrived at the spot.

> The Cemetery, which had been fought over, bore many scars of war [with] craters filled with water and trees splintered and broken off. The fence and rustic gateway put up had disappeared. Ronald's grave was uninjured, although there were four shell-holes within a few feet of it; the oak cross was intact save for two scratches from shell splinters.

One of the earlier crosses erected to Ronald's memory was also there and Sir Edward placed it at the foot of his son's grave before leaving.

At Armentières as elsewhere the flotsam of war lay everywhere, with the ghastlier evidence of the bitter fighting all too evident if one cared to look. And in those early days there were still to be seen poignant personal reminders, for there were fragments of letters to be found and family photographs of women with their children. One of the visitors, six months after the guns stopped firing, was Lady Londonderry. In April 1919 she spent five days touring the battlefields. 'Destruction on every side, and an atmosphere of death pervading everything,' she wrote.

The only signs of life were salvage parties of men exhuming dead bodies, or burying them, or else digging cemeteries. Two bright splotches of colour caught the eye in the near distance. Flags! Yes. They were Union Jacks which lay over the floor of two wagons, they covered poor shapeless lumps of clay carefully placed in sacks, the remains of those who had fought their last fight on this famous field. I would have preferred myself that the dead had been left to lie in peace where they fell . . .

In another place, evidently a machine gun emplacement, lay skulls cut in half, teeth, bones and broken rifles, with belts of cartridges and portions of clothes and bones mixed. The punishment all along the slope must have been deadly. It seemed impossible to realize on this quiet spring evening what a hell the countryside had been so recently.

Even two years later, the dead remained in view.

In shell holes we saw plenty of human bones; and in Delville Wood [on the Somme] there were boots with mummified feet within them. Our guide warned us what to expect, since it gave one a distinct shock to realize that the bones and fragments were human.

Mrs L. M. Orton, who had travelled from Bredhurst in Kent, took a trip among the shattered tree stumps of Delville Wood. In the autumn of 1921 she visited the Western Front for the first time, ostensibly to see the grave of her brother Christopher Wicks, killed in April 1918 while serving with the Army Service Corps. Her memories of the trip were then submitted for publication in her local newspaper the *East Kent Gazette*.

Her party was staying at a hostel, about thirty people in total, 'all on the same errand to visit a grave,' wrote Mrs Orton. Her group was being led by a former army officer, Mr Coles, 'the most sympathetic, tactful and patient official, a man who had served on the Somme Battlefields and so could answer questions with first-hand knowledge'.

Of course even a small knowledge of French is wonderfully help-ful, and so we needed less shepherding than most; and we were equipped with all particulars concerning the grave we sought before we left England. We learned that some people arrive with no particulars, and no memory for regimental ranks or numbers, or cemeteries, and expect the YMCA to find out on the spot in which of the three thousand odd military cemeteries in France and Belgium their relative is buried. That is so British and insular, and the YMCA, Salvation Army, and Church Army officials surely need to be the most tactful of men in the universe.

To give an idea of the numbers travelling, the Church Army took 5,000 family members in the months to June 1919, the Salvation Army another 18,500 visitors between 1920 and 1923, while the YMCA helped 60,000 people between 1919 and 1923. Interest in the battlefields dropped appreciably from 1925 onwards, although the decline in numbers was periodically arrested when great monu-ments, such as those to the missing, were unveiled. The publication at the end of the 1920s of some of the classic First War memoirs, such as Robert Graves' *Goodbye To All That*, also renewed interest. Overall, the declining numbers reflected the fact that most of the bereaved relatives who wished to visit the Western Front had done so, and most chose for reasons of stress, financial or emotional or more likely both, never to visit again.

'We found the cemetery, and a gardener in charge,' wrote Mrs Orton.

> We could easily pick out my brother's cross, as we had had a photograph of it months before. I enquired why my brother's cross was so much larger and of a different wood to very nearly all the others, and we were told that when a single casualty took place, such as my brother's death, the comrades had a special cross made, and the printing was very clear and well executed. So that was very comforting.
>
> Three-and-a-half years have elapsed since Christopher was put in that narrow military grave, but memory is very keen, and it only seemed to us, as we stood there, a few days since we heard of his death. The well-kept cemetery with its neat flowerbeds was all that we could have desired for a last resting place for him. If anyone who reads this has relatives buried in St Pierre Cemetery, Amiens, they may rest assured that the work done by the War Graves Commission is beyond reproach.

Visiting the Western Front allowed grieving relatives, if not to come to terms with their loss, at least to feel that they were confronting their feelings in such a way that they might be able to continue their lives when they got home. They never forgot, but they were at peace inasmuch as they had done all that they could. For some, coping with bereavement meant returning year after year. Charles and Annie Taylor, the parents of Second Lieutenant Ernest Taylor of the Lincolnshire Regiment, returned to Varennes Military Cemetery annually until 1939. They left to posterity a poignant photograph album that chronicled their trips, containing dozens of images of the cemetery and of the grave, images that also captured the passing years in their own countenance and bearing. For others, one trip was enough to settle

their minds. This was how one bereaved wife felt after her trip in
October 1919.

Angela Farmer was the sister of the writer Wilfrid Ewart, a
former officer in the Scots Guards, who accompanied her back to
the Somme to find her husband's grave. As they travelled together,
he noticed how she changed.

> The laughter had faded from the blue eyes that had always laughed:
> the lips wore no smile, but the rose had not died from her cheeks,
> nor the gold from her hair. How inadequate she was – unequal in
> years to the burden of sorrow.

When they arrived on the Somme, the sight of the battlefield
took her completely by surprise.

'I never expected this,' Angela said.

> I have tried to think of it, and of him in it, and of what hell looks like.
> But I never imagined such loneliness and dreadfulness and sadness in
> any one place in the world. One cannot imagine it. I thought I knew
> what it was like, but I only thought. I never felt until now.

There were no tears, recalled Ewart, for tears were 'inadequate
to the immensity of the tragedy printed here upon the earth'.

Angela had brought with her a wreath to lay at the grave and,
to make the connection with her husband more tangible, she had
also brought his letters. His name was Charles Farmer, and in
1916 he was a thirty-year-old lieutenant serving with the 7th
King's Royal Rifle Corps close to the then German-held village of
Longueval. The letters Angela brought included his last, written
an hour before he was killed:

> It is very cold for the time of year. I am wearing your woollen scarf
> which keeps me warm. It is raining, but I am crouching under a
> piece of corrugated iron . . . The Germans are about a hundred

yards away, but I can see nothing except an apple tree just above their trench. Our line cuts across a road into a wood where there are a lot of German crosses. Just behind are the remains of a village, with a chateau sort of upside down . . . Shells are buzzing overhead. We go for the apple tree at dusk this evening . . . Already it is getting dark. I think of you again and again – I know you'll give me strength – and of the little Pamela, though I've never seen her, and of the day that must come when we three shall be together . . .

It was this detailed information and the knowledge that he was buried by the apple tree that Angela and Wilfrid Ewart would use to find the grave near the razed village of Ginchy. 'What is the satisfaction of our search?' Wilfrid asked himself.

What do we expect to find, and what to feel? It is as though some magnet, some occult, refined sense drew us on. This we could not explain . . . the reality is underground – a skull, a few bones, a wisp or two of hair, a shred or two of khaki cloth. But to that we cling.

They looked around for the landmarks: the village ruins and wood, a German graveyard, a fork in the road. 'Here even was the apple tree and there – yes, distinctly enough – a trench.' But, sadly, no grave, only several square yards of disturbed earth.

A dugout had fallen in. A spade lay. A rusted rifle was half buried in a shell-hole: a steel helmet in a pool of water. Of a grave there was no sign nor any cross near.

Angela knelt down beside the apple tree and, making the Sign of the Cross, laid at its foot the laurel-wreath. It is probable she said some prayer, for vaguely, disjointedly, Angela believed in God. Rising, she said: 'If only one could know – if only one could *know* – that some day we three shall be together again.' With that we went back into the world again.

For the rest – well it was ended! Of that Angela spoke no more.

She laughed – her little pretty face all over. She chatted blithely all the way to London. Her mind was her own, and it was possible that none should ever peep into it again . . . She went laughing into the world again: and people say, 'Does she care so very much?' – for she dances and sings, dances to sound of piano and violin. Nor had the dancing light ever left her gay blue eyes. Her heart responds; she loves; she lives . . .

Some people, like Angela, felt oddly reinvigorated by what they had seen on the battlefields; she less by the deep faith that fortified others like Harry Lauder, more by an acceptance that she had done all she could. Still in her twenties, she could now come home and live happily as she felt her husband might have wished. Harry's mindset was also positive. His visit to his son's grave at Pozières had been traumatic but cathartic, too. He had to drag himself away and was torn between two emotions: one to stay, the other to return to his wife and tell her what he had seen and felt.

I felt that I was bearing a message to her. A message from our boy. I felt – and I still feel – that I could tell her that all was well with him, and with all the other soldiers of Britain, who sleep, like him, in the land of the bleeding lily. They died for humanity, and God will not forget.

And I think there is something for me to say to all those who are to know a grief such as I knew. Every mother and father who loves a son in this war must have a strong, unbreakable faith in the future life, in the world beyond, where you will see your son again. Do not give way to grief. Instead, keep your gaze and your faith firmly fixed on the world beyond, and regard your boy's absence as though he were but on a journey.

My whole perspective was changed by my visit to the front. Never again shall I know those moments of black despair that used to come to me. In my thoughts I shall never be far away from the little cemetery hard by the Bapaume road.

And life would not be worth the living for me did I not believe that each day brings me nearer to seeing him again.

I am going back to France to visit again and again that grave where he lies buried. So long as I live myself that hill will be the shrine to which my many pilgrimages will be directed. The time will come again when I may take his mother with me, and when we may kneel together at that spot.

And meanwhile the wild flowers and the long grasses and all the little shrubs will keep watch and ward over him there, and over all the other brave soldiers who lie hard by, who died for God and for their flag.

*   *   *

The British cemeteries, just as the government and IWGC had hoped, soon began to appear like oases in a barren landscape, with lawns gradually covering the mud, and flowers and bushes and rapidly growing saplings planted among the graves. During the early 1920s, the IWGC gradually replaced all the wooden crosses with markers made out of white Portland stone and the result, with the graves in neat, serried rows, seemed parade-ground-like: impressive yet heartrending at the same time.

With the design of the headstone, the British and Empire forces stole an irrevocable march on both their allies and foes. It was true that the production of the ubiquitous stone slab was not a seamless transition from original inception to final creation; a few critics were appalled at a gravestone that incorporated, but was not intrinsically, a Christian cross. Nevertheless, the final result is today considered a masterpiece of creativity. Other nations, most notably the French and the Germans, opted for the cross, but in doing so they depersonalised the grave, as the shape limited the space for additional information, other than name, number and regiment. By contrast, the British stone, gleaming white, was in many ways spiritually uplifting, and because of its size it could incorporate further details including the engraved regimental cap badge, the soldier's age and bestowed military honours. There was even room, at the bottom of the stone, for a carved message composed by the family in honour of their dead.

No one was careless when it came to the words, although cost might have limited what was said. As every vowel and syllable was paid for, at three and a half old pence a letter, poorer families often resorted to RIP as the best they could afford; others, better off, had more opportunity for eloquence though space was officially limited to sixty-six letters, although in reality this was not strictly enforced. Some families chose the parting words of the dead soldier, some the memory of a parting kiss. Others preferred a statement of fact, others the age-old prayer that God knew best. There are patriotic phrases and staggeringly personal tributes. Not all dedications appeal to modern sentiments and there are those that have greater literary merit than others that scan poorly, but that did not matter. Behind every inscription there was a story, most now lost to posterity.

Knowing that there was a grave to visit, even though it was overseas, gave some crumb of consolation to grieving families. By contrast, for those families whose loved ones were missing, the torture of not knowing could be open-ended. Peter and Lizzie Miller had repeatedly enquired whether their son's body had been found. His friend, Raymond Singleton, had written to say that Peter had received a rudimentary burial and that his body lay around 100 yards north-east of the north-eastern corner of High Wood. Then, in January 1918, the Millers received a message of regret from the War Office informing the family that despite a working party's 'thorough and methodical re-search' of the area, Peter's body had not been found and that his grave must have been obliterated by shelling. The story appeared closed. Then, occasionally, in the months and years after the war, new information trickled in, although in most cases it merely confirmed what the families already knew with certainty.

Emily Miller's parents were both dead before anything more was heard of their son Peter. The news partly confirmed the information already received from Raymond Singleton, but with a terrible twist, as Emily discovered.

After the war a memorial at Hornchurch was dedicated to local men who'd died, including Peter's name. And we discovered a young man used to go on every anniversary of my brother's death and lay flowers on the memorial. We never knew the reason. Then many years later this man's mother and sister asked me to their house at Manor Park in London. While I was there I decided to visit the memorial, which was some twelve miles away. I had my dog with me and thought I would take him for a walk, and the man insisted that he walked with me all twelve miles – he said we would go by bus on the way back but we never did.

We put flowers on the memorial and then walked eleven and a half miles back before he said anything about my brother. My brother had been killed helping someone else – him. A machine gun had started firing and Peter and three friends were in a bunch together. They all got into shell-holes, and this man in a shell-hole on Peter's right went into a panic. He screamed for my brother to come and Peter got out of his safe shell-hole to help but as he did so a sniper shot him and he fell, dead.

How could I react to this revelation? I just took it calmly, you couldn't alter anything.

Most such eyewitness accounts were accepted, although with hindsight, when they were held up to scrutiny, they were often anything but accurate. It was rare that the evidence would be as unequivocal as that received by Emily Miller. In September 1919 the family of one missing officer received news of their son not from a British soldier but from a German.

In August 1917, Second Lieutenant Raymond Wilson disappeared in fighting near Inverness Copse in the Ypres Salient. Nothing concrete had been known about him for over two years when his family received a letter from a British sergeant, Henry

Bourne, serving with the British Army of Occupation at Solingen, near Cologne. The sergeant had met a former German soldier named Emil Loose and the news was startling. Their beloved son had died in Emil's arms.

Emil Loose had possession of Raymond's Pocket Testament as well as a photograph of the nineteen-year-old officer. Emil did not speak English and all correspondence was transmitted through the sergeant. Times were quickly changing, it seemed. Bourne referred to Emil Loose as his friend, which would have shocked many families at home still embittered by the war but not, apparently, the Wilsons.

Emil, as explained, was one of five brothers who had served in the war, two on the Russian, three on the Western Front. Emil was slightly gassed and one brother had been badly wounded in the legs while serving on the Somme in 1916, but all had returned home.

In August 1917, Emil had been serving with No. 239 Badische Infantry Regiment, and his company was in position near the Menin road just outside Ypres. It was while they were there that the British attacked but after severe fighting the Germans forced them to retire. 'At this time I saw your son, who with a few soldiers had bravely defended himself, but who had been wounded by a gunshot, while the other soldiers were able to escape,' remembered Emil Loose.

I at once jumped to your son and saw, after I had opened his coat, that he was hit on the abdomen. I drew him into a shell-hole, in order to be safer from the bullets, and could at once bandage him.

Your son spoke in a very broken tone to me, unfortunately I could not understand him. He delivered to me his pouch, and I found in it 'Identity card', 'The Testament', and the 'Photograph' also a visiting card with the inscription, 'Mr Ernest E. Wilson, 1 The Sycamores, Wimbledon Common', from which I obtained your address. Afterwards your son lived about fifteen minutes and then died, when he threw his head back into my hands . . . I buried with him comrades wrapped in their waterproof sheets. I could not make another grave on account of the severe fighting all round.

Emil Loose then included a sketch of where he had buried Raymond on the northern edge of a wood known to the British as Inverness Copse.

And so began a remarkable correspondence in which Emil Loose and Ernest Wilson exchanged letters on a regular basis. Ernest Wilson, chief accountant at Barclays Bank, took up Emil's map and financed a search for his son. He kept Emil informed of progress, although in the end no body was ever found. In turn, Emil sent a photograph of himself so that Ernest and his family could get an impression of the man they were writing to, while Ernest's young daughter designed a calendar that was sent to Germany with good wishes for the New Year. In time even an offer to visit Germany was extended to the Wilson family.

Emil made frequent references to Raymond. 'I give you once again the assurance that your son Raymond found a tranquil and honourable death and be consoled with that, that he was not alone in his dying hour, that a German soldier cared for him.' In another letter he continued: 'I only did my duty as a soldier to my wounded opponent, no longer as an enemy, but as a friend in need and treated him as a man.'

While Emil talked of Raymond, both sides were on safe ground but, although the friendly tone did not change, Emil began to take a risk, probably unconsciously, when he referred to the recent Versailles Peace Treaty.

'We Germans are now condemned to pay the heinous war indemnity, and I shall hope that Germany will succeed in this in spite of her internal troubles, so that a lasting peace shall be assured.' And in another letter he wrote: 'Unfortunately we have still in Germany a very bad time for the stipulation of the Versailles Treaty weighs too severely upon the population . . .'

Perhaps the friendship had run its natural course, and when

Raymond Wilson was no longer the focus of the letters, both sides might have politely drawn an end to the discourse. Did it irk Mr Wilson at all that Emil and all four brothers returned from the Great War while his only serving son did not? It is impossible to say. What is clear, albeit from Emil's letters only, is that when Emil began to write of his business ambitions in South America, Mr Wilson took great umbrage. Reading between the lines, it is clear that Ernest Wilson felt it was Emil's duty, along with all Germans, to pay reparations and not, in effect, to sidestep his responsibility. As Barclays' chief accountant, Ernest Wilson would in all likelihood have had very definite views on the issue.

Dear Mr Wilson

. . . Up to now I have only received letters from you with pleasant contents and I must express my sorrow at the strange contents of your last letter. It has painfully moved me that you should have taken such a view of my plans to emigrate to America.

What the French are starting with us means oppressing the German people: certainly I am of the opinion that the wounds inflicted by the war must be healed again and in the making good by German coin I would gladly assist . . . I hope Mr Wilson you will understand these few words and perhaps also the reason, which has made me wish to seek a new home in Brazil – I also hope to find friends who will support my plan. It would grieve me very much if through the knowledge of this, our friendship should be saddened . . .

Even allowing for the slight vagaries in translation, the phrase 'the strange contents of your last letter' strongly suggests that there was an anger that went beyond a simple academic disagreement with Emil Loose's intentions; all contact between the two men apparently ended.

The evident fallout between Ernest Wilson and Emil Loose

showed how easily deep emotions thought to be dormant could still manifest themselves as anger through someone else's wrong word or ill-considered thought. Even long-established relationships could be ended in a moment if the occasion required bitter words between close friends. This is precisely what happened between Hazel Macnaghten and a friend known only as Enid, who, rather stupidly though probably absent-mindedly, set in train Hazel's default mechanism to search for her husband on the pretext of new evidence, however vague and unlikely.

'I am sorry, dear Hazel, that our long, delightful friendship is at an end,' wrote Enid. The date: December 1931. It was a full seventeen years since Hazel's husband Angus had disappeared in fighting near Ypres but still Hazel would not entirely give up.

It had been only a little over two months since she had written to a man named in the press as John Gouldney. He had been reported as having lost his memory entirely during the fighting of 1914 and only regained his 'original personality' in 1930. If he had been effectively 'lost' for all this time, could not Angus be in the same position? Hazel quizzed Gouldney as to what had happened but his answer was necessarily vague. 'Trusting you may yet get some good news relative to your husband,' he replied, 'I remain dear Madam, yours truly, John Gouldney.' Quite what Hazel hoped to glean from her letter that could facilitate her search for Angus is unclear, not least because it was probably unclear to Hazel herself. But as she had followed up every lead for nearly two decades, she probably felt compelled to follow this one. She had, after all, both the contacts and the finances with which to pursue the most tenuous of leads, an advantage once but now more akin to a curse than a help.

Which is why the next and last piece of 'evidence' concerning Angus caused her such unnecessary anxiety and strife, ending only with the breakup of a close friendship, as Hazel's son, also named Angus, recalled.

One of my mother's most intimate friends was a well-educated, much travelled woman, whom my mother had known since their girlhood days together . . . I remember so well in 1931, when she was staying with us at Windsor, that she mentioned, quite casually, her impression of having caught a glimpse of my father when she was travelling in the Balkans in 1922. Her story was that her train had stopped one night at 'an unknown railway station either in Serbia or one of those countries between Bulgaria and Trieste'. She had looked up and thought she had a fleeting glimpse of 'dear old Angus' in a train standing on the adjoining track . . .

It was a comment she regretted when Hazel asked her to write down exactly what she had seen. Even at the time Enid seemed to backtrack on her story, playing down the evidence. She was, she said, in a very dazed, ill condition and frightfully overtired at the time, and the glimpse she had was probably only a 'likeness' . . .

'I will not attempt to describe my mother's feelings at hearing the news,' remembered Angus. 'Needless to say, she immediately started putting enquiries in motion.'

The Foreign Office was contacted, as was the German chargé d'affaires who in turn wrote to the German office concerned with answering questions to do with the missing. Was it possible that British prisoners might have been sent to Bulgaria? The British legation at Sofia was asked to follow up the story and the International Committee of the Red Cross in Geneva was approached with pictures and detailed particulars. Even the Bulgarian police were asked to investigate, all to no avail. The sighting of a man in Sofia who happened to look like Angus in 1922 was hardly likely to yield results in 1931. Hazel's long search was finally abandoned, as was her friendship with Enid.

10

'Least Said, Soonest Mended'

'As he bravely died
So I must live.
From his wife'

3/8190 *Company Sergeant Major Reginald Page MM*
8th Norfolk Regiment
Killed in action 21 July 1916, aged thirty-three
Buried Delville Wood Cemetery, Longueval

In November 1918 no one would seriously have suggested that *men* should not take the plaudits for winning the war, or that it was essentially for them that the great monuments of commemoration and remembrance would be built in Britain and abroad. No one would query why homes were being built for heroes, not heroines – though some might come to question whether they were being built at all – or in the years to come that it was primarily for the sacrifices of men that the nation came to a halt for two minutes of respectful silence and contemplation.

It was a man's world, in as much as men occupied almost every significant position in business and in government. The case of Mary Morton's mother had shown that her self-evident 'infidelity', though she honestly believed her husband was dead (and presumably, owing to the passage of time, she had been officially so informed), ensured that the law backed the man and delivered custody of the children automatically to the father.

In general, the state's attitude to women was largely

paternalistic. There was every assumption that, once the war was over, women would retreat to the home, giving up the jobs that had once been a male preserve, and in the main that took place. As early as October 1916, *The Times* acknowledged the importance of women's war work; it even went as far as to say that 'wages of an adequate character, and the new opportunities they bring, are revolutionizing women's outlook on industry', yet in the same breath it cautioned that 'whatever new industrial realms throw open, home and motherhood remain as women's great and unique work . . . the pledges given as to the restoration of pre-war conditions [i.e. returning jobs to returning men] must, of course, be completely kept', except, the newspaper went on to mention, where men decided that women could continue. A woman, regardless of class, was defined in Britain by her relationship to men, whether it was as wife, sweetheart, sister, daughter or mother, and little over the course of the war did much to alter that fact.

When the total number of memorials to army divisions, battalions or battles is calculated, it can only be said that there is an utter dearth of memorials to women. In an alcove in York Minster, an unobtrusive memorial commemorates the death of women in the services and those employed in war work: wooden panels list the names of those killed. But how many other such memorials exist?

It should not have required death by volume to underscore the sacrifice of women in the Great War, in particular the work of women not engaged directly in any war work but who by their extraordinary efforts kept the home fires burning. They kept children warm in spite of bitter weather outside, often empty stomachs inside, and bleak war news that made life appear at times unbearable. The nation took the domestic work of these women for granted; it handed out pitiful Separation Allowances and then monitored the way these were spent in order to withdraw them if they were deemed incorrectly used. Additionally, the daily fear of the knock on the door, the news that might come by telegram or letter, eroded confidence and even sanity and then, when it arrived . . .

Did the pressure on women surviving on the Home Front in any way counterbalance the pressure on men serving on the Western Front? Who knows? What is evident is that neither side could ever understand what the other was suffering. Many couples had married just prior to the war, or in the heady days following its outbreak, only later to discover when the war ended and families were reunited that one partner hardly knew the other. Others had grown apart and held different priorities or ambitions. Accusations of infidelity made against wives by returning soldiers were rife, as was domestic violence as soldiers struggled to come to terms with what they had seen and sometimes done. It could be hard to fit back into families that had learned to live without them and to adjust to children too young to remember a time when their fathers were there. Was it any wonder that in the year after the war divorces tripled in number compared with 1914, although the overall figure was still low?

And then there were the children, and not just the children removed prematurely from school and engaged in industry and agriculture, but the growing numbers working in the home, children like Clara Whitefield and Donald Overall, who took pride in their cooking and cleaning, even in the back-breaking scrubbing of fireplaces and floors. It was their contribution to the war effort, although they rarely saw it in such terms. Rather, it was their support for Daddy at the front and, even more so when he was gone, for Mummy at home, keeping the house together in adversity. The tears Doris Davies shed in 2004, when she finally saw her father's grave near Ypres, were not just for him, she realised, but for what his death had cost her mother, Daisy, left with three children aged six, four and two. The war had also cost her mother two of her three brothers.

'She said she would never remarry,' recalled Doris.

I know when I was getting married she was very upset; she had lost what I was going to get. In fact I don't think she ever forgave me for getting married so young. She never gave her grandchildren hugs. I think she lost a lot of feeling when she lost her husband; she just went sort of dead. She lived for us and that was about the limit of her life.

Other than the financial support payable to all whose husbands were serving in the forces, wives were largely left to fend for themselves when war broke out. They were not only emotionally vulnerable, fearing that any day they might receive calamitous news from the War Office, but also financially vulnerable, having to make all the decisions that would keep a roof over the family's head and the children fed and clothed. Of course a few found the experience liberating, especially those escaping rotten husbands who had abused their position in the household and kept their wives on a tight financial shoestring. One woman who spoke about her husband quite freely admitted she wished he would be killed. 'But I 'spose he'll be spared, and others as'd be missed 'll be taken, for that's the way of things. It's the only time since I've been married as I and the children's 'ad peace. The war's been a 'appy time for us.'

Yet this was a minority view. The war had been an extraordinarily tough time in women's lives and for none more than the women who, through the death of their husbands, were left alone. In crude figures, married soldiers numbered just over 28 per cent of the army's fatalities. They left behind over 190,000 widows, of whom fewer than a quarter were childless. This meant that 145,000 widows were raising almost 360,000 children under the age of sixteen and, of these women, over 53,000 were struggling to bring up three or more children on their own. It is unsurprising that many war widows chose to remarry, craving the financial security that marriage brought both for themselves and for their children. According to official figures released in 1932 by the

Registrar General, the immediate post-war marriage rate was 30 per cent higher in 1919 and 1920 than the pre-war rate, while remarriages among widows aged 20–45 shot up by 50 per cent. Love was not always the primary motivation.

Financial security appeared to have been on the mind of George Musgrave's mother when she spoke to her son about a proposal she had received. It was made by a butcher whose shop was opposite the Musgraves' home, and George had already noticed how this man had always been very pleased to see his mother and gave her extra bits of meat when she made her purchases. George had noticed something else, too. The butcher was extremely fat, 'laughably fat', according to George. Then one day he came to the house very smartly dressed.

> I was in the kitchen and she had an interview with this man in the other room and after he'd gone she came and asked me, 'Would you like Mr Mortimer as a father?' I could not bear the thought as he was so large and I knew I would be laughed at, so she closed her mind to the idea. He was well off but she looked after my interests first and not hers. But she had obviously considered it for my sake.

Violet Baker's father, Sam, had been killed on the Somme in 1916. Four years later her mother married again, when Violet was seven. The marriage lasted two years before her husband died and she remarried once more. Both marriages, according to Violet, were principally for the security of the children and not for love.

> I asked my mum sometimes, 'Oh why did you marry again?' and she used to say, 'Well, I had to do something or we would have landed up in a home.' Years later, when my mother was in her late eighties and in a nursing home, she still explained what she did by saying, 'Well, I tried my best for you.'

There was and there would remain a serious problem for the men who proposed to these widows. Inevitably the new suitor had much to live up to. Although there had clearly been women locked into loveless marriages, marriages blighted by domestic violence, there were far more wives whose husbands had been hard-working, kind and considerate.

The men who fought the Great War were young, for nearly three-quarters of those killed had been aged thirty or less. These men left a large group of young widows, many married perhaps for just a year or two before the war broke out, women whose marriages had not grown stale, women who were not exhausted by looking after endless children. Their husbands had patriotically gone to war and had not returned, nobly sacrificing their lives for their country.

Whether to remarry or not was a question that could tear at the heartstrings, for to marry meant to break with the past, the consigning of a first marriage to memory. After accepting a proposal of marriage after the war, Vera Brittain began to consider her feelings at length. She realised that to stay unmarried, wed only to the memory of her fiancé Roland, would consign her to the past, whereas to marry would offer her the future. 'Should I, then, submit myself to that pain of a future so completely out of tune with the past? Should I, who had once dedicated myself to the dead, assume yet further responsibilities towards the living?' She asked herself whether she could withstand further blows, should anything happen to her husband and in time, their children. She doubted it.

As with many of her contemporaries, she struggled with feelings of guilt.

There remained now only one final and acute question of loyalty to the dead; of how far I and the other women of my generation who deliberately accepted a new series of emotional relationships thereby destroyed yet again the men who had once uncomplainingly died for them in the flesh.

As she walked through Regent's Park she thought long and hard, asking herself what Roland would say if he could return. Would he think her forgetful and unfaithful? Would any of those she had loved and lost argue that she should remain beholden to them in death? Life, after all, was there to be lived, 'so long as I am in the world, how can I ignore the obligation to be part of it?' she asked herself.

Vera Brittain analysed, probably overly, her predicament, certainly in comparison with others living in poverty who, by dint of hardship and uncertainty, were forced to make more practical decisions. Yet she asked questions that many other women, much less eloquent, posed for themselves, and not all of them ever resolved the issues in such a way as to ensure their lasting contentment.

The risk would remain that the dead would be eulogised to the detriment of new relationships. For all their faults, and these could be quickly forgotten, the dead could never again blot their copybook. First marriages had not failed: they were abruptly and cruelly ended by bomb and bullet. Consequently, any faults within the marriage, if they were remembered, were often downplayed, times of happiness recalled with greater, perhaps exaggerated, fondness. Equally, if there were difficulties within a second marriage there would be a natural propensity to contrast and compare them with the past, magnifying the current problems, as Violet Baker saw.

> Mum never showed any emotion with her third husband, and I never saw them holding hands or having a kiss. I don't think she loved him, or in fact either husband really. She was still talking about Sam. Mother used to say, 'Sam did this' and 'Sam did that,' and my stepfather used to say, 'Oh it's always Sam!'

Charles Chilton went to live with his grandmother after his father was killed in 1918 and then his mother died. He remembered how his grandmother worshipped the memory of the son who was killed, but argued frequently with another much younger son.

She often talked about my father, she thought he was a saint and quite often she'd have a row with my father's younger brother and she'd say terrible things, 'I wish it had been you that had gone and not him', which led to him bursting into tears, it was awful. But then because he was dead she thought much more of him, of course. She had thirteen children in all so she had to spread her love around them a bit but my father was the only one she lost in the war.

Even when mothers decided to remarry, there were likely to be other issues that needed resolving. Children, particularly those who had clear and fond memories of their father, were less likely to accept a new one. Violet Baker had had two 'new' fathers by the time she was ten and she cared for neither.

I never forgot Dad, there was nobody to replace him and so I never really understood why my mother married again because she doted on my father, and always spoke about him and kept so many photos. That second husband was a widower and lived in the same area. Mother had been forced to work on the land as she only got ten shillings widow's pension for me, and 7s. 6d. for my brother, and he worked on the land too and that is how she met him.

I didn't take to him and would never have said he was my dad and I don't think he liked me very much either. He hadn't got any time for us. There were no hugs, no bedtime stories, goodness gracious no. My stepfather was quite harsh. In fact he was horrible. Whatever went wrong it was always me that did it, and my mum would stick up for me. There was a cane resting on a couple of hooks underneath the dining table, and the threat was there, you wouldn't dare to speak out of turn: seen and not heard, that was his idea. I know he gave me the stick one day, caught me with a cane, and Mum was furious. I hated him from that moment on.

Understandably, it must have been difficult for any man to accept that he was not the only man in his wife's life, though it could be done. Harry Patch, the last survivor of the trenches, married Ada Billington after he was demobbed in 1919. He was aware that her first love, a man called Harold Thomas, had been killed and the pain of that loss made Ada determined not to commit to anyone else until the war was over and she was certain that her man was coming home. Harry and Ada were happily married for nearly sixty years, but the engagement ring from her first love sat on her dressing table for many years, and Harry accepted that; not all men would have done so.

Ada had not married Harold Thomas and there were no children. Children brought an entirely different dynamic into the relationship. Not only had the new husband to accept that he would help bring up children who were not his own, but he had to be 'father' to children who were a daily reminder to him that the spirit of someone else remained a party to the new relationship. If that was not difficult enough, children were far from dispassionate bystanders. When it came to accepting the new status quo, they would decide for themselves whether the new man in their lives would be accepted or rejected. Even when the new marriage was happy, there was a natural inclination among children to resist any pressure to accept the newcomer as 'father'.

Lily Jones's mother, Sophia, kept her husband's memory alive for a while but then she married Mr Dunford, a collier who lived in an adjacent road with his grown up son and daughter, and it seemed prudent not to harp on about the man she had loved and lost. Lily never believed it was a love match, more, she thought, a case of companionship. Mr Dunford was kind to Sophia and was good with her two youngest children with whom he formed a solid bond.

In order to relieve the strain on her mother when bringing up children on her own, Lily had been moved to Urdsley to live with a relative but after the marriage she came back to the family home in Blackwood.

I would find Mr Dunford going round the living room carrying Wyndham and Vera [born 1918] on his back, growling as if he was a lion, and he'd say, 'Lily, won't you come on my back as well?' And I'd say 'no', I didn't want to. He wasn't Daddy, though my brother seemed to accept him, I think because he was another male in a house of girls. Mummy tried hard to get me to call him grancher [Welsh for grandfather] but I refused, I wouldn't accept it, and always called him Mr Dunford. To me he didn't really belong there. He had moved into Mummy's house.

For years, Lily clung to the idea that the army had made a mistake, that perhaps one day her father would suddenly walk through the door and everything would return to normal. It was an extremely common fantasy among children, a comforting albeit fleeting thought. It was hard for a child to imagine that the father they had had, and whom they had worshipped, could be done down by anyone, least of all a German. Then, in 1919, Lily's family received final and incontrovertible evidence that John Jones was dead when Sophia received a letter from a man who, as a prisoner of war in 1918, had found and buried her husband in Bourlon Wood. Even then Lily harboured some hope.

I found a magazine in which I saw this photograph of somebody in America and I thought, 'Gosh, he looks like Daddy, could it be him?' I took it home for the family to see but they said, 'No, it is not your father.' And I was really disappointed, same dark brown hair, moustache. I thought that was him.

Mabel Hunter had had just the same daydream as Lily but when her mother remarried in 1919 the dream more or less evaporated. Mabel's mother married Tom Fawcett, a man she had known as an acquaintance for a number of years, and Mabel accepted the situation with equanimity.

I knew then that Dad was not coming back and that Tom Fawcett was standing in for him and I had to make the best of life because Mum was happy enough and my brother accepted him as his dad. As far as I was concerned Tom wasn't my dad, he was my mother's husband, and Dad was, and still is, in my heart. I missed him but I accepted that all I had of my dad was the picture in the postcard.

Mabel could remember her father, her younger brother could not, and that made a great deal of difference as to whether Tom Fawcett was going to be called 'Dad' or not. Not that Mabel had anything against the man – on the contrary.

Tom was a lovely person and she could not have picked a better father figure for us for he was a kind gentle soul, he spoke well and never swore. Mother took me aside one time and said, 'He's your dad now and I want you to call him Dad if you can, he's part of the family and we are living all together and he's the breadwinner and we have to be thankful that we have someone to look after us.' It was only in later years that I appreciated his kindness. He was the best dad I could ever have had besides my own.

Lily Jones's brother Wyndham had only vague memories of his father. He had wept and clung on to his father when John left for France for the last time and he had exhibited great emotional stress at the news that his father had gone missing. Yet he had been so young that the memories of these events were, if anything, more Lily's than his own, and he had taken to Mr Dunford. Having a father figure was important to a young boy's development. Donald Overall and his younger brother had worshipped their father. On his death, Donald became the man of the house and adopted the position with pride, but he was still not even seven when the war finished and he wanted a father figure, a new role model he could look up to. It was Donald rather than his mother who suggested she marry again, and who better than another soldier who had served with his father?

When the war was over the Regimental Sergeant Major in Dad's battalion came to see mother. He was ever such a nice fellow called Cecil Picken. He wanted to marry my mother, he loved her a lot, and she had a little affection for him but she wouldn't marry because as she said to me on many occasions, 'Your father was my man.' I wanted Cecil to marry Mum, and he wanted to be our father. He used to take me out to the football matches, to Madame Tussaud's and to Church parades. He even took me up to the Sergeants' Mess in the drill hall on Farringdon Road and we played on the snooker table there.

He was a Bluecoat boy, so he was an educated chap. My brother and I chivvied Mother, 'Why don't you marry uncle Cecil?' I would have liked to have had that man as a father because he was a man I could touch and see, and he talked to us and took us out. He was a good friend to us but he eventually moved away and married someone else.

The loss of Cecil Picken was a blow to Donald who was intelligent and fascinated by the world around him. He needed someone like Cecil, the former Bluecoat boy, to nurture him and answer his many questions.

When I was eleven years old I was swotting for a scholarship to the London Technical College and Mother dearly wanted me to win it. I had been taught algebra and trigonometry in those days; Mum couldn't even spell the words, but it was difficult to keep going on my own. I had an uncle who had been a machine-gunner in the war and he had got shot in the mouth and his face was all destroyed. He was a clerk, but he did not understand the modern techniques that kids were being taught. I went to him with questions and it was double Dutch as far as he was concerned.

I used to get so frustrated with homework, with these problems at weekends and I would nearly be in tears with frustration because I had nobody to ask, I had to work it all out on my own.

Eventually I sat for this exam and I was the only boy in Bermondsey to be awarded a scholarship and the headmaster, he was an ex-naval man, he called all the boys into the school hall to attention. He had Mother up there with me and I was awarded a prize with a little metal plate and that was presented to my mother in front of all the kids at school and with me there feeling so proud.

Girls might not have needed dads as role models in the same way as boys, but they still missed a father figure. Joan Healey 'longed to be like other little girls who had their dad to put them on their shoulder', and later in life, like Donald Overall, she yearned for the help she would otherwise have received with her homework; she missed his attendance at school open days, too. Joan had grown to understand that she was very like her father, interested in sport and in art, and school open days would have presented the perfect opportunity to share her interests with him.

There was another issue, too.

I never had the confidence in meeting boys because I felt somehow that I didn't have the self-assurance to handle the opposite sex, because we didn't have a man in the household; it was just me, my mother and my grandmother all the time.

Her mother, Ethel, had decided not to remarry.

We had heard of someone whose children were very unhappy with the new father they had, and Mum said to me, 'That's why I never remarried.' I was quite a cheeky girl and for fun I said, 'Perhaps you didn't get the chance!' She was very indignant at the suggestion, and I can only think she must have had the opportunity but hadn't taken it.

Try as they might, many wives simply could not envisage living with anyone else. Their first husband would be their last and, no matter how difficult the struggle would become, they were prepared to make the necessary sacrifice. Any thought of marrying again would require too great a shift emotionally and psychologically. It might also entail the wholesale clear out of personal treasures and keepsakes, perhaps consigning the first marriage to little more than a dream. George Musgrave's father had travelled extensively and had brought back many small presents that, after his death, meant even more to his wife.

There was a cupboard in our bed/sitting room and in there mother stored things my father had brought back from all over the world from his sailing days. There was a mandolin and bits of clothing, pictures; every trip he brought something. In the kitchen above the stove, there was a clock that he had brought home and his photograph was always to be seen on the mantelpiece in the kitchen, a sort of memory corner.

Jettisoning these items would have been traumatic; besides, it made good sense when there was a boy in the house, and when money was tight, to keep items such as her husband's old clothes. Reusing material, no matter what its original purpose, was essential. A kilt made a useful underlay for stair carpets; old army blankets, as Donald Overall's mother found, could be dyed, cut up and made into clothes for her sons, or sold. A war widow might use the buttons from her husband's uniform to make a brooch or use them on coats or jackets. Women, especially those who chose not to remarry, went out of their way to reflect their continued pride in their late husbands and the regiments with which they had served, as Donald Overall witnessed.

The buttons of my father's regiment were black with a bugle, and Mum used to write to the regimental headquarters in Farringdon Road and get stacks of these buttons because all her dresses were covered in black buttons of my father's regiment, on the cuffs, down the front, she never forgot my father, never.

Donald's mother had picked up her former profession as a seamstress to work all the hours she could in order to provide for her two boys. Nevertheless, balancing work with the protection and welfare of children made life extremely difficult for those who chose not to remarry and who had to manage without the support of family nearby. George Musgrave was an only child in London, and yet his world was no greater than the sitting room in which he was left for many hours of each day to entertain himself. His mother, Louisa, had to go out and work at a doctor's house, answering the door and the telephone, cooking and cleaning.

Treats were rare. It was a great thing to go on a bus ride to see the river in London because she had not the money, even a few pennies. Well, you have to decide whether that is pennies on me or pennies on clothes. The government's intention to help us was there, until they found that the arithmetic didn't work out.

She got a small pension, thirty shillings a week perhaps, but the amount was trivial, it never replaced the money Dad would have brought in and of course she had to pay the rent and also pay the landlady to keep an eye on me while she was out. In the normal way a family would be in the same street and would look after each other, but in Mum's case her sisters were in different parts of London, her father was dead and my grandmother was in desperate financial straits herself.

After a very long day working she would come back to the house to put me to bed and then she would start doing the day's chores late at night, so much of it by candlelight as we only had a single gas mantle in the kitchen.

Mum was a very good seamstress and there came a time when all the other boys in the school had long trousers and I didn't have long trousers, because Mum had to make all my clothes. I told her the boys had long trousers and she said: 'I've been waiting for you to say that,' and she went to the cupboard in the corner of the room. She'd saved my father's trousers, tailoring them to my size. I tried them on and they fitted.

They were drainpipes, out of fashion, and I was the laughing stock of the school. I didn't want other children to know my difficulties and for that reason I went into my shell, I didn't want to be seen. I didn't feel I had anyone to talk to so I had to fend for myself. I had grown up an isolated child playing on the floor; I had my own world so I could easily retire into it as I became an adult, either as a writer or as an artist.

Money remained tight for Donald's mother, too, although when time and money permitted she would make every effort to take the children up to town and give them a day away from the daily grind at home.

We always had clean clothes, kid gloves, collar and tie, all very neat and tidy. We used to go to the Cenotaph and the City of London Memorial by the Stock Exchange dedicated to the London Brigades and then she would show us round the town because she was well up on those things. Often, when she had sufficient money, we would go into an Express Dairy shop and we would get a cream bun and a cup of tea, tuppence each. My brother and I used to sit there like kings eating this cream bun and we thought it was a wonderful treat and she used to sit there watching us; she was so proud of us two kids.

The children of servicemen killed in the war were not entirely forgotten by the outside world. Doris Davies's mum subscribed to a special country holiday fund set up for widows and costing a shilling a week. The money saved would enable her daughter to visit the country for a few days once a year. Elsewhere, the British Legion organised parties at Christmas, held in churches or drill halls, and invited children such as George Musgrave and Charles Chilton. There might be a clown who would put on a show, followed by lemon curd sandwiches, as Charles Chilton recalled, and a Father Christmas to hand out small gifts as the children left, such as a scarf with an apple or an orange, or perhaps a small bag of sweets. These parties gave children a welcome escape, but they also helped them to understand that they were not alone, that there were others in exactly the same position. But participation in these parties did not alter or ameliorate the feelings many widows had about the war or make them any less bitter. Their feelings of resentment were not going to be assuaged in any way by periodic kindness towards themselves or their children.

Government-inspired tokens of appreciation, such as the so-called 'death penny' or bronze plaque announced in 1918 and finally distributed in 1919 to next of kin, were not always accepted with the gratitude expected. Violet Baker had lost her beloved husband, Sam, and she was in no mood to be thankful. 'My mother was given the death penny and I know that she was disgusted,' recalled Violet. '"That for a husband," she said.' Doris Davies's mother felt the same about the pension.

> She always used to call the pension 'blood money'. She would say, 'I don't want their blood money', but she had not the wherewithal to say no and so she had to accept it. She was so angry. She never wore her husband's medals, in fact I never even saw them and there were no pictures of him around the house, as a constant reminder of what she lost; she didn't want to see.

Annual commemorations of the Armistice only turned the screw on these women's emotions. Every family had its own way of dealing with the day. Some joined in the communal commemorations, others hid away and remembered in solemn and private silence; such was the case with Louisa Musgrave:

> Mum would wear black with perhaps a white blouse and his medals. A maroon sounded and we would look out of the window

and we'd see all the vehicles come to a stop, and all the horses and carts and all the people would stand there, and the two of us would look down from our room on to the trams and tram wires and she would shed a tear and grab me and say, 'You are all I have.'

'On Armistice Day my grandmother and Mrs Morgan [grandmother of the future comic actor Kenneth Williams] used to get together at our house and cry,' recalls Charles Chilton.

Each time she would bring a picture of my father and her son together, taken before they went overseas, and she would give it to me; she seemed to have endless copies. I was in the Boys' Brigade so we would march down to a monument at King's Cross Station and have a special service and I would play the bugle, then we would march through the streets back to our headquarters.

Charles Chilton's mother remarried shortly after the war, but not until she died in 1924 did he fully comprehend that his biological father was in fact dead. His stepfather had always been as loving to Charles as to his own sons and daughters. Then, after the death of Charles's mother, his 'father' suddenly left with his own children and seven-year-old Charles went to live with his father's mother.

'I was just an appendage at the end of several of my father's siblings, all living in the same house. I was a bit of a nuisance to them because my grandmother seemed to favour me above her own children because she would say "because he's my boy's boy", and that made me very precious to her though I couldn't relate to her loss at all. I'd never met my father and although I had affection for my mother, she had had to pay her attention to the two younger boys of my stepfather and then, by the time I was seven, she herself was dead. When I was alone I used to cry for my mother and think about her. Then, as I grew older, I cried less and my memory of her just faded into the distance and now I find it hard even to visualise her.'

In the years ahead, it was up to the families to keep alive the memory of 'Dad', or 'brother', or, in Charles's case, his mother. Some chose to pass on all the stories they could to their children, some understandably felt it was impossible to mention their loved one ever again. Letitia Sherington simply could not speak of her son for fear of what the memory of Arthur would do to her fragile emotions and the 'tight band', as she called it, that gripped her head. Instead, she threw herself into her family and her work, and her surviving children knew never to mention their sibling again.

Mabel Hunter's mother remarried and, though she did not forget Ernest, she never actively reminded herself of him either. Memories and mementos were placed out of sight. Mabel's mother also believed in the widespread ethos that children were better off being encouraged to look to the future and not to live in the past.

After he'd died nobody would talk to us about it, they probably thought, 'least said, soonest mended'. In those days it wasn't explained why he wasn't coming home. We would understand more when we were older, and we just had to carry on. My uncles came home and they were in uniform and I used to wonder why they could come back and had not brought my dad with them. I asked my mother's youngest brother and he said that he wasn't fighting where my dad was and that I just had to accept the fact that my father had given his life. I remember him saying, 'Don't worry, we'll look after you, you won't go short of anything, we'll all look after you and see that you won't miss out.' And that was how it was left.

Mum never talked about our father and she seemed very remote about ever bringing him back into our lives. It was my grandmother who told us the few things my brother and I knew about Dad, such as how he had first met Mum.

The family of Harry Farr, shot at dawn for cowardice in 1916, kept the story secret, such was the shame attached to the conviction. The episode was a stain on the family name that nobody wished to revisit and after Harry's death the desire to forget slowly drove a wedge between his side of the family and his wife and only daughter, Gertrude. Gertrude grew up with no idea of what had happened. She believed that her father had died in the war, in action, like the fathers or brothers of everyone else. That was until late in the 1950s and a family reunion.

We never met up with the rest of my father's family really for forty years. There were eight boys in my father's family and one girl. The girl went to America as a nanny when she was eighteen and she never came back except once when I was forty and she returned to visit everyone. She was talking to me at a family gathering and said, 'Is this true what I hear about how Harry died?' The rest of the family turned round and said, 'We don't talk about Harry.' I looked at her. I didn't know what she was talking about at first. So when I came home I spoke to my mother, and I said, 'Is that right, what Auntie Nellie said?' And she said, 'Yes it's true. Your father was shot for cowardice and the family disowned him.' Mum was very upset that it was all coming out in the open, but once the floodgates were open she just spoke all about it. She did not cry; I never ever saw her cry, my mum was too strong a person.

Children learnt about their missing father or brother only when 'Mum' found the strength to open up about her life with those who had died. Donald Overall and his younger brother pieced together their dad's story on the basis of snippets garnered over many years.

My mother and father were very close, she told me. They were always together. When he was gone she used to tell me how easy it was to live with him and how he loved his hockey and he loved his pipe.

She told me about the snipers and how they went over the top and how scared they were and how, when his mates were killed, he had to carry on. That's why he wouldn't take corporal's stripes on his arm because he didn't want to be separated from his mates, what were left of them. I was really proud of my dad and I always wished I could be like him.

I didn't know his faults, he must have had them, but I didn't know them. He must have had weaknesses, but I didn't know them either, I only knew what my mother told me.

Although George Musgrave had no memory of his father, he had the picture of the train his father had drawn for him in the trenches, and in George's mind that sealed forever the bond between father and son. He was eager to learn as much as he could about his father.

He had served in the Merchant Navy and had travelled the world. Mum was proud of her marriage and every now and then little bits would come out about Alf, that he was always joking, that he was a good mimic and that he was always the centre of attraction; she would talk about him as if she was talking about a film star. But he was only home for a few days and then he would be off again to Australia, or Canada, so what married life they had was very fragmented. Then she told me how he was on a boat, the SS *Minnetonka*, that was torpedoed and sunk during the war and they all had to jump ship. When he came back with no ship to go back to, he was unemployed. So he would go off at 4 a.m. to the docks to see if someone would offer him work. It was a sad but a proud reflection of what he meant to her.

The parents of Joan Healey had long spoken about their hopes and dreams for their young daughter. Her memory of her father was scant, one very distinct recollection of his arrival home on leave but nothing more. However, the hopes and dreams her father had for his daughter lived on.

I was always told by my mother, or perhaps an uncle or aunt, that when I joined something or I did something good, or well, they would say, 'Your daddy would have wanted you to do that,' or 'Your daddy would have been proud of you,' and that followed me all through my younger life. Everything I did as a young girl was connected to my father, it kept my father alive for me.

ENDPIECE

In 1943 Donald Overall was married and the father of two sons. He was also in the Royal Air Force and had just been sent to No. 4 Group, Bomber Command, in Yorkshire as a flight engineer. The men with whom he would serve on a Halifax bomber were being sent up on training flights, known as circuits and bumps. On board, taking Donald's place as flight engineer, was the 'spare bod', an experienced airman who would oversee the flight while Donald retreated to stand underneath the astrodome overlooking the wings.

On this occasion, returning to the airfield, the pilot hit the ground heavily, throwing the Halifax back into the air. As it did so the plane turned at an acute angle so that the starboard wing nearly touched the ground. The 'spare bod' snatched the controls, flew the plane round and landed safely.

If that wing had touched the ground it would have been ripped off, igniting the petrol fumes inside. In this situation the flames would have come straight through the plane where I was standing and fried me alive. In that critical moment it flashed through my mind that my wife would have a sergeant's pension on which to live while my two boys would have their education paid for, that's what was agreed when I signed up.

You have to understand that all this went through my mind in an instant before the plane was brought under control. Then the reaction set in and I was frightened, and the sweat came out of every pore of my body and I could hardly keep my hands still for a few seconds. Nobody spoke about the incident afterwards, we just got on with our job, yet I was wracked with the knowledge that I had come perilously close to leaving my sons and at roughly the same age as when my father had died and left my brother Cecil and me.

At the end of the war when my demob number was up, I was asked if I had thought about signing on for a further four years. I did not want to. I felt like a civilian in an air force uniform but I was then a flight sergeant and they were offering a crown on my stripes and a £2,500 bounty. It was a bloody fortune and could really have helped set my family up.

I came home to Ada to talk it over. I was out in the kitchen and she was sitting in an armchair; and I was telling her about this job. She let me have my own way in a lot of things, so I explained things to her and she never said anything until I'd finished. 'Well, love,' she said, 'the two boys need their father.' Now how could I answer that when I had never had a father? I couldn't sign on for another four years. I would have loved to, but the kids come first, don't they?

ACKNOWLEDGEMENTS

I would like to thank the kind and supportive staff at Bloomsbury, particularly Bill Swainson, the senior commissioning editor, for his continued support and unwavering belief in my books. I am also very grateful to Nick Humphrey, Ruth Logan, Anna Simpson, Anya Rosenberg, Emily Sweet, David Mann, Paul Nash, Polly Napper and Andrew Tennant for the great team effort of bringing *The Quick and the Dead* to publication. Once again I would also like to express my gratitude to Richard Collins for his astute editorial comments. This is the fourth of my books he has worked on and I appreciate his obvious interest and precision.

I should especially like to thank David Faulder and his family for their kind permission to use the image of their father, Harold Faulder, taken at Tyne Cot Cemetery in the 1920s, which has given this book its very moving cover image. Furthermore, as always I am indebted to my great friend Taff Gillingham for reading through the text and picking up a number of small errors; his knowledge is invaluable and much appreciated.

Especial mention should be made of my excellent agent, Jane Turnbull, whose professional help, support and friendship I value in equal measure: thank you, Jane.

My warmest thanks must go to my family: to my mother, Joan van Emden, who, as always, has been of inestimable support, using her wonderful command of English grammar to great effect, normally at short notice! I remain always in debt to my wife, Anna, who remains a sea of calm when the work files and paperwork drift out of my office and downstairs as deadlines loom, and to our wonderful four-year-old son Benjamin, who is cottoning on to what soldiers are but still does not fully appreciate why Daddy cannot always come and play at the drop of a hat.

I would like to thank the following people for permission to reproduce photographs, extracts from diaries, letters or memoirs: Dave Empson, who has been incredibly kind and generous over the years in letting me use some wonderful material from his extensive collection, in this case the story of Lieutenant Raymond Wilson, as well as some remarkable images taken from post-war pilgrimages to the battlefields; Stuart Arrowsmith, who has been very generous in lending me yet more photographs from his collection, taken by Sergeant Harold Bisgood, 2nd London Regiment; Emma Hamlett, Museum Manager at the Durham Light Infantry Museum, for her kindness in allowing me to reproduce the letter in a bottle dropped overboard by Private Thomas Hughes while on his way to France; and Elizabeth and Ken Pretty for the image of Thomas Hughes with his family. I am also grateful to Laurence Martin for an extract from the diary of Sapper Jack Martin; Jean Wade for the information regarding her grandfather, Lance Corporal William Swann; Mary Greenwood for paperwork concerning her father, Lance Corporal William Plant; the friends of Emily Miller for the pictures and letters belonging to her family; David Sweetnam for the letter picked up from the battlefield by the Reverend Andrew E. Boyce. I am also very grateful to Nicolas Ridley for the Arnold Ridley quotation from *Godfrey's Ghost*.

As always, I am very grateful to the families of those I have interviewed who have also been most kind in forwarding precious family photographs and documents. In particular, I would like to thank Rob Crow and Alizon Jones for items relating to Arthur Sherington, as well as Sylvia Barcock and Daphne Geal, the daughters of Violet Downer, for their kind assistance and permission to use the image of Private Samuel Baker's family.

My gratitude for help and advice goes to William Spencer at the National Archives; Ian Hook, Keeper of the Essex Regiment Museum, for valuable information on the Essex Regiment; Roy Hemington at the Commonwealth War Graves Commission for his kindness and support; Gordon Small for details concerning the Newport-on-Tay war memorial; and my good friends Mary Freeman, for details on the death of Billy Congreve, Lawrence Brown, Vic and Diane Piuk, Jeremy Banning, Mark Banning, Peter Barton, and David and Judith Cohen. My gratitude too goes to Thames fisherman Steve Gowan, and to Maurice Turner and Steve Williams. I should also like to thank Barrie Thorpe for his generous advice and permission to quote from his excellent book, *Private Memorials of the Great War on the Western Front*, all the profits from which go to the Western Front Association's Battlefield Project Memorial Fund.

Lastly, I would like to thank all the 'children' of the Great War, those who are still alive, all aged between 95 and 109, who have been willing to subject themselves to my questioning, and those who have died since the inception of this project. I am forever grateful to them all for remembering events, now almost a hundred years in the past, which were painful, disorientating and sometimes deeply traumatic.

Sources and Credits for Text and Photographs

Text

Extracts from Vera Brittain's *Testament of Youth* (1933) are included by permission of Mark Bostridge and T. J. Brittain-Catlin, Literary Executors for the Estate of Vera Brittain 1970.

Commonwealth War Graves Commission: By kind permission of the Commonwealth War Graves Commission, 2 Marlow Road, Maidenhead, Berkshire, SL6 7DX. With grateful thanks to CWGC Archives Supervisor, Roy Hemington.

Files: 26 GRC 1 Narrative Letters and Reports (correspondence with R. Cecil mentioning exhumation of Lt W.G.C. Gladstone, 26 April and 5 May 1915). 30 GRC 5 Section for dealing with photographs and enquiries, 1915. 142 WG 237/2 Advertisement by Mr R. Kipling – suggestions by the public concerning headstones and a letter concerning the vision of dead son (with a proposal for monument), 18 February 1919. 153 WG 783 Pt 1 War Graves Association (file including the issue of the repatriation of the dead including the formation of the British War Graves Association and the work of Mrs S. A. Smith). 268 WG 1294/3 Pt 3 Exhumations – France and Belgium – General File, 13 January 1918–19 November 1919. 269 1294/3/Pt 4 Exhumations – France and Belgium – General File, 20 November 1919–30 July 1920, including correspondence from Ruth Jervis, Henry Cook and William Dawson. 280 ACON 167 Exhumations – France and Belgium – *Sunday Express*: article alleging bodies had been privately exhumed and repatriated; list of successful and unsuccessful exhumation attempts 1919–1925. 899 WG 1606 Memorials – UK – General File.

Letter from R. Lorimer to Director of Works re controversy over inclusion of executed man on war memorial (Newport-on-Tay), with reply, 29 November 1921.

Imperial War Museum: By kind permission of the Department of Documents, Imperial War Museum, Lambeth Road, London SE1 6HZ. With grateful thanks to Roderick Suddaby, Anthony Richards and Simon Offord from the Department of Documents.

Frank Bracey – 94/46/1; Francis Herbert Gautier – 86/19/1; Lady Londonderry – 06/128/1; Captain A.C.R.S. Macnaghten – 96/2/1; H. A. Mortlock – 06/91/1; Nelson Newman – 96/57/1; Harry Wakeman – 67/305/1.

Every effort has been made to trace copyright holders, and the author and the Imperial War Museum would be grateful for any information which might help to trace those whose identities or addresses are not currently known.

The National Archives, Kew, Richmond, Surrey, TW9 4DU, www.nationalarchives.gov.uk

In the 1920s Lieutenant Colonel Robert Fitzpatrick corresponded with the Great War's official historian, Brigadier-General Sir James E. Edmonds (Cab45), and extracts from his letters have been used in the book.

FO (Foreign Office files): FO383/47/48/50/177/296 files concerning Edward Page Gaston; FO383/180 Case of Captain Roser and Captain H. T. Maffett. WO (War Office files): WO32/5846 Graves Registration Commission; WO32/4841 Rudyard Kipling's message of sympathy for relatives; WO32/4675 Method of reporting a soldier's execution to relatives. WO71 Court Martial Papers: WO71/502 Peter Black. WO95 War Diaries: WO95/2929 1/5th South Lancashire Regiment; WO95/2247 2nd Royal Irish Rifles; WO95/2694 6th Sherwood Foresters; WO95/3148 A&Q Branch, July 1918, details on battlefield burials. WO339 Officers' Files concerning: Percy Boswell WO339/44267; Valentine A. Braithwaite WO339/11125; William L. Congreve WO339/7831; E.F.C. Colquhoun WO339/67169; Harold W. Cottrell WO339/66926; A.A.K.C. Conan Doyle WO339/26137; W.G.C. Gladstone WO339/23298; Raymond Lodge WO339/29968; Charles May WO339/17649; Harold Perks WO339/30294; John Vernon F. Prestidge WO339/46531; John N. F. Pixley WO339/59588; Arthur Prosser WO339/35727; Angus Macnaghten WO339/15594; George Smith-Masters WO339/11453; Evelyn M. Southwell

WO339/690; Herbert Vacher WO339/63999; Hubert R. White WO339/29008; Raymond E. Wilson WO339/72719. WO363 Army Service Records: WO363/478 George William Dorrington. PIN (Ministry of Pensions): PIN 15/336 Establishment of the Ministry of Pensions.

Soldiers of Gloucestershire Museum: Letters from J. C. Proctor – Acc. No. 4762.

Trustees of the Army Medical Services Museum: Diary of Captain Henry Wynyard Kaye, MD, RAMC. RAMC/739.

www.thetimes.co.uk

Bibliography
Memoirs

Andrews, William Linton, *Haunting Years*, Naval & Military Press

Anonymous, *To My Unknown Warrior, November 11 1920*, privately published

Banks, Thomas, and Randolph Chell, *With the 10th Essex in France*, 1921

Bickersteth, Stanley, *The Bickersteth Diaries*, Pen & Sword, 1998

Brittain, Vera, *Testament of Youth*, Virago, 1982

Buxton, Andrew, *The Rifle Brigade, A Memoir*, Robert Scott, 1918

Carr, William, *A Time to Leave the Ploughshares*, Robert Hale, 1985

Carrington, Charles, *Soldier from the Wars Returning*, Hutchinson, 1965

Cliff, Norman, *To Hell and Back with the Guards*, Merlin Books, 1988

Collins, Norman, *Last Man Standing*, Pen & Sword, 2002

Cook, Walter, *Reflections on 'Raymond'*, Grant Richards, 1917

Ewart, Wilfrid, *Scots Guard*, Strong Oak Press, 2001

Gillespie, Alexander, *Letters from Flanders*, Smith, Elder & Co., 1916

Gladstone, Viscount, *Gladstone, William G. C. 1885–1915*, Nisbet & Co., 1918

Glubb, John, *Into Battle*, Book Club Associates, 1978

Fielding, Rowland, *War Letters to a Wife*, Spellmount Classics, 2001

Fildes, G.P.A., *Iron Times with the Guards*, John Murray, 1918

Graham, Stephen, *A Private in the Guards*, William Heinemann, 1928

Graves, Robert, *Goodbye to All That*, Penguin, 1984

Griffith, Wyn, *Up to Mametz*, Gliddon Books, 1981

Hodges, Frederick James, *Men of 18 in 1918*, Arthur H. Stockwell Ltd, 1988

Hope, T. S., *The Winding Road Unfolds*, Putnam, 1937

Howson, Hugh, *Two Men: A Memoir* [Evelyn Southwell 1886–1916 and Malcolm White 1887–1916], Oxford University Press, 1919

Kehoe, Thomas Joseph, *The Fighting Mascot*, Dodd, Mead & Co., 1918

Kiernan, R. H., *Little Brother Goes Soldiering*, Constable & Co. Ltd, 1930

Lauder, Harry, *A Minstrel in France*, Hearst's International Library, 1918

Lawson, Henry, *Vignettes of the Western Front*, Positif Press, 1979

Leighton, Marie, *Boy of My Heart*, Hodder & Stoughton, 1918

Lodge, Sir Oliver, *Raymond or Life After Death*, Methuen & Co. Ltd, 1916

Lucy, John, *There's a Devil in the Drum*, The Naval and Military Press, 1993

Macnaghten, Angus, *Missing*, Dragon Books, 1970

Martin, Sapper, *The Secret War Diary of Jack Martin*, Bloomsbury, 2009

McClintock, Alexander, *Best o'Luck*, George H. Doran, 1917

Morgan, Hugo, *Life Amongst The Sandbags*, Hodder & Stoughton, 1916

Morton, Mary, *A Cinder Grows*, Eric Dobby Publishing, 1993

Nicholson, Walter, *Behind the Lines*, Cape, 1939

Noakes, Frederick, *The Distant Drum*, Pen & Sword, 2010

Parker, E. W., *Into Battle*, Leo Cooper, 1994

Patch, Harry, *The Last Fighting Tommy*, Bloomsbury, 2007

Peel, Mrs C., *How We Lived Then*, Bodley Head, 1929

Pixley, Olive, *Listening In: A Record of a Singular Experience*, LSA Publications, 1930

Poulton, Sir Edward B., *The Life of Ronald Poulton*, Sidgwick & Jackson, 1919

Quiller-Couch, Bevil, *The Tears of War*, Cavalier Books, 2000

Rathbone, Basil, *In and Out of Character*, Garden City, 1962

Rogerson, Sidney, *Twelve Days*, Barker, 1933

Sanders, Leslie, *A Soldier of England*, J. Maxwell & Son, 1920

Sassoon, Siegfried, *Diaries 1915–1918*, Faber & Faber, 1983

Scott, Canon Frederick, *The Great War As I Saw It*, The Naval and Military Press

Scott, Ralph (Atkinson, George), *A Soldier's Diary*, W. Collins

Thomas, Alan, *A Life Apart*, Gollancz, 1968

Vernede, Robert, *Letters to His Wife*, Collins, 1917

Voigt, F. A., *Combed Out*, Jonathan Cape, 1929

Williamson, Benedict, *'Happy Days' in France and Flanders*, The Naval and Military Press

Other Reading

Barton Peter, with Jeremy Banning, *The Somme: A New Panoramic Perspective*, Constable, 2006

Brown, Malcolm, *Tommy Goes to War*, J. M. Dent & Sons, 1986

Clifford, Colin, *The Asquiths*, John Murray, 2003

Cooksey, Jon, *Pals, 13th and 14th York and Lancaster Rgt*, Pen & Sword, 1986

DeGroot, Gerard, *Blighty: British Society in the Era of the Great War*, Longman, 1996

Lellenberg, Jon, *Arthur Conan Doyle: A Life in Letters*, Penguin Press, 2007

Lloyd, David W., *Battlefield Tourism*, Berg, 1998

Messenger, Charles, *Call to Arms*, Weidenfeld & Nicolson, 2005

Milner, Laurie, *Leeds Pals*, Pen & Sword, 1998

Small, Gordon, *The Newport on Tay and Wormit War Memorial*, privately published, 2008

Spagnoly, Tony, and Ted Smith, *Cameos of the Western Front 4*, Pen & Sword, 2004

Thorpe, Barrie, *Private Memorials of the Great War on the Western Front*, The Trustees of the Western Front Association, 1999

Turner, E. S., *Dear Old Blighty*, Michael Joseph, 1980

van Emden, Richard, *Boy Soldiers of the Great War*, Headline, 2005

van Emden, Richard, *Prisoners of the Kaiser*, Pen & Sword, 2000

van Emden, *Sapper Martin: The Secret Great War Diary*, Bloomsbury, 2009

Winter, J. M., *The Great War and the British People*, Macmillan, 1987

Winter, Jay, *Sites of Memory, Sites of Mourning*, Cambridge University Press, 2010

Winter, John, *Death's Men*, Allen Lane, 1978

Interviews conducted by the author with the following seven Great War veterans:

Arthur Barraclough

Norman Collins

Hal Kerridge

Harry Patch

Robert Renwick

Jack Rogers

Ernest Stevens

I would like to thank the following twenty-three Great War civilians for their kind help with my research:

Lily Baron, née Jones, born August 1912, daughter of Lance Corporal John Jones, killed in action 22 November 1917

Florence Billington, born December 1898, girlfriend of Private Edward Felton, killed in action 16 May 1915

*Edith Cackett, born 1912, daughter of Gunner Arthur Knight, died of flu 21 November 1918

*Kathleen Calderbank, born May 1916, daughter of Private Henry Calderbank, killed in action 3 August 1917

Joan Carter, née Healey, born July 1914, daughter of Rifleman Albert Healey, killed in action 28 March 1918

*Charles Chilton, born June 1917, son of Private Charles Chilton, killed in action 21 March 1918

*Grace Cox, née Hewett, born February 1902, sister of Private Albert Hewett, killed in action 18 October 1918

Joyce Crow, née Sherington, born February 1909, sister of Rifleman Robert Arthur Sherington, killed in action 9 October 1916

*Emily Crowhurst, née Hughes, born August 1912, daughter of Private Thomas Hughes, killed in action 21 September 1914

*Doris Davies, born August 1910, daughter of Corporal Nelson Charles Davies, died of wounds 6 February 1916

*Violet Downer, née Baker, born August 1913, daughter of Private Samuel Baker, killed in action 22 October 1916

Ellen Elston, née Tanner, born August 1908, daughter of Sergeant John Tanner, killed in action 6 August 1917

*Gertrude Harris, née Farr, born October 1913, daughter of Private Harry T. Farr, executed 18 October 1916

Emily Galbraith, née Miller, born July 1895, sister of Private Peter Miller, killed in action 9 September 1916

Dennis Gilfeather, born 1907, brother of Private John Gilfeather, killed in action 25 September 1915

*Mabel Howatt, née Hunter, born July 1912, daughter of Corporal Ernest Hunter, killed in action 22 June 1917

Madge Maindonald, born December 1905, sister of Private Edwin Maindonald, killed in action 7 October 1916

*Clara Middleton, née Whitefield, born January 1907, daughter of Private Richard Whitefield, died of wounds 13 February 1917

*George Musgrave, born October 1915, son of Private Alfred Musgrave, died of wounds 11 December 1917

*Donald Overall, born April 1913, son of Rifleman Harry Overall, died of wounds 15 June 1917

Lucy Walter, née Neale, born April 1907, daughter of Sergeant Harold Neale, died of dysentery 15 October 1917

Leonard Whitehead, born June 1907, brother of Private George W. Whitehead, killed in action 29 October 1915

George Wilson, born December 1905, brother of Private Hubert Wilson, killed in action August 1915

* Denotes still alive at the time of writing, June 2011.

Photographs

Imperial War Museum, London: By kind permission of the picture library of the Imperial War Museum, Lambeth Road, London, SE1 6HZ.
Q5242, Q8346, Q11281, Q3096, Q10329, Q110570J, CO1066, HU83788, Q23688, Q13521, Q54588, Q31131, Q31041, Q30238, Q109794, Q31514, Q14965, Q109517.

Durham Light Infantry Museum, Durham: Private Thomas Hughes' message in a bottle, courtesy of the DLI Museum, copyright John Attle.

Getty Images: Permission to reproduce the following images:
90740803 (soldier leaving for the First World War); 64331 (postwoman): 3286745 (flowers at the Cenotaph); 3277584 (Armistice Day); 3286704 (unknown warrior).

INDEX